PROGRESSIVE

GUITAR
CHORDS

BY GARY TURNER AND BRENTON WHITE

Distributed by

AUSTRALIA
Koala Publications Pty. Ltd.
37 Orsmond Street,
Hindmarsh 5007
South Australia
Ph: (08) 346 5366
Fax: 61-8-340 9040

USA
Koala Publications Inc.
3001 Redhill Ave.
Bldg 2#109
Costa Mesa
CA. 92626
Ph: (714) 546 2743
Fax: 1-714-546 2749

U.K. and Europe
Music Exchange,
Mail Order Dept,
Claverton Rd, Wythenshawe,
Manchester M23 9ZA
Ph: (0161) 946 1234
Fax: (0161) 946 1195

Reorder code KP-CH

ISBN 0 947 183 09 4

CONTENTS

4

SECTION THREE: CHORD/KEY RELATIONSHIPS

INTRODUCTION

PROGRESSIVE GUITAR CHORDS has been specifically designed for players of three different levels:

THE BEGINNER, who will mainly use the **OPEN CHORD SECTIONS**. These contain the simplest and most widely used chord shapes in all keys. **THE SEMI-ADVANCED PLAYER**, who will need a thorough knowledge of **BAR CHORD** shapes in all positions. These are particularly useful for rock guitarists.

THE ADVANCED PLAYER, who will refer to the **MOVEABLE SHAPES** for chords widely used by jazz guitarists.

There are three main sections in Progressive Guitar Chords. **SECTION ONE** gives a systematic and concise listing of chord shapes, arranged in order of chord type. These chords are organised for the three levels of guitar players, as described above.

SECTION TWO contains important music theory for guitarists. It provides a thorough knowledge of scales, keys and chord construction, enabling the student to understand (and construct) any chord.

SECTION THREE presents a complete listing of the most common chords in every key, together with example progressions. These "scale tone" chords are extremely useful for choosing the correct backing chords of a song (or melody).

HOW TO USE THIS BOOK

OPEN CHORD SECTIONS

A CHORD can be defined as a group of three or more different notes played together. Chords can be illustrated by the use of **CHORD DIAGRAMS** (at right), which involve a grid pattern of strings (vertical lines) and frets (horizontal lines).

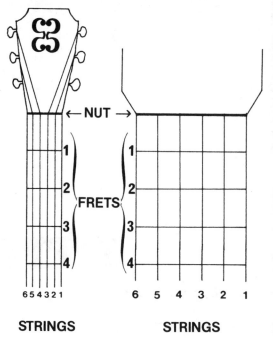

Upon chord diagrams dots are written to indicate the positioning of the left hand fingers, which are numbered as such:

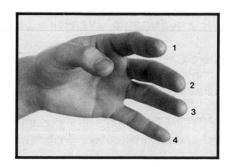

A **BROKEN LINE** indicates that a string is not to be strummed:

DO NOT STRUM THIS STRING →

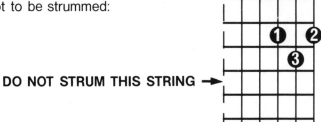

A **CROSS**, placed by the nut, indicates that a string's sound is to be **DEADENED**. In the example given, the 5th string is deadened by the second finger **LIGHTLY** touching it.

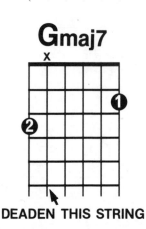

DEADEN THIS STRING

The notes contained in each chord are written below the chord box. For more advanced students, the chord formula notes have been included:

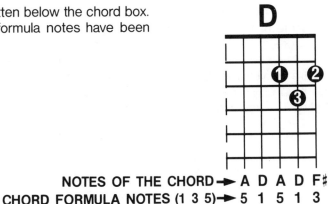

NOTES OF THE CHORD ➤ A D A D F♯
CHORD FORMULA NOTES (1 3 5) ➤ 5 1 5 1 3

When the same finger is used to play more than one note, it is indicated by a line joining the notes:

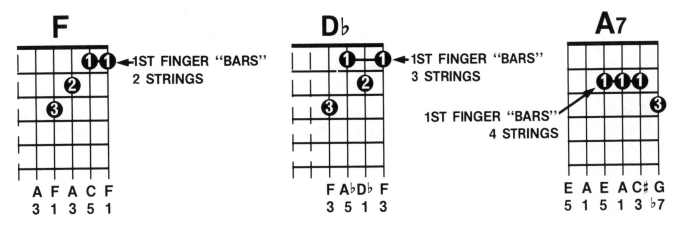

There are many different ways of playing the same chord, and where two or more shapes are given, either may be used. In the **OPEN CHORD** section of this book, where two or more shapes are given the most popular one will be **SHADED**.

It is not necessary to learn all of the open chord shapes in this book before commencing the study of bar chords. There are many situations where a bar chord shape will be more convenient, once the barring technique has been mastered. The most important open chords for you to learn are outlined in section I of **PROGRESSIVE RHYTHM GUITAR**.

The fingerings indicated are the most commonly used for each chord shape, however in certain situations (eg for ease of chord changing) you may wish to alter the standard fingering.

Beginning students should read through the theory sections on **SUBSTITUTION** (see the table on pge 153) and **TRANSPOSING** (pge 154). The information contained in these sections will help you to play songs which would otherwise be too difficult (ie eliminating difficult chords and transposing to an "easy" key).

BAR CHORD SECTIONS* — FOR SEMI ADVANCED PLAYERS.
Most rock guitarists use **BAR CHORDS**, which involve the first finger **BARRING** across 4, 5 or 6 strings. No open strings are used in bar chords. Here are 3 examples:

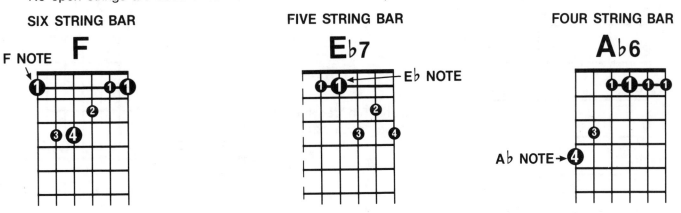

*Before commencing the study of bar chords, you should be thoroughly familiar with basic open chord shapes.

In each of these chord diagrams the **LARGE DOTS** are the **ROOT NOTES** of the chord. The root note is the note with the same name as the chord, thus F is the root note of F major, E♭ is the root note of E♭7 and A♭ is the root note of A♭6.

All bar chords are derived from open chord shapes moved up the fretboard, with the first finger barring to replace the nut. Thus if an open E major chord is moved up one fret and the first finger bars across all six strings at the 1st fret, and F major chord is formed:

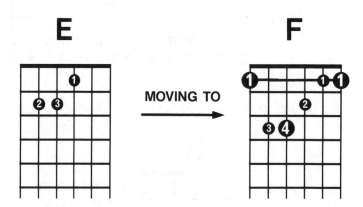

The lowest root note of this chord is located on the **6TH STRING**, and thus the chord is often referred to as a **ROOT 6 BAR CHORD**. It can also be called an **E FORMATION BAR CHORD**, because of its relationship to the open E shape.

If the F root 6 bar chord is moved up one fret (barring the 2nd fret) it becomes F♯ or (G♭); if it is moved up another fret it becomes G; another fret Ab and so on. The name of the chord is always taken from the note on the 6th string, summarized below:

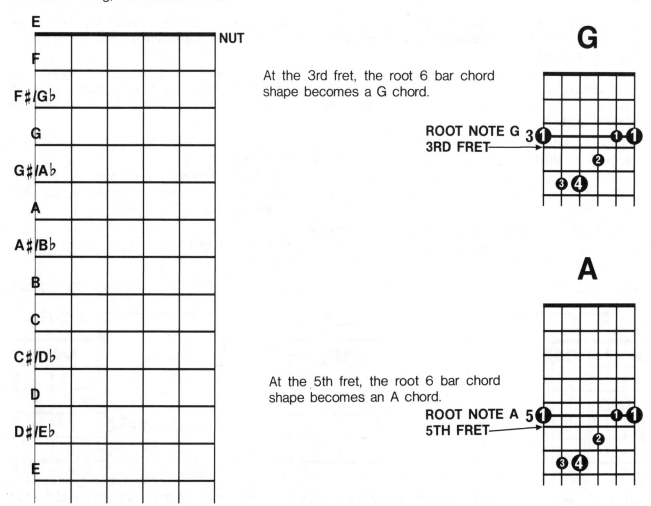

At the 3rd fret, the root 6 bar chord shape becomes a G chord.

ROOT NOTE G 3RD FRET

At the 5th fret, the root 6 bar chord shape becomes an A chord.

ROOT NOTE A 5TH FRET

As the chord shape moves up the neck, its **NAME** changes but its **TYPE** (major) does not. It will always remain a major chord.

In this book each bar chord shape is taken up to the 12th fret, however the actual number of bar chords you can play will depend on the type of guitar you have. On a classical guitar you may only be able to bar up to the 8th fret, whereas on an electric guitar you should be able to play up to the 12th fret.

The notes on the guitar start repeating from the 12th fret on (ie 13th fret notes = 1st fret notes, 14th fret notes = 2nd fret notes etc); hence **ANY** chord shape (open, bar or moveable) can be played as written or 12 frets higher.

Other root 6 bar chords use the same principle as described above. For example, if the E minor open chord shape is moved up one fret, it becomes F minor:

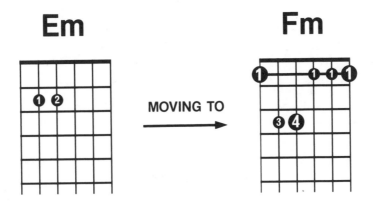

Once again, the **NAME** of this root 6 bar chord changes as it moves up the neck, but its **TYPE** does not. ie. it is always a minor chord. Because the shape is based on an open E minor chord, it can also be referred to as "**E FORMATION**".

Another common form of bar chord has its lowest root note on the **5TH STRING** and is thus referred to as a **ROOT 5 BAR CHORD**. It can be illustrated by moving an open A chord shape up the neck, thus:

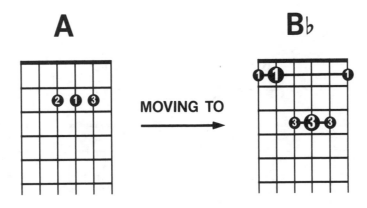

The chord name is taken from its root note, located on the 5th string:

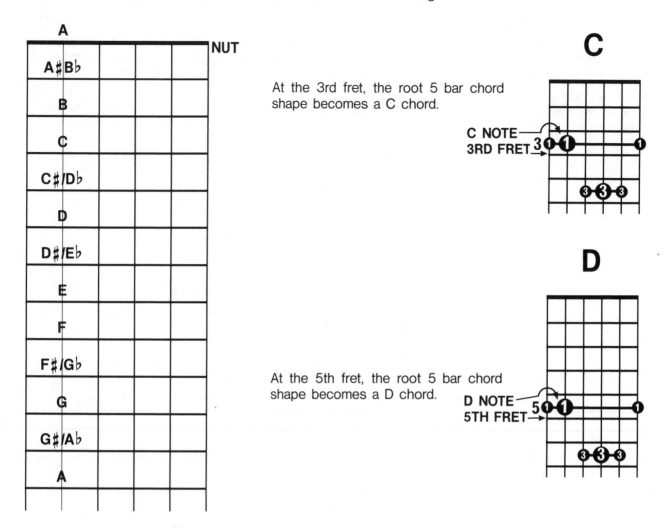

At the 3rd fret, the root 5 bar chord shape becomes a C chord.

At the 5th fret, the root 5 bar chord shape becomes a D chord.

These chords can also be referred to as "**A FORMATION BAR CHORDS**".

Root 6 and root 5 are the most popular bar chords, however there are useful bar chord shapes with their root notes located on the other four strings, and these are also presented in this book. For example:

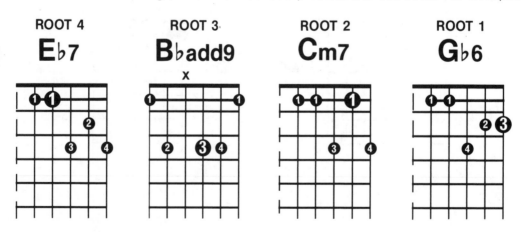

Once again, all of these bar chords are derived from open chord shapes.

MOVEABLE SHAPE SECTIONS — FOR ADVANCED PLAYERS

Any chord that involves no open strings can be regarded as a moveable chord; it does not necessarily need to be a bar chord. In the Gmajor 7 chord below, the 5th and 1st strings are deadened (by the first finger) as indicated by the cross signs:

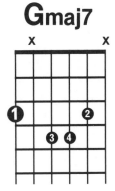

Gmaj7

If this shape were played at the 5th fret it would be an A maj7 chord, and so on. It is thus a root 6 moveable chord shape, but not a bar chord.

The moveable shapes presented in this book are mainly used by jazz guitarists and other advanced players. They are all given in the **FIRST POSITION**, but can be moved up the neck in the same manner as bar chords. You may find some of the shapes difficult to play in first position, but they will be easier when moved up the neck. Once again, root notes (where present) are indicated by larger dots.

Many chord shapes which contain all the notes in a given chord formula can be impossible or impracticable to play on guitar. These shapes can be simplified by omitting certain notes of the chord. The least important notes of a chord are the first and the fifth; all others are essential to maintain its characteristic sound. For example, in a 9th chord the third determines whether it is major or minor; the 7th determines whether it is major 7th or dominant 7th and the 9th is the essential note which gives the chord its name. This leaves the root and fifth, which may be omitted, **EXCEPT** where the fifth occurs as an **ALTERED** note in the chord formula. eg chords such as $7\flat5$ and $9\sharp5$ must contain the fifth.

When chord notes are omitted, you are actually playing a **SUBSTITUTION**. For example, if you omit the root note of, say, C9, then you are left with the notes of Gm6:

C9:	C	E	G	Bb	D
Gm6:	G	Bb	D	E	

Thus many of the moveable 9th chord shapes are identical to the m6 shapes. This substitution principle is very common and is outlined in the boxes placed at the beginning of each moveable shape. For the example above:

> I9 (No Root)=Vm6
> e.g. C9 (No C)=Gm6

In moveable shapes deadened strings (x) are used exclusively to indicate notes that are not in the chord. These may be deadened by either the left hand fingers or the thumb (for the 6th string). In some instances you may wish to avoid strumming the string.

SECTION ONE

OPEN CHORDS
(Beginners)

BAR CHORD SHAPES
(Semi-Advanced Players)

MOVEABLE SHAPES
(Advanced Players)

13

MAJOR
Open Chords

maj

1 3 5

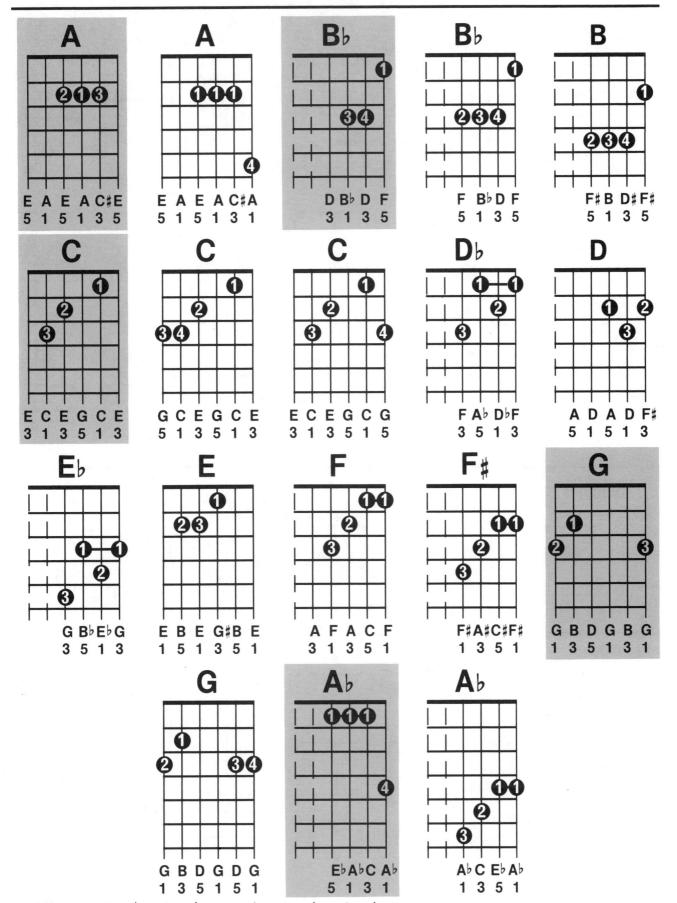

A — E A E A C#E / 5 1 5 1 3 5

A — E A E A C#A / 5 1 5 1 3 1

Bb — D Bb D F / 3 1 3 5

Bb — F Bb D F / 5 1 3 5

B — F# B D# F# / 5 1 3 5

C — E C E G C E / 3 1 3 5 1 3

C — G C E G C E / 5 1 3 5 1 3

C — E C E G C G / 3 1 3 5 1 5

Db — F Ab Db F / 3 5 1 3

D — A D A D F# / 5 1 5 1 3

Eb — G Bb Eb G / 3 5 1 3

E — E B E G# B E / 1 5 1 3 5 1

F — A F A C F / 3 1 3 5 1

F# — F# A# C# F# / 1 3 5 1

G — G B D G B G / 1 3 5 1 3 1

G — G B D G D G / 1 3 5 1 5 1

Ab — Eb Ab C Ab / 5 1 3 1

Ab — Ab C Eb Ab / 1 3 5 1

REMEMBER A# =Bb, C# =Db, D# =Eb, F# =Gb, G# =Ab. **SEE ENHARMONICS** on page 138.

maj

MAJOR
Bar Chord Shapes

1 3 5

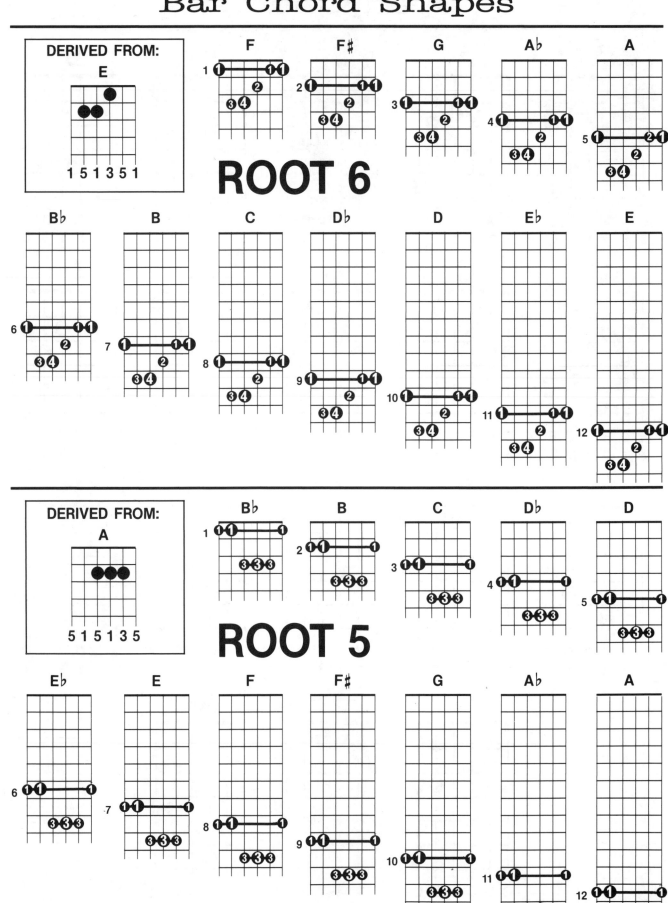

DERIVED FROM: E

1 5 1 3 5 1

ROOT 6

DERIVED FROM: A

5 1 5 1 3 5

ROOT 5

maj | MAJOR | 1 3 5
Bar Chord Shapes (Cont.)

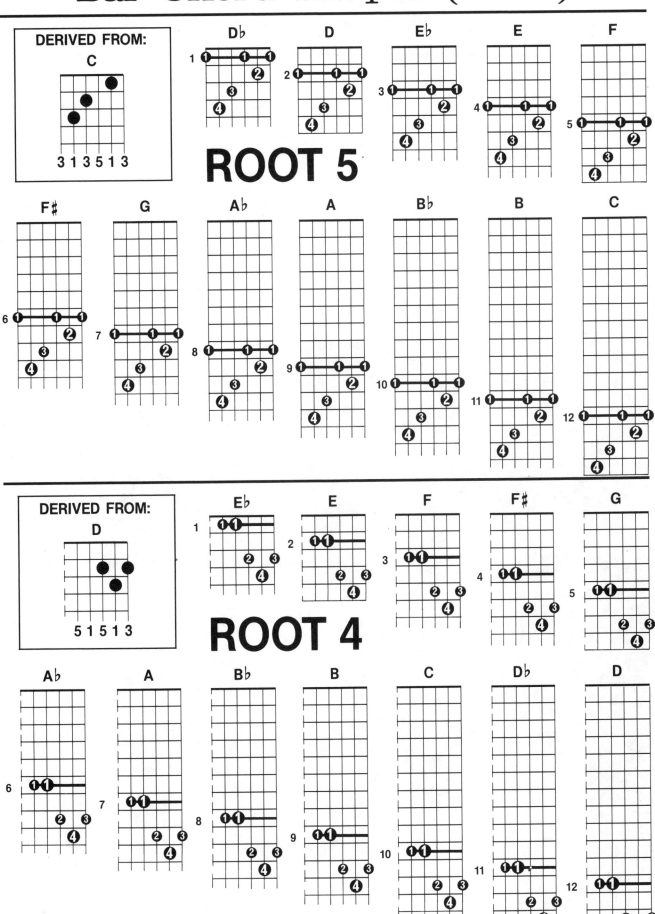

DERIVED FROM: C — 3 1 3 5 1 3

ROOT 5

Db · D · Eb · E · F · F# · G · Ab · A · Bb · B · C

DERIVED FROM: D — 5 1 5 1 3

ROOT 4

Eb · E · F · F# · G · Ab · A · Bb · B · C · Db · D

maj		

MAJOR
Moveable Shapes

	1 3 5

All moveable chord shapes are shown in first position only but may be moved up the fretboard in the same manner as Bar Chords.

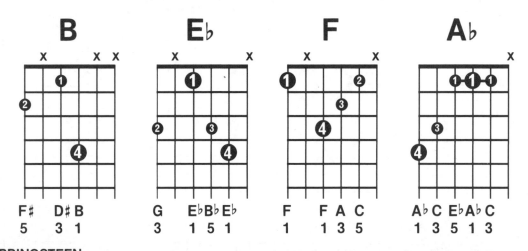

BRUCE SPRINGSTEEN

sus

SUSPENDED
Open Chords

1 4 5

The suspended chord is often written as "sus4" in sheet music.

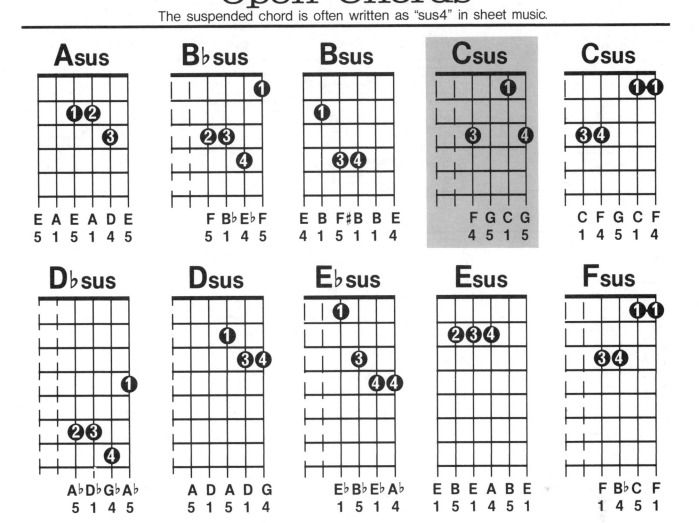

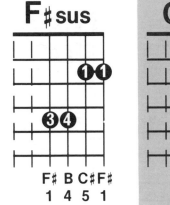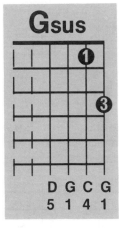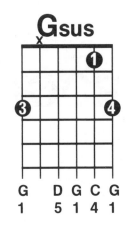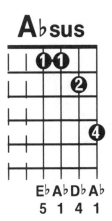

sus

SUSPENDED
Bar Chord Shapes

1 4 5

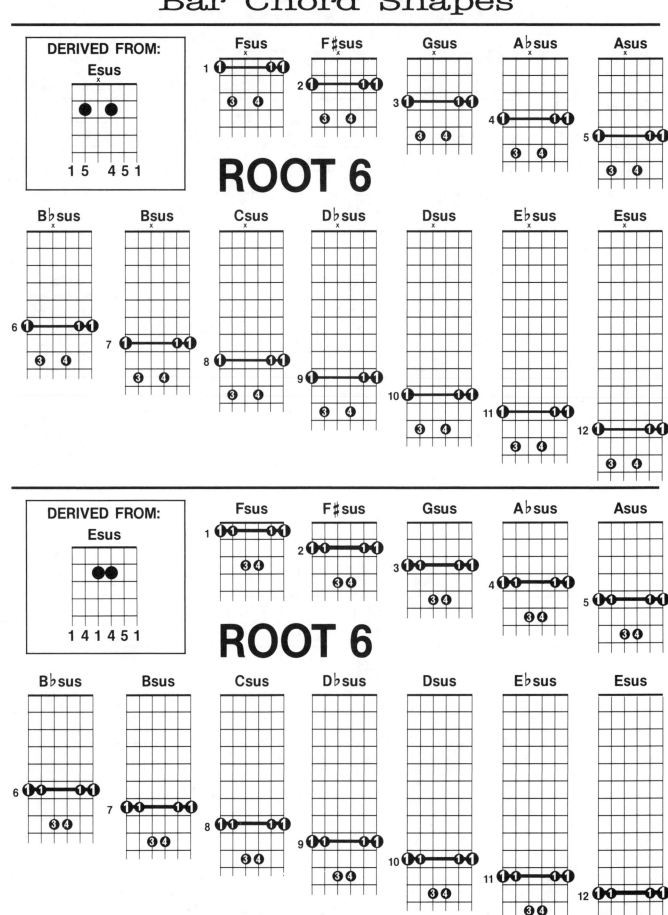

SUSPENDED
Bar Chord Shapes (Cont.)

sus | 1 4 5

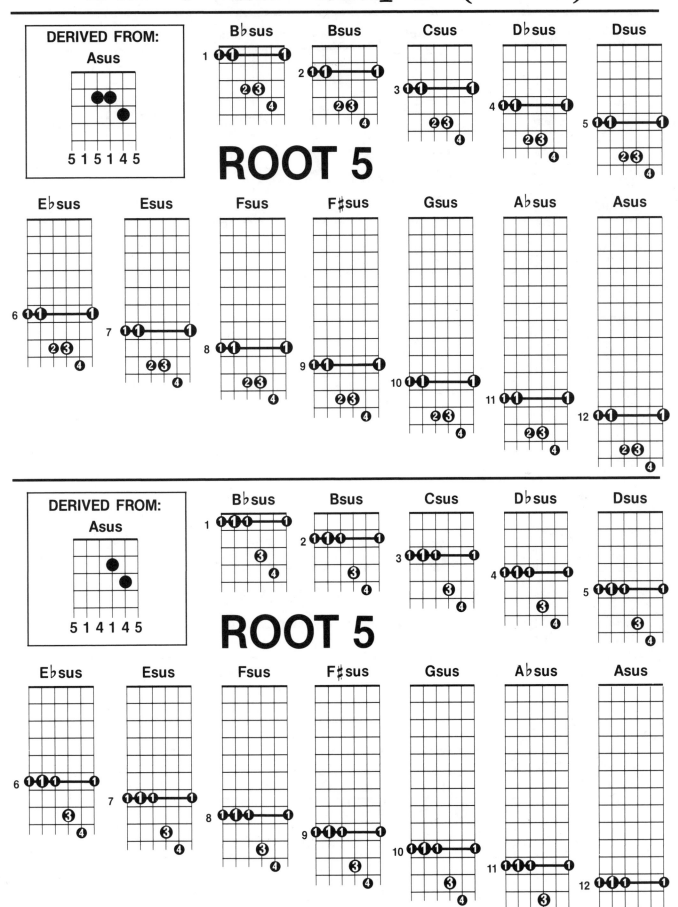

sus	**SUSPENDED**	1 4 5

Bar Chord Shapes

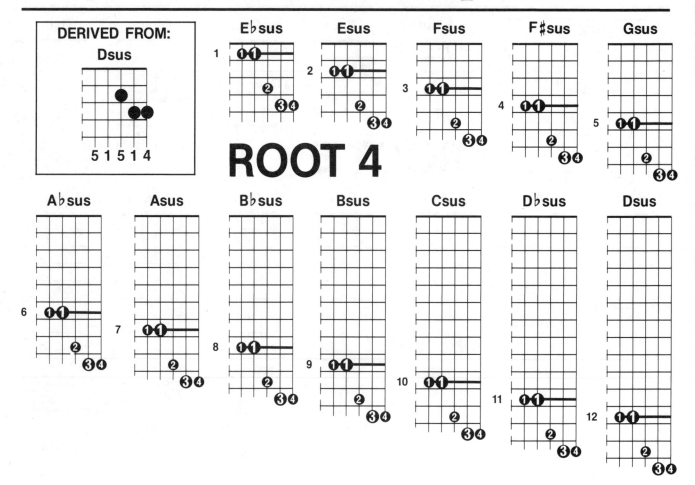

DERIVED FROM:
Dsus
5 1 5 1 4

Ebsus   Esus   Fsus   F#sus   Gsus

ROOT 4

Absus   Asus   Bbsus   Bsus   Csus   Dbsus   Dsus

sus	**SUSPENDED**	1 4 5

Moveable Shapes

All moveable chord shapes are shown in first position only but may be moved up the fretboard in the same manner as Bar Chords.

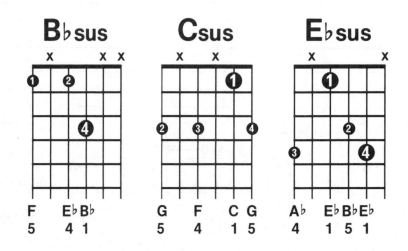

Bbsus   Csus   Ebsus

maj-5   MAJOR FLAT FIVE   1 3 ♭5
(or Major Diminished Fifth)

Open Chords

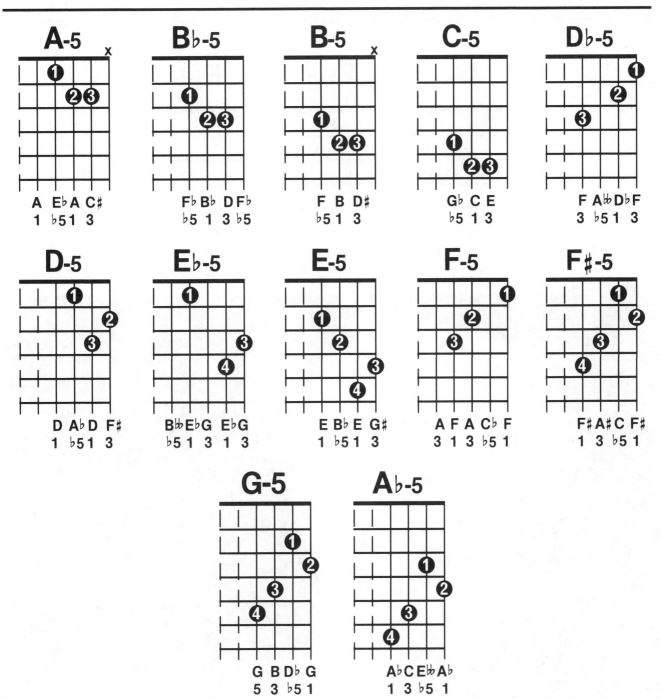

-5

MAJOR FLAT FIVE

1 3 ♭5

Moveable Shapes
This chord type has no useful bar chord shapes.

All moveable chord shapes are shown in first position only but may be moved up the fretboard in the same manner as Bar Chords.

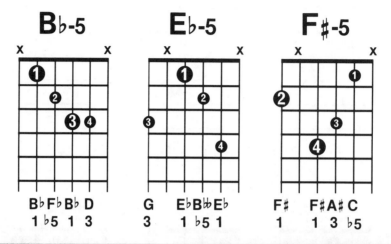

B♭-5

B♭ F♭ B♭ D
1 ♭5 1 3

E♭-5

G   E♭ B♭♭ E♭
3   1 ♭5 1

F♯-5

F♯   F♯ A♯ C
1   1 3 ♭5

DAVID BOWIE

add9 | MAJOR ADD NINE | 1 3 5 9
Open Chords

Aadd9

E A E B C# E
5 1 5 9 3 5

B♭add9
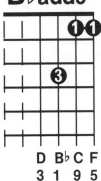

D B♭ C F
3 1 9 5

Badd9
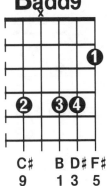

C#   B D# F#
9   1 3 5

Cadd9
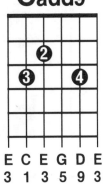

E C E G D E
3 1 3 5 9 3

C#add9
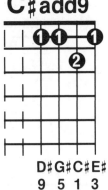

D#G#C#E#
9 5 1 3

Dadd9
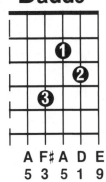

A F# A D E
5 3 5 1 9

E♭add9
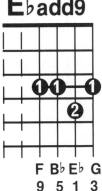

F B♭ E♭ G
9 5 1 3

Eadd9
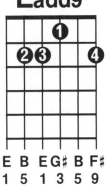

E B E G# B F#
1 5 1 3 5 9

Fadd9
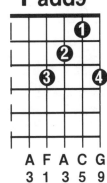

A F A C G
3 1 3 5 9

F#add9
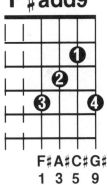

F#A#C#G#
1 3 5 9

Gadd9
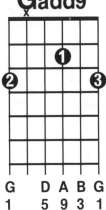

G   D A B G
1   5 9 3 1

A♭add9
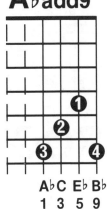

A♭C E♭ B♭
1 3 5 9

add9 | MAJOR ADD NINE | 1 3 5 9
Bar Chord Shapes

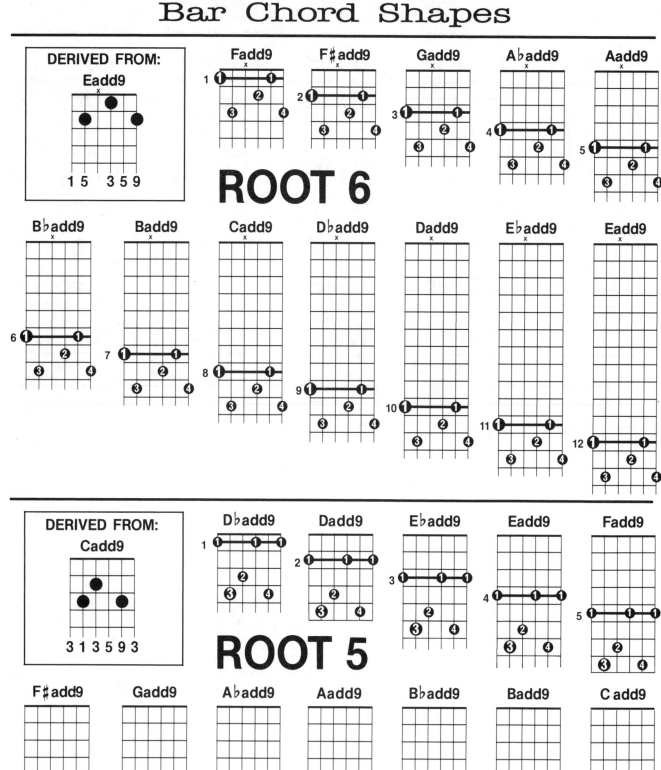

ROOT 6

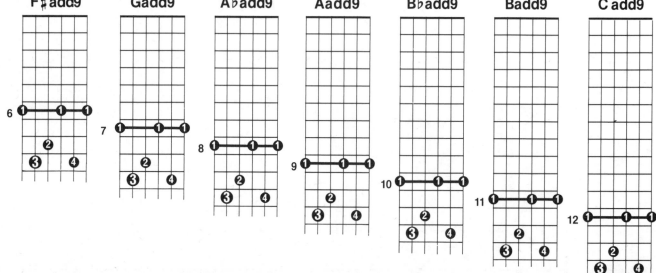

ROOT 5

add9 MAJOR ADD NINE 1 3 5 9
Bar Chord Shapes(cont.)

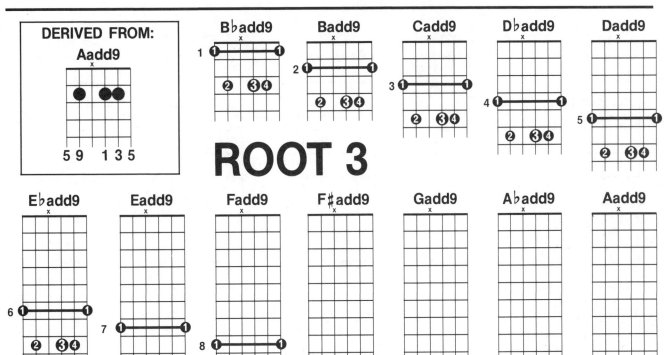

ROOT 3

add9 MAJOR ADD NINE 1 3 5 9
Moveable Shapes

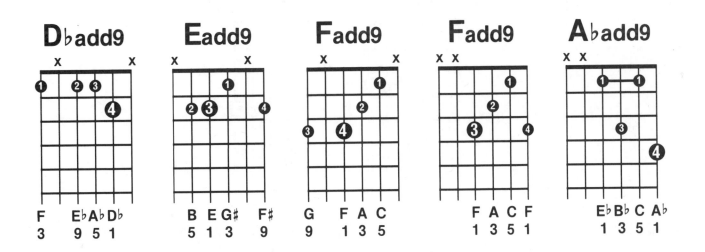

MINOR
Open Chords

m

1 ♭3 5

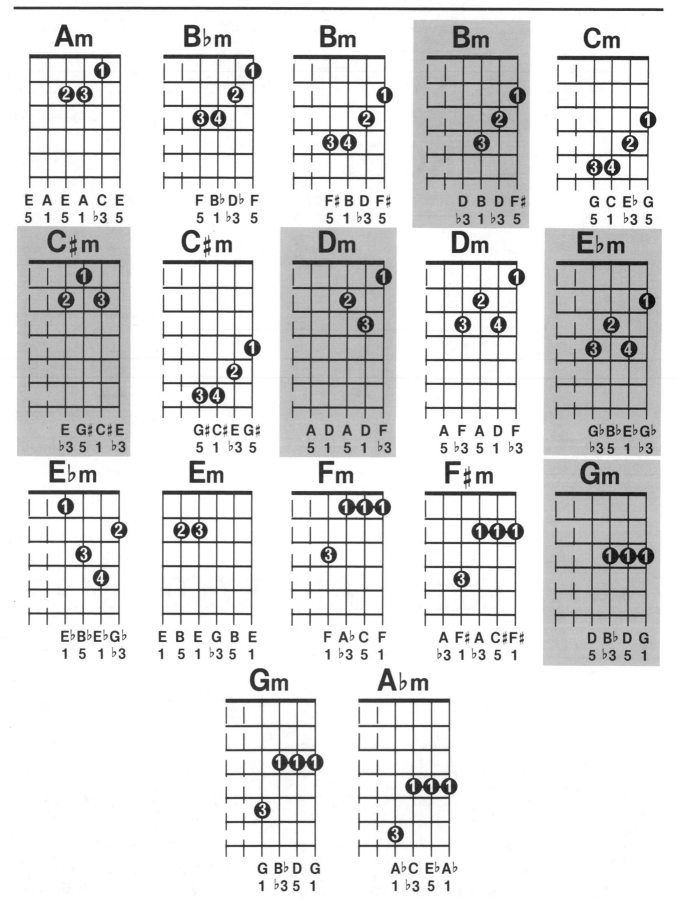

REMEMBER, A♯=B♭, C♯=D♭, D♯=E♭, F♯=G♭, G♯=A♭. **SEE ENHARMONICS** on page 138.

MINOR
Bar Chord Shapes

m

1 ♭3 5

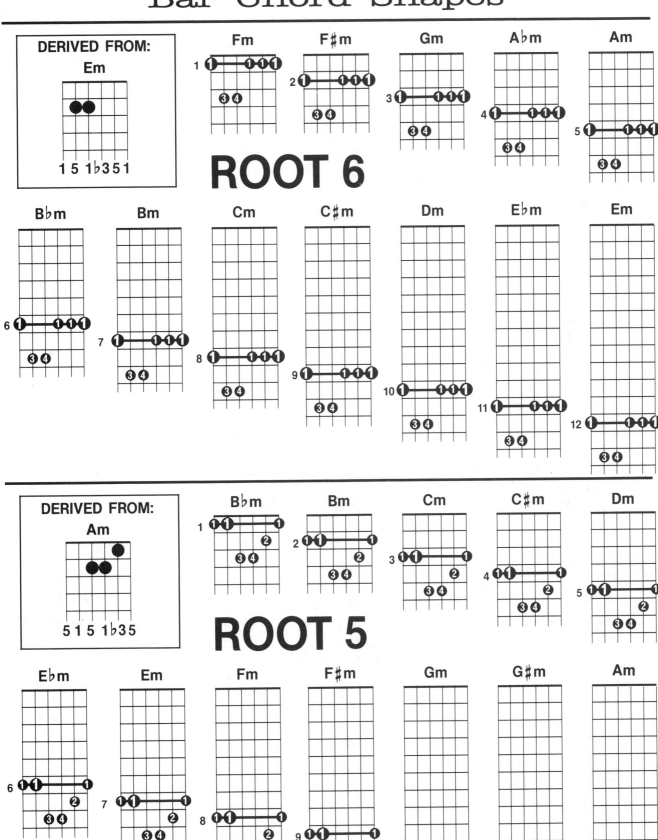

ROOT 6

ROOT 5

MINOR

m   **1 ♭3 5**

Bar Chord Shapes (Cont.)

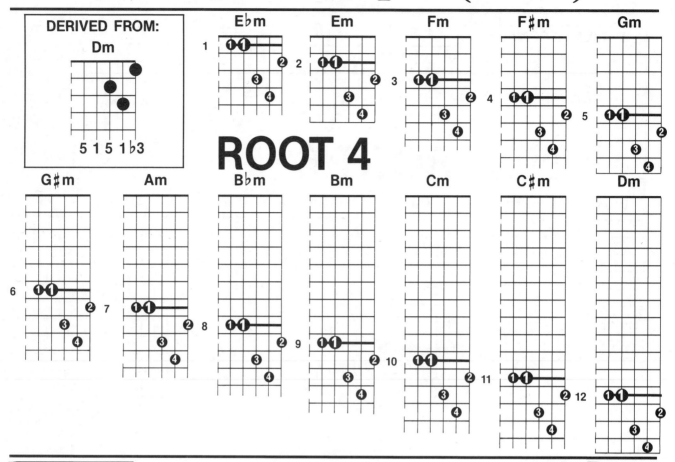

ROOT 4

MINOR

m   **1 ♭3 5**

Moveable Shapes

All moveable chord shapes are shown in first position only but may be moved up the fretboard in the same manner as Bar Chords.

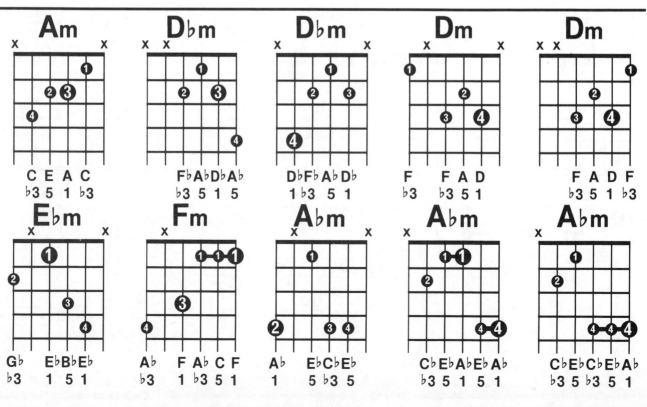

+

AUGMENTED
Open Chords

1 3 #5

A+
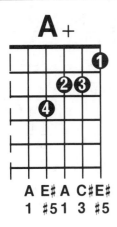

A E# A C#E#
1 #51 3 #5

Bb+
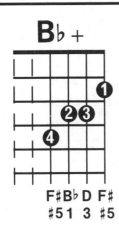

F#Bb D F#
#51 3 #5

B+
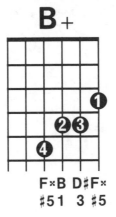

F× B D#F×
#51 3 #5

C+
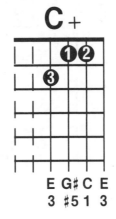

E G# C E
3 #51 3

Db+
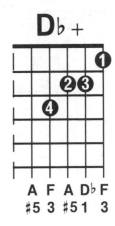

A F A Db F
#5 3 #51 3

D+
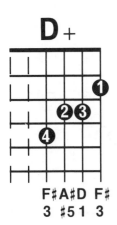

F#A#D F#
3 #51 3

Eb+
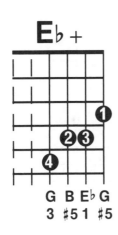

G B Eb G
3 #51 #5

E+
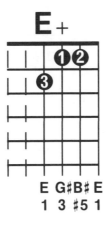

E G#B# E
1 3 #5 1

F+
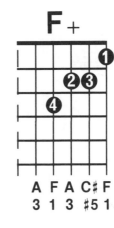

A F A C# F
3 1 3 #5 1

F#+
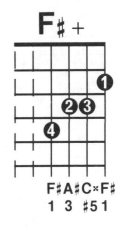

F#A#C×F#
1 3 #51

G+
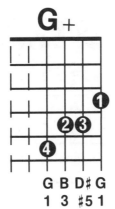

G B D# G
1 3 #5 1

Ab+
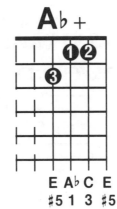

E Ab C E
#5 1 3 #5

+

AUGMENTED
Bar Chord Shapes

1 3 ♯5

Each augmented chord has 3 different names; the names being taken from each of the 3 notes in the chord.

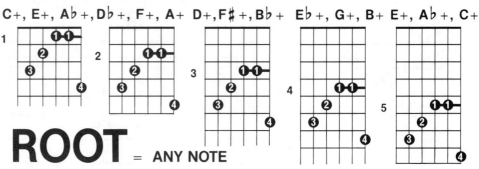

DERIVED FROM:
B+, E♭+, G+

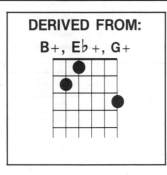

C+, E+, A♭+, D♭+, F+, A+ D+, F♯+, B♭+ E♭+, G+, B+ E+, A♭+, C+

ROOT = ANY NOTE

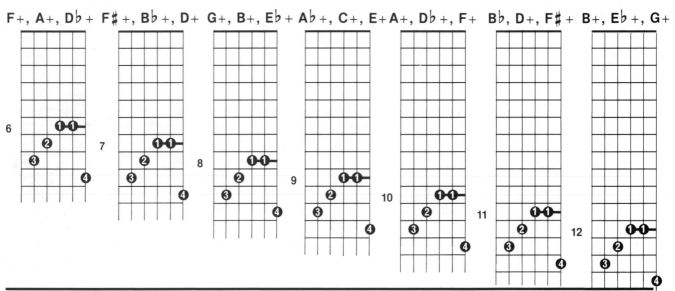

F+, A+, D♭+ F♯+, B♭+, D+ G+, B+, E♭+ A♭+, C+, E+ A+, D♭+, F+ B♭, D+, F♯+ B+, E♭+, G+

+

AUGMENTED
Moveable Shapes

1 3 ♯5

I+ = III+ = VI+
e.g. C+ = E+ = A♭+

All moveable chord shapes are shown in first position only but may be moved up the fretboard in the same manner as Bar Chords.

A♭+, C+, E+   F+, A+, D♭+   G+, E♭+, B+

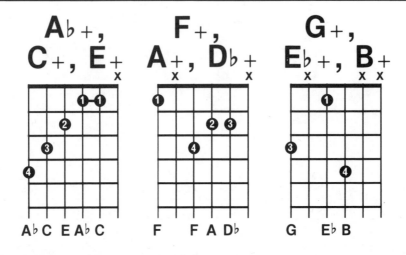

A♭ C E A♭ C   F   F A D♭   G   E♭ B

MAJOR SIX
Open Chords

6   1 3 5 6

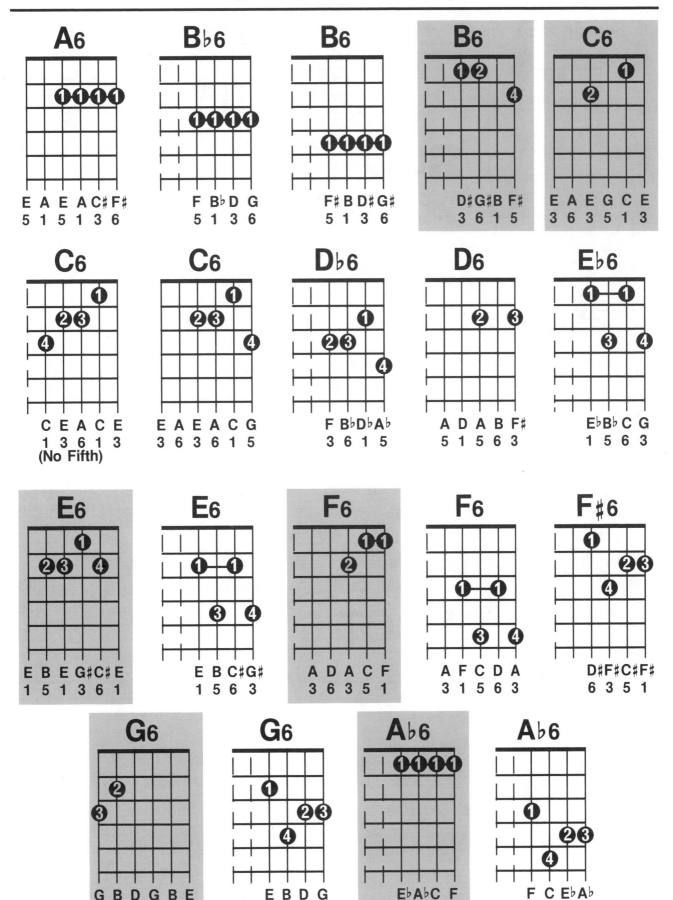

6   MAJOR SIX   1 3 5 6
Bar Chord Shapes

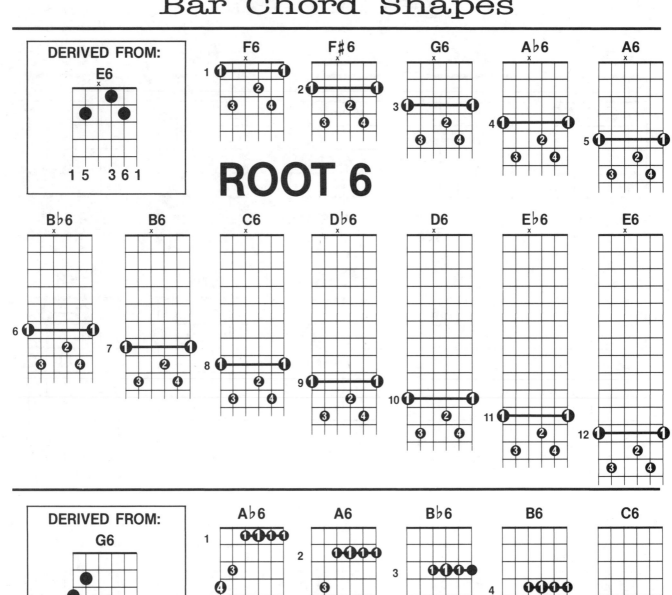

ROOT 6

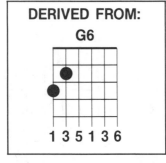

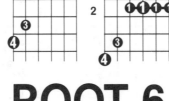

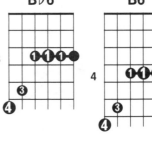

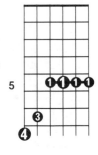

ROOT 6

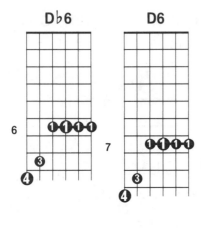

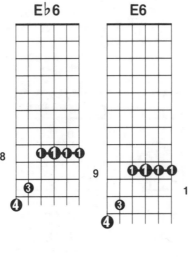

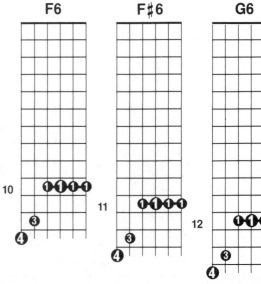

MAJOR SIX

6   **1 3 5 6**

Bar Chord Shapes (Cont.)

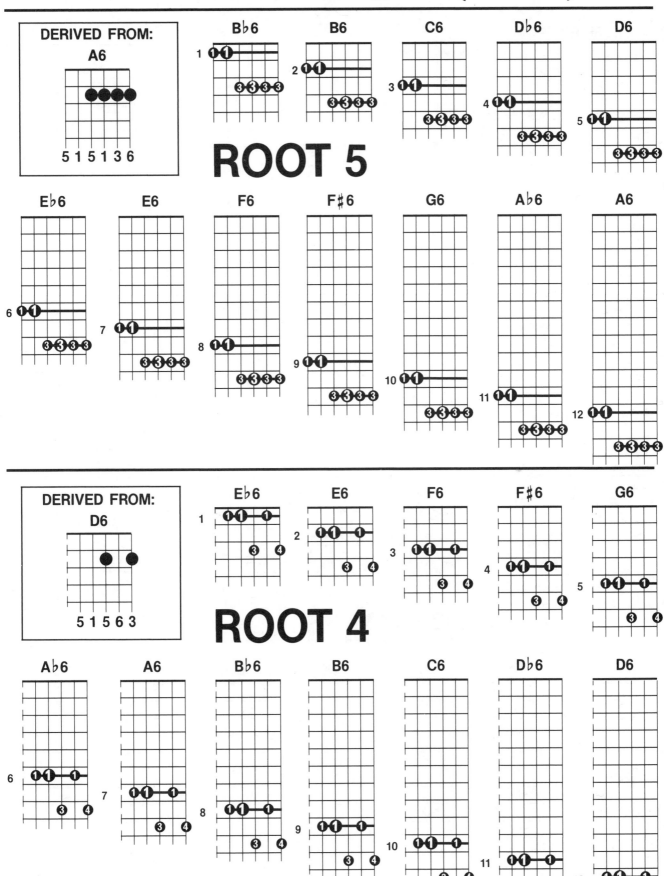

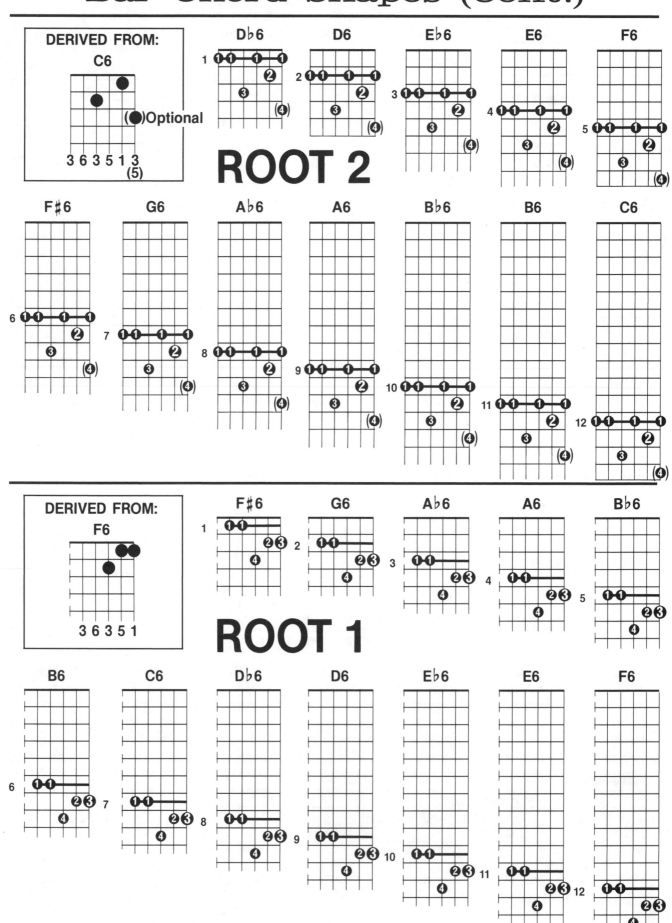

MAJOR SIX

Bar Chord Shapes (Cont.)

6 | 1 3 5 6

MAJOR SIX
Moveable Shapes

| 6 | | **1 3 5 6** |

I6 = VIm7
e.g. C6 = Am7

For any Major Six chord, a minor seven chord based upon the sixth note of the scale may be used e.g. for C6 use Am7 (see page 53).

All moveable chord shapes are shown in first position only but may be moved up the fretboard in the same manner as Bar Chords.

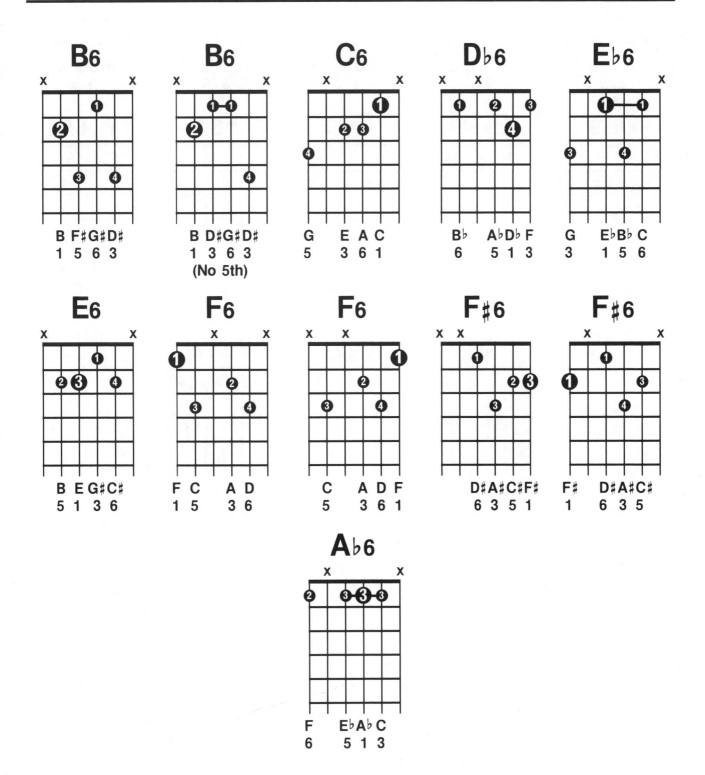

6/9   MAJOR SIX ADD NINE   1 3 5 6 9
Open Chords

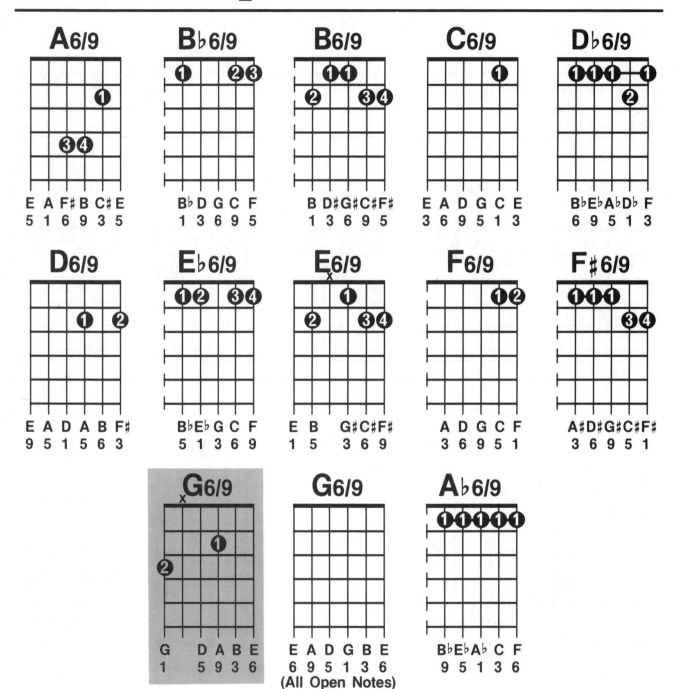

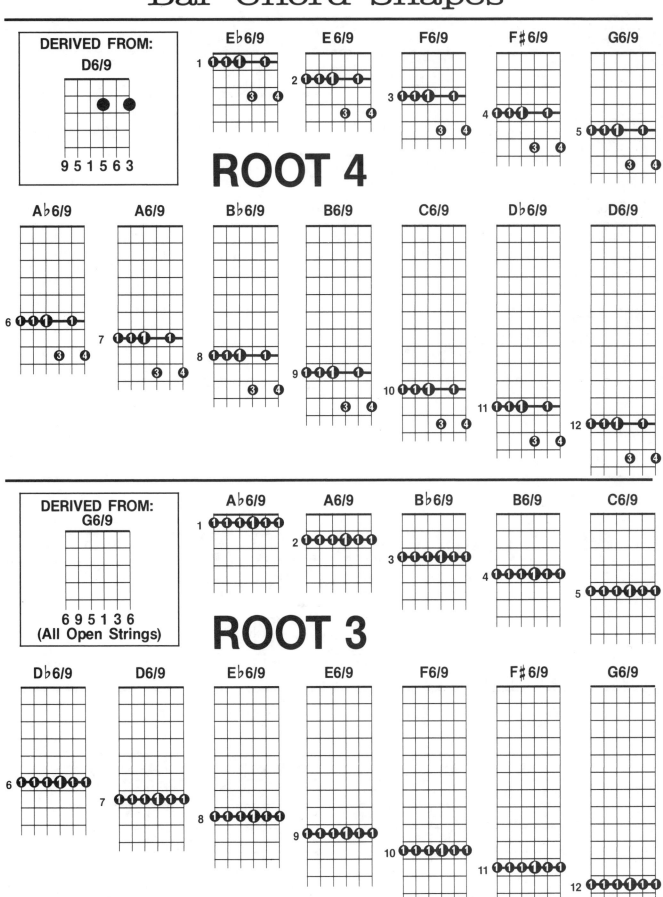

| 6/9 | **MAJOR SIX ADD NINE** | **1 3 5 6 9** |

Bar Chord Shapes (Cont.)

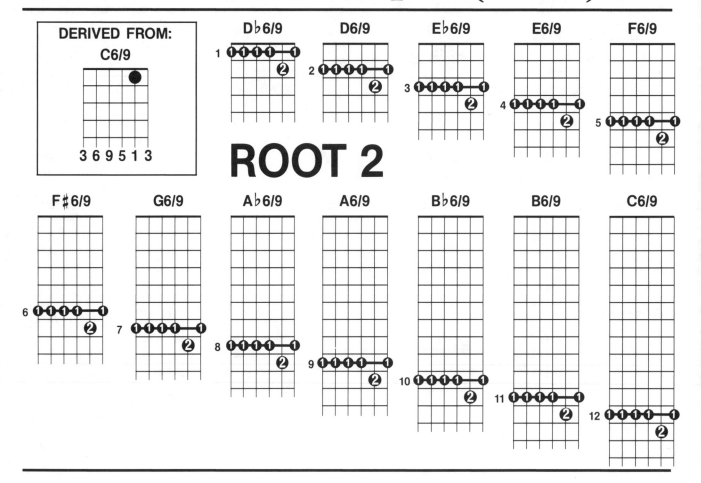

ROOT 2

| 6/9 | **MAJOR SIX ADD NINE** | **1 3 5 6 9** |

Moveable Shapes

$I^{6/9} = II11$ **(No 3rd)**
e.g. $C^{6/9} = D11$ **(No F♯)**

For any Major Six Add Nine chord, an Eleventh chord (without 3rd) based upon the second note of the scale may be used e.g. for C6/9 use D11 (No F♯) (see page 112).

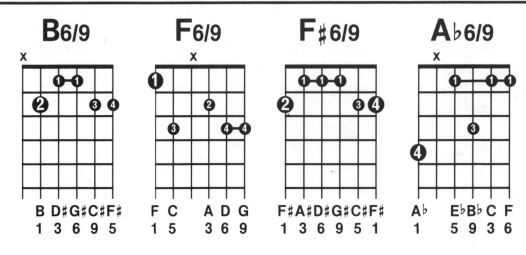

MINOR SIX
Open Chords

m6

1 ♭3 5 6

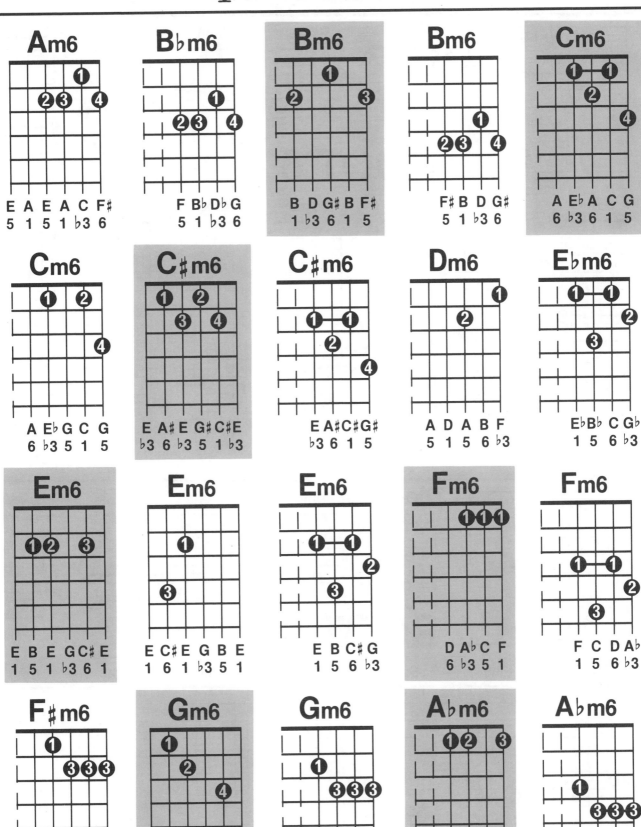

m6

MINOR SIX
Bar Chord Shapes

1 ♭3 5 6

DERIVED FROM:

Em6

1 5 ♭3 6 1

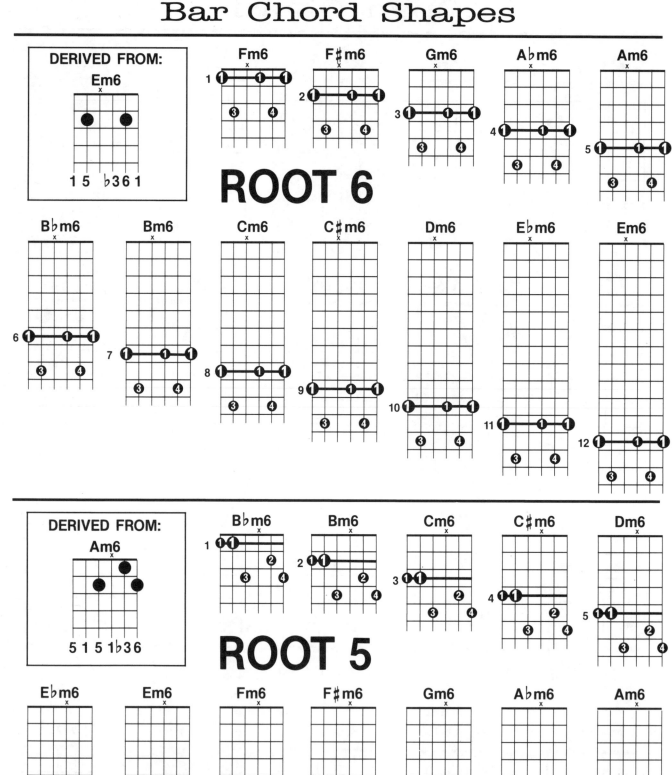

ROOT 6

DERIVED FROM:

Am6

5 1 5 1 ♭3 6

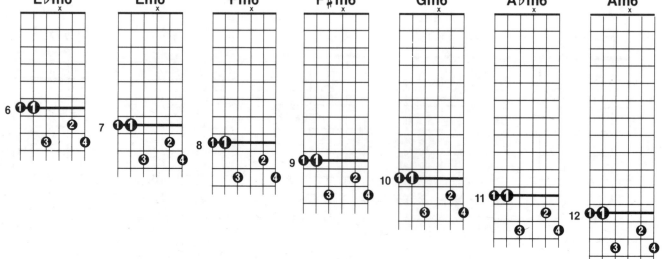

ROOT 5

m6   MINOR SIX   1 ♭3 5 6
Bar Chord Shapes (Cont.)

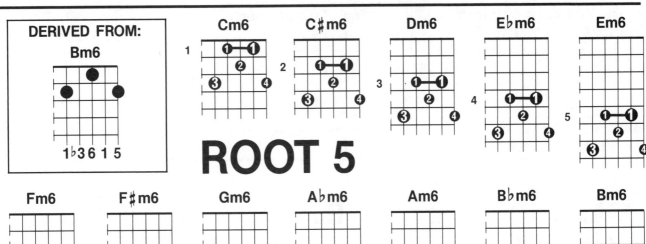

ROOT 5

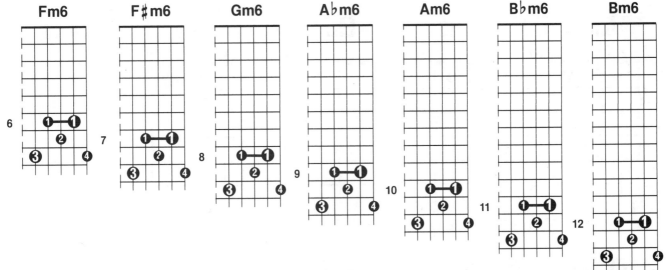

ROOT 4

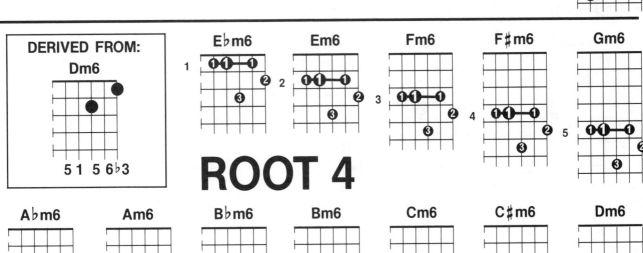

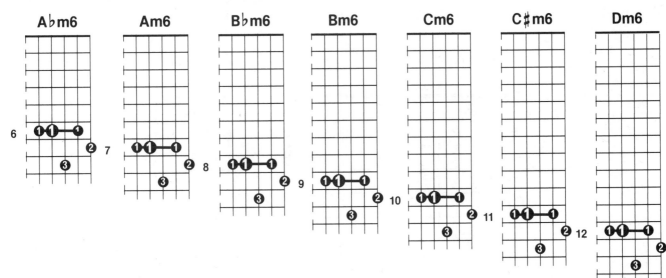

m6　**MINOR SIX**　1 ♭3 5 6
Moveable Shapes

1. | Im6=VII7♯5♭9 (No Root) | e.g. Cm6=B7♯5♭9 (No B)

2. | Im6=IV9 (No Root) | e.g. Cm6=F9 (No F)

3. | Im6=VIm7♭5 | e.g. Cm6=Am7♭5

1. For any m6 chord, a 7♯5♭9 chord (without the root note) based upon the seventh note of the scale may be used e.g. for Cm6 use B7♯5♭9 (No B note) (see page 84).
2. For any m6 chord, a 9 chord (with no root note) based upon the seventh note of the scale may be used e.g. for Cm6 use B7♯5♭9 (No B note) (see page 84).
3. For any m6 chord, a m7♭5 chord based upon the sixth note of the scale may be used e.g. for Cm6 use Am7♭5 (see page 58).

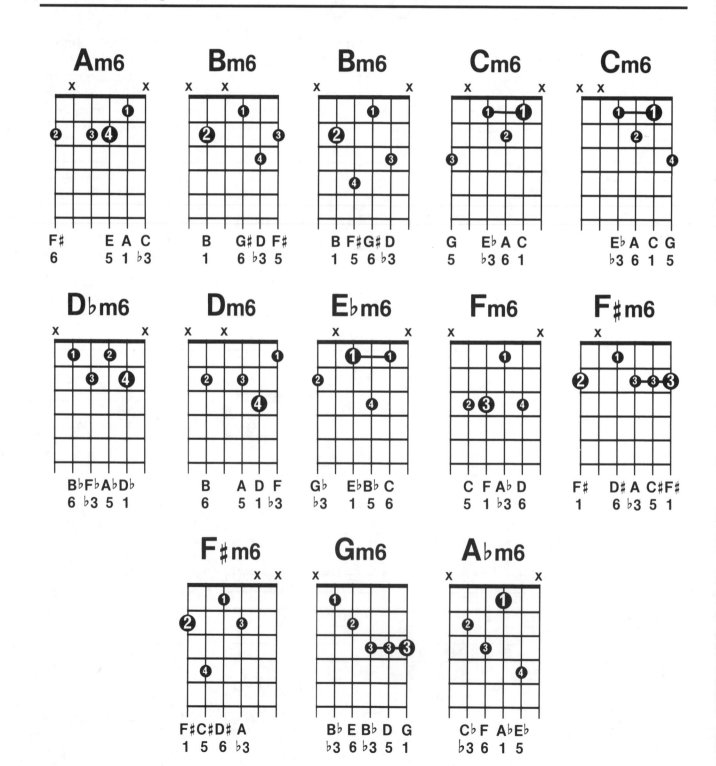

m6/9   MINOR SIX ADD NINE   1♭3569
Open Chords

Am6/9
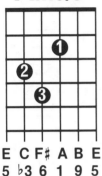

E C F# A B E
5 ♭3 6 1 9 5

B♭m6/9
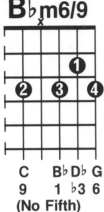

C   B♭D♭ G
9   1 ♭3 6
(No Fifth)

Bm6/9
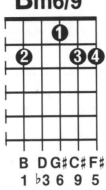

B D G#C# F#
1 ♭3 6 9 5

Cm6/9
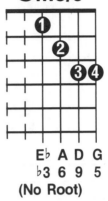

E♭ A D G
♭3 6 9 5
(No Root)

D♭m6/9
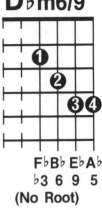

F♭B♭ E♭A♭
♭3 6 9 5
(No Root)

Dm6/9
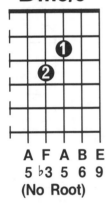

A F A B E
5 ♭3 5 6 9
(No Root)

E♭m6/9
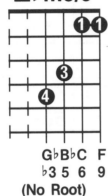

G♭B♭C F
♭3 5 6 9
(No Root)

Em6/9
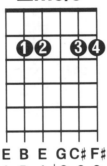

E B E GC# F#
1 5 1 ♭3 6 9

Fm6/9
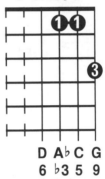

D A♭ C G
6 ♭3 5 9
(No Root)

F#m6/9
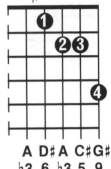

A D# A C#G#
♭3 6 ♭3 5 9
(No Root)

Gm6/9
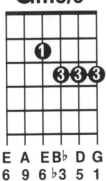

E A EB♭ D G
6 9 6♭3 5 1

A♭m6/9
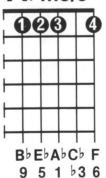

B♭E♭A♭C♭ F
9 5 1 ♭3 6

44

m6/9	**MINOR SIX ADD NINE**	1 ♭3 5 6 9

Bar Chord Shapes

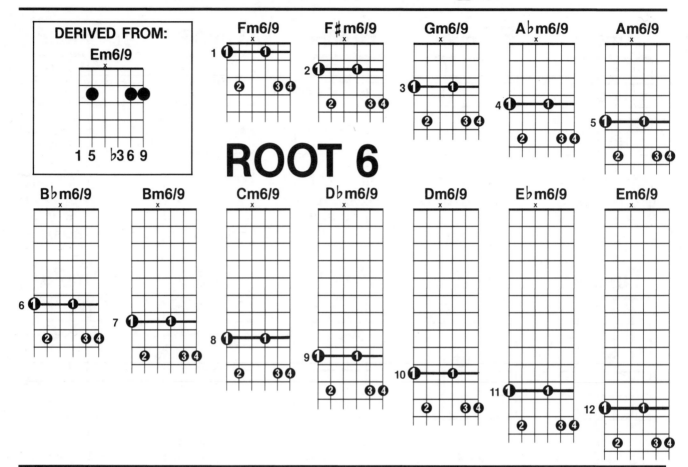

ROOT 6

m6/9	**MINOR SIX ADD NINE**	1 ♭3 6 9

Moveable Shapes

> Im⁶/₉ = IV13 (No Root)
> e.g. Cm⁶/₉ = F13 (No F)

For any Minor Six Add Nine chord, a Thirteenth chord (without root note) based upon the fourth note of the scale may be used e.g. for Cm6/9 use F13 (No F note) (see page 120).
All moveable chord shapes are shown in first position only but may be moved up the fretboard in the same manner as Bar Chords.

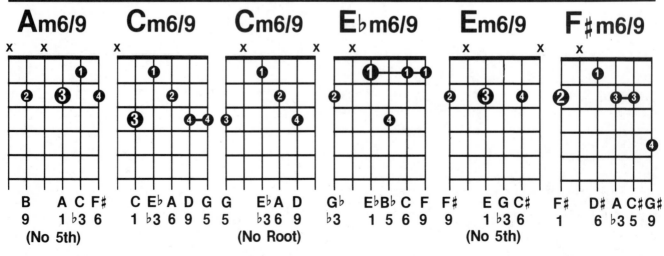

7 DOMINANT SEVEN 1 3 5 ♭7
Open Chords

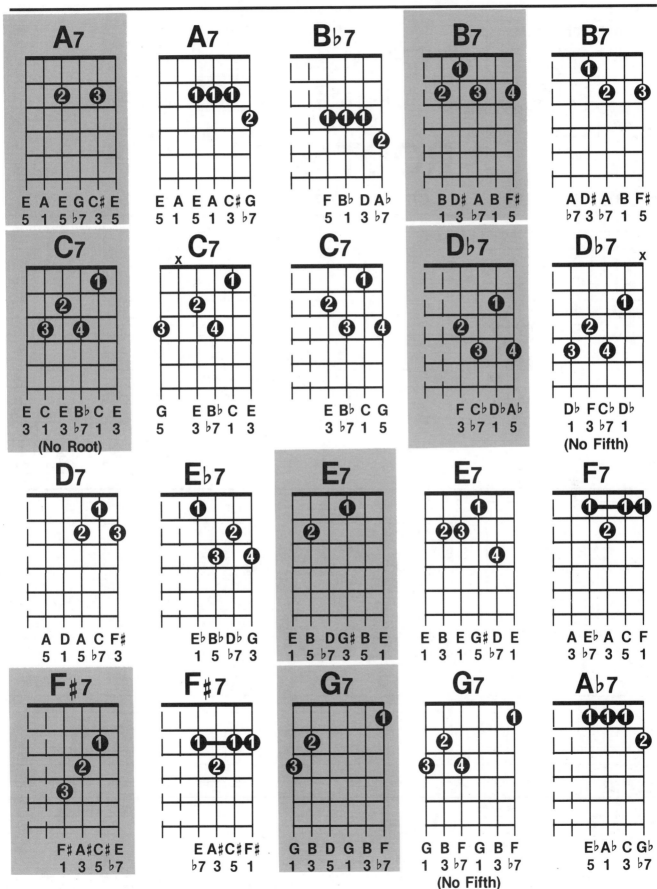

REMEMBER A♯=B♭, C♯=D♭, D♯=E♭, F♯=G♭, G♯=A♭. **SEE ENHARMONICS** on page 138.

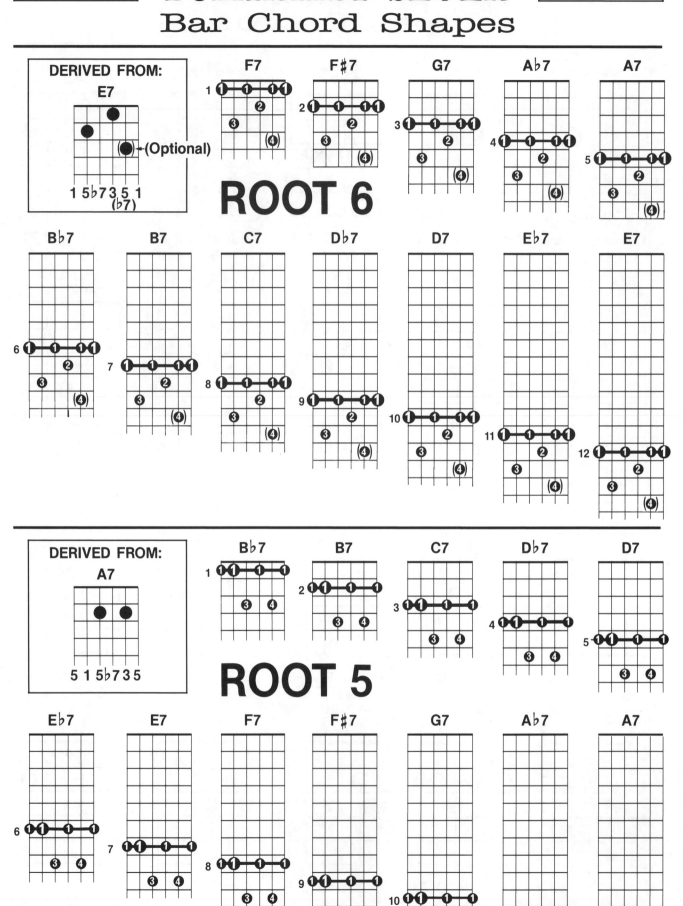

7 DOMINANT SEVEN 1 3 5 ♭7

Bar Chord Shapes (Cont.)

DERIVED FROM:

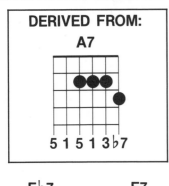

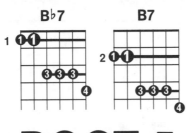

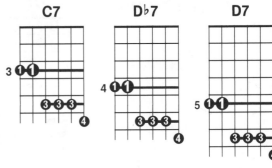

ROOT 5

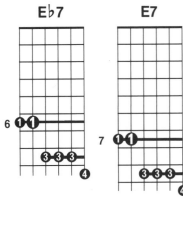

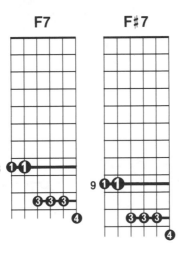

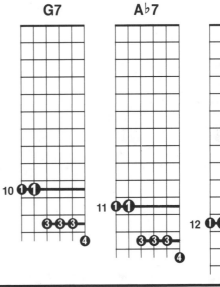

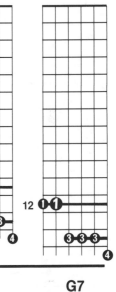

DERIVED FROM:

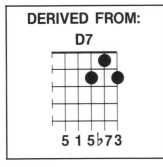

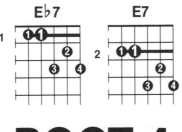

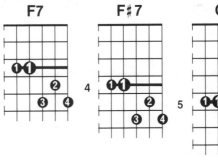

ROOT 4

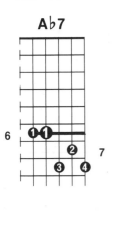

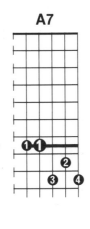

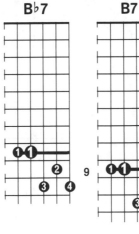

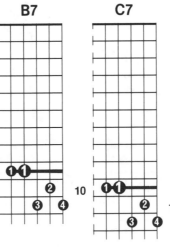

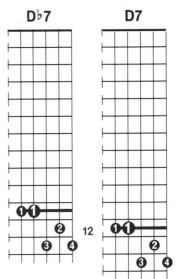

48

7 DOMINANT SEVEN 1 3 5 ♭7
Bar Chord Shapes (Cont.)

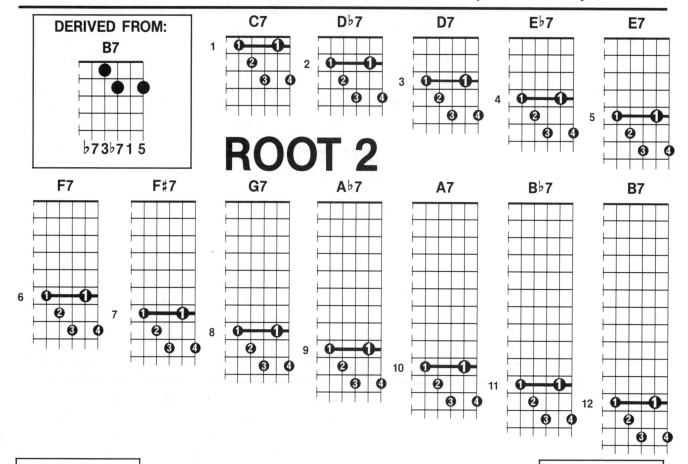

ROOT 2

7 DOMINANT SEVEN 1 3 5 ♭7
Moveable Shapes

All moveable chord shapes are shown in first position only but may be moved up the fretboard in the same manner as Bar Chords.

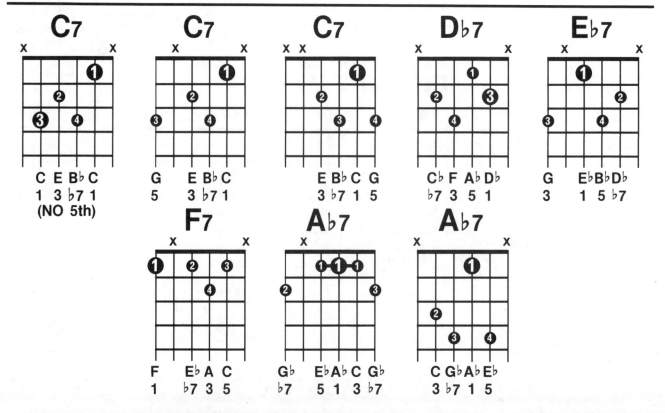

7sus | SEVEN SUSPENEDED | 1 4 5 ♭7
Open Chords

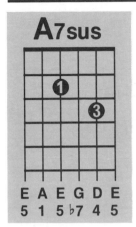
A7sus

E A E G D E
5 1 5 ♭7 4 5

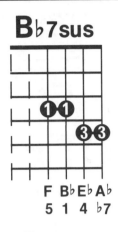
A7sus

E A E A D G
5 1 5 1 4 ♭7

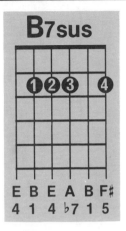
B♭7sus

F B♭ E♭ A♭
5 1 4 ♭7

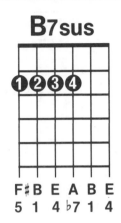
B7sus

E B E A B F♯
4 1 4 ♭7 1 5

B7sus

F♯ B E A B E
5 1 4 ♭7 1 4

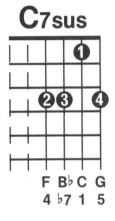
C7sus

F B♭ C G
4 ♭7 1 5

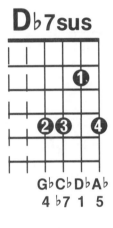
D♭7sus

G♭ C♭ D♭ A♭
4 ♭7 1 5

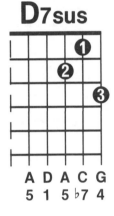
D7sus

A D A C G
5 1 5 ♭7 4

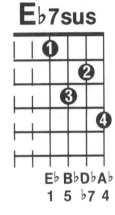
E♭7sus

E♭ B♭ D♭ A♭
1 5 ♭7 4

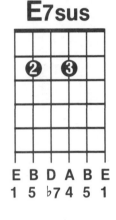
E7sus

E B D A B E
1 5 ♭7 4 5 1

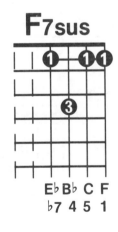
F7sus

E♭ B♭ C F
♭7 4 5 1

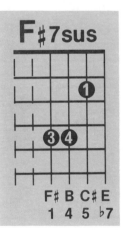
F♯7sus

F♯ B C♯ E
1 4 5 ♭7

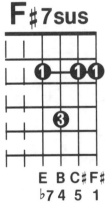
F♯7sus

E B C♯ F♯
♭7 4 5 1

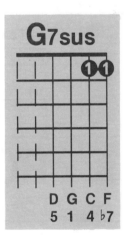
G7sus

D G C F
5 1 4 ♭7

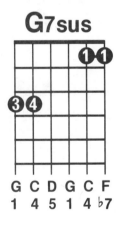
G7sus

G C D G C F
1 4 5 1 4 ♭7

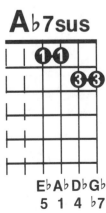
A♭7sus

E♭ A♭ D♭ G♭
5 1 4 ♭7

7sus | SEVEN SUSPENDED | 1 4 5 ♭7
Bar Chord Shapes

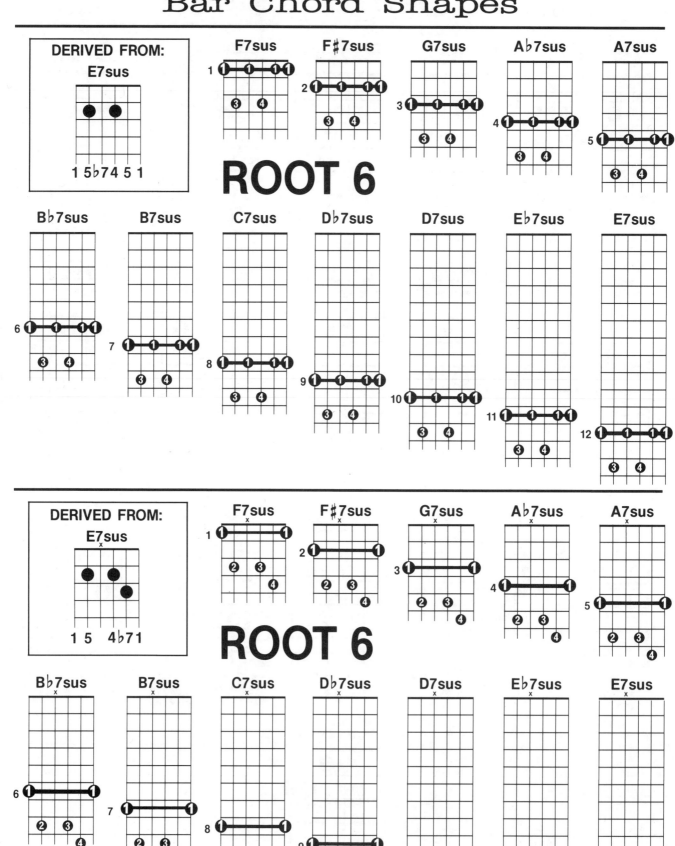

DERIVED FROM:
E7sus
1 5♭74 5 1

F7sus · F♯7sus · G7sus · A♭7sus · A7sus

ROOT 6

B♭7sus · B7sus · C7sus · D♭7sus · D7sus · E♭7sus · E7sus

DERIVED FROM:
E7sus
1 5 4♭71

F7sus · F♯7sus · G7sus · A♭7sus · A7sus

ROOT 6

B♭7sus · B7sus · C7sus · D♭7sus · D7sus · E♭7sus · E7sus

7sus — SEVEN SUSPENDED — 1 4 5 ♭7
Bar Chord Shapes (Cont.)

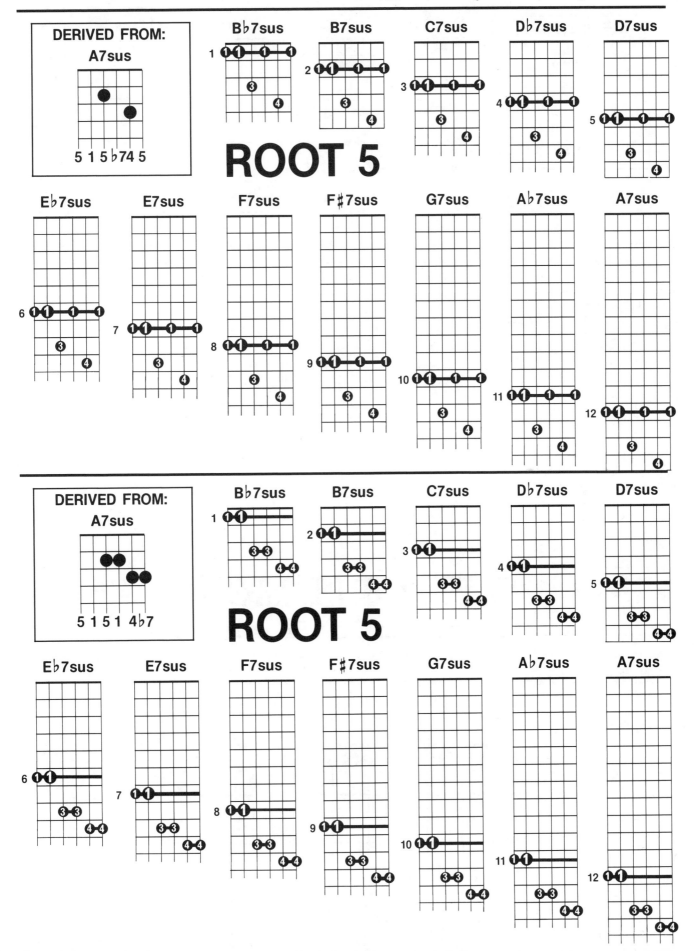

7sus	SEVEN SUSPENDED	1 4 5 ♭7

Bar Chord Shapes

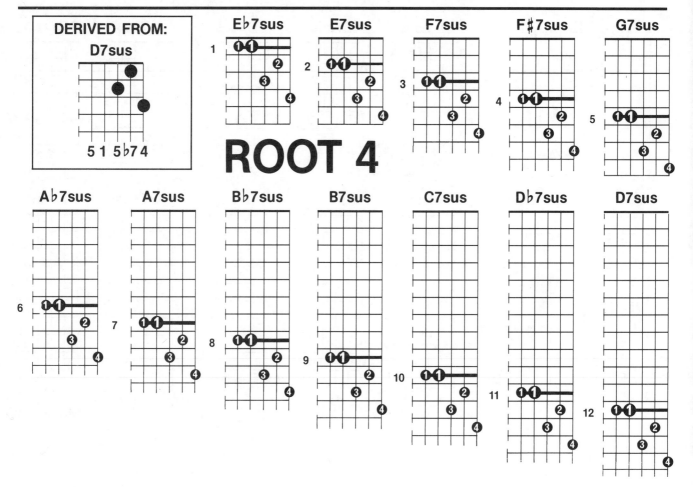

DERIVED FROM: D7sus — 5 1 5 ♭7 4

Eb7sus, E7sus, F7sus, F#7sus, G7sus — **ROOT 4**

Ab7sus, A7sus, Bb7sus, B7sus, C7sus, Db7sus, D7sus

7sus	SEVEN SUSPENDED	1 4 5 ♭7

Moveable Shapes

All moveable chord shapes are shown in first position only but may be moved up the fretboard in the same manner as Bar Chords.

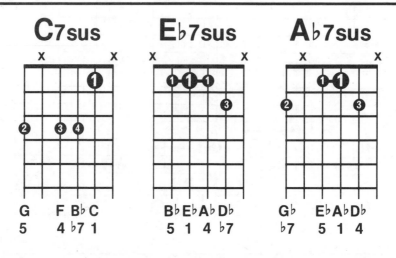

C7sus — G F Bb C / 5 4 ♭7 1

Eb7sus — Bb Eb Ab Db / 5 1 4 ♭7

Ab7sus — Gb Eb Ab Db / ♭7 5 1 4

MINOR SEVEN
Open Chords

m7

1 ♭3 5 ♭7

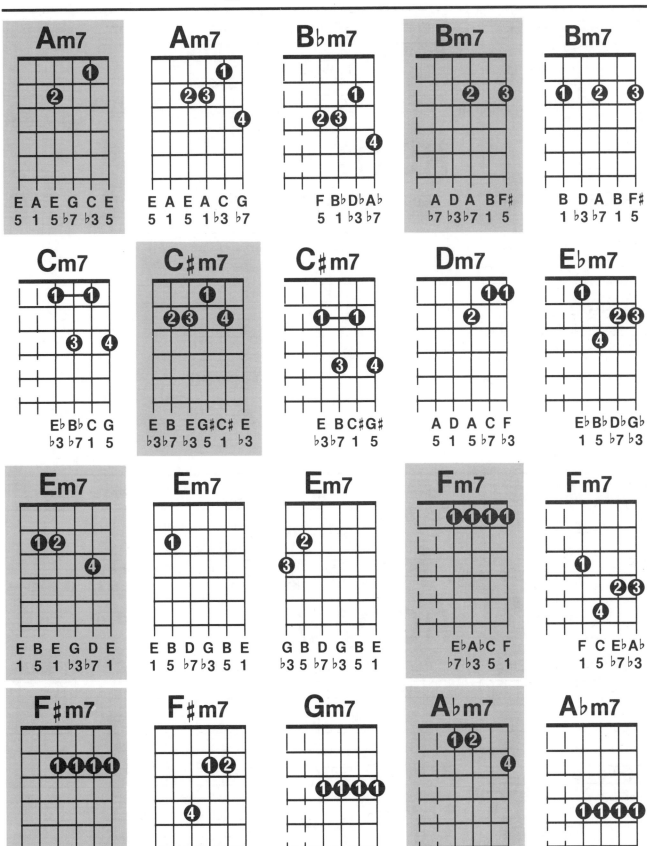

MINOR SEVEN
Bar Chord Shapes

m7

1 b3 5 b7

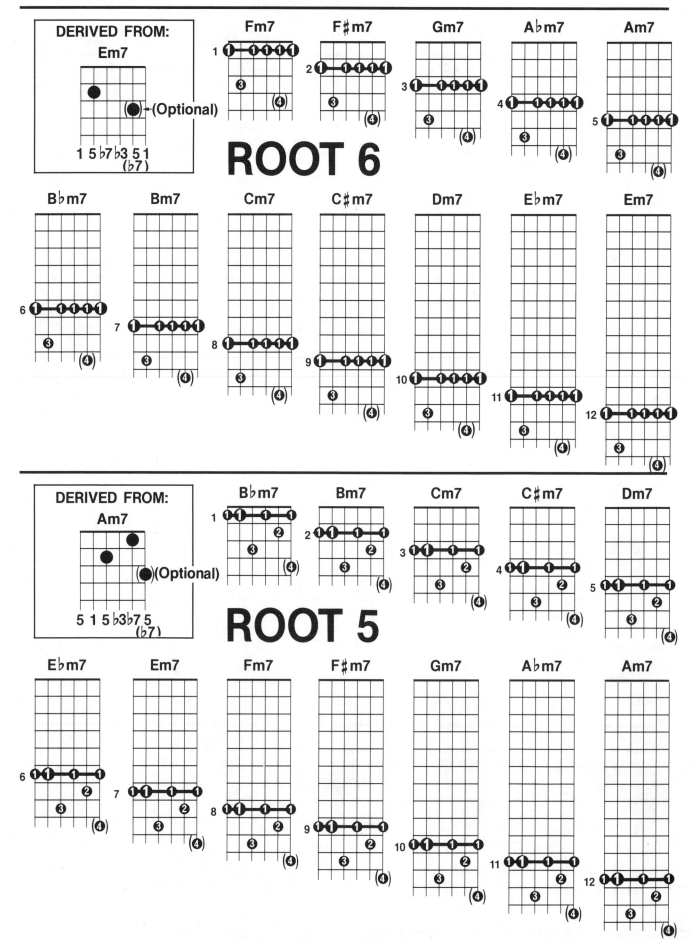

m7 MINOR SEVEN 1♭3 5♭7
Bar Chord Shapes (Cont.)

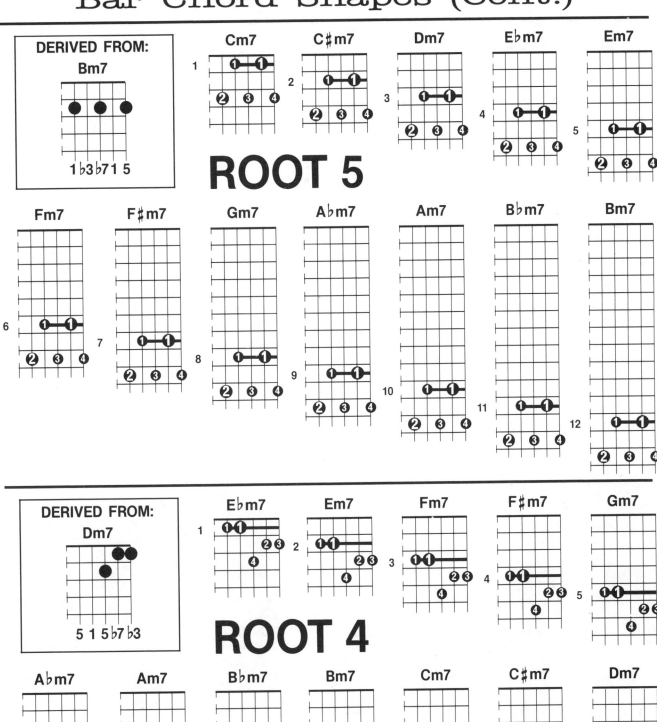

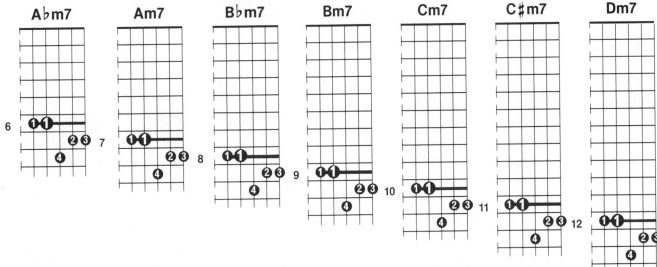

MINOR SEVEN

| m7 | | 1 ♭3 5 ♭7 |

Bar Chord Shapes (Cont.)

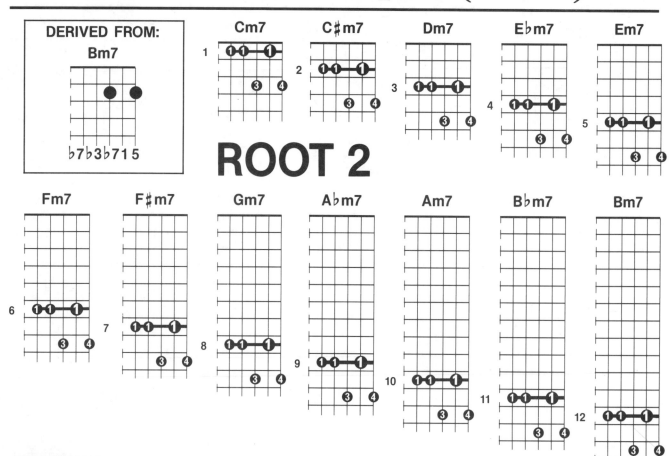

DERIVED FROM: Bm7 — ♭7 ♭3 ♭7 1 5

Cm7, C♯m7, Dm7, E♭m7, Em7

ROOT 2

Fm7, F♯m7, Gm7, A♭m7, Am7, B♭m7, Bm7

THE BEATLES

MINOR SEVEN
Moveable Shapes

| m7 | | 1 ♭3 5 ♭7 |

> Im7 = ♭III6
> **e.g. Cm7 = E♭6**

For any Minor Seven chord, a Major Sixth chord based upon the Flattened Third note of the scale may be used e.g. for Cm7 use E♭6 (see page 31).

All moveable chord shapes are shown in first position only but may be moved up the fretboard in the same manner as Bar Chords.

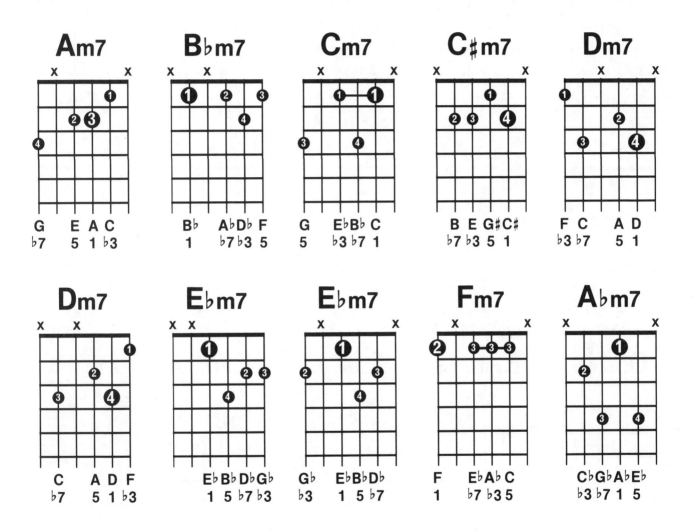

58

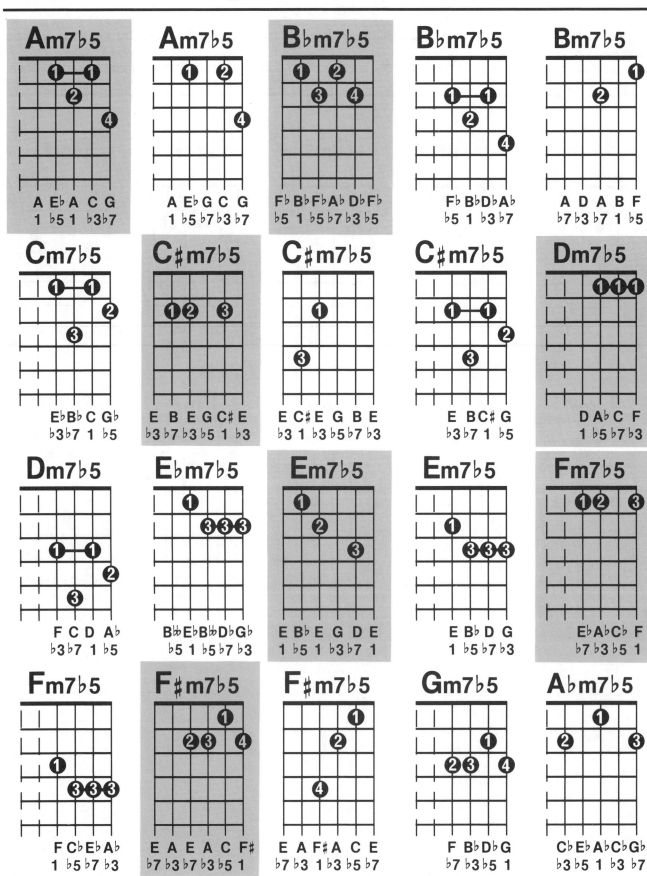

59

m7♭5 | MINOR SEVEN FLAT FIVE | 1♭3♭5♭7
Bar Chord Shapes

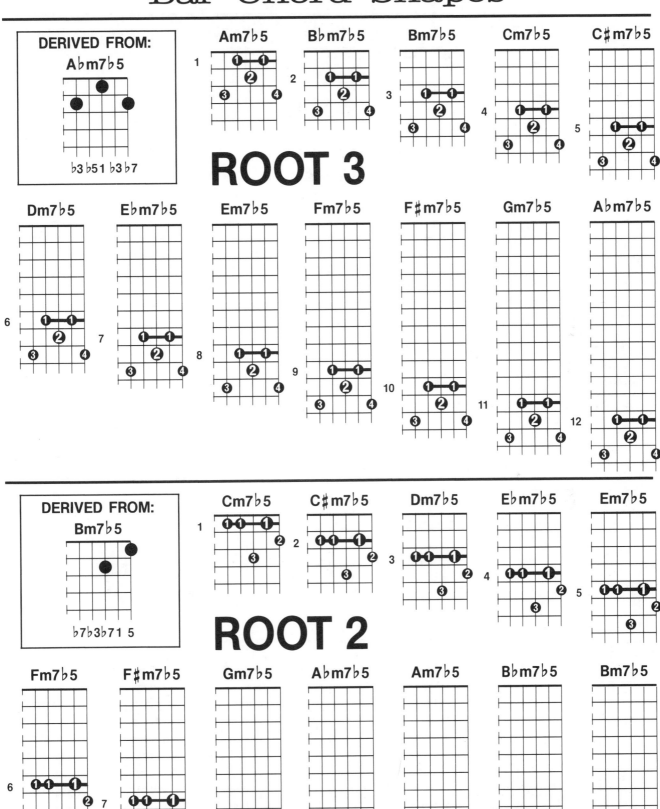

m7b5 MINOR SEVEN FLAT FIVE 1 b3 b5 b7
Bar Chord Shapes (Cont.)

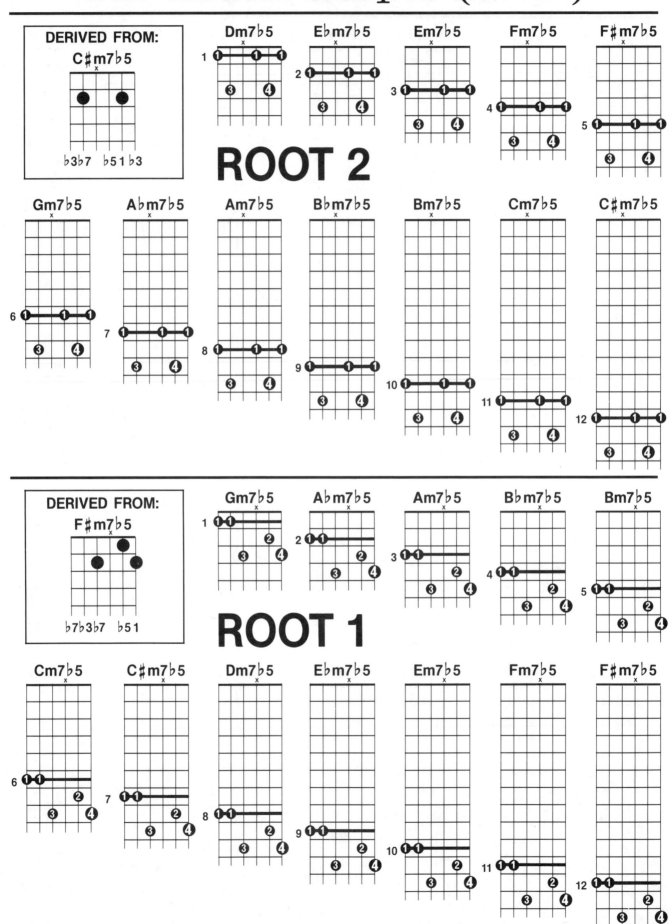

m7♭5 | MINOR SEVEN FLAT FIVE | 1♭3♭5♭7

(Also Called Minor Seventh Diminished Fifth or Half-Diminished Seven)

Moveable Shapes

1.
Im7♭5 = ♭IIIm6
e.g. Cm7♭5 = E♭m6

2.
Im7♭5 = ♭VI9 (No Root)
e.g. Cm7♭5 = A♭9 (No A♭)

1. For any Minor Seven Flat Five chord, a Minor Six chord based upon the Flattened third note of the scale may be used e.g. for Cm7♭5 use E♭m6 (see page 39).

2. For any Minor Seven Flat Five chord, a Ninth chord (with no root) based upon the Flattened Sixth note of the scale may be used e.g. for Cm7♭5 use A♭9 (without A♭ note) (see page 87).

All moveable chord shapes are shown in first position only but may be moved up the fretboard in the same manner as Bar Chords.

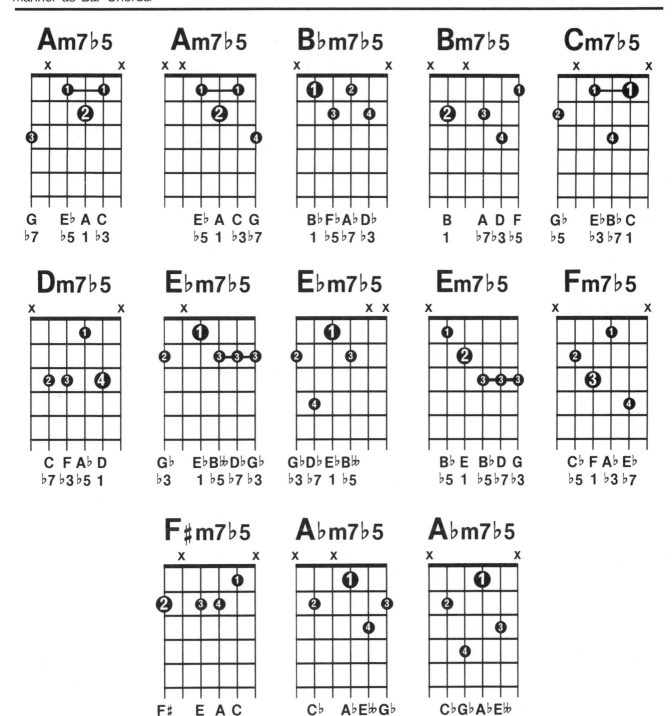

62

° or °7 **DIMINISHED SEVEN** 1♭3♭5♭♭7
(Or Diminished)

Open Chords

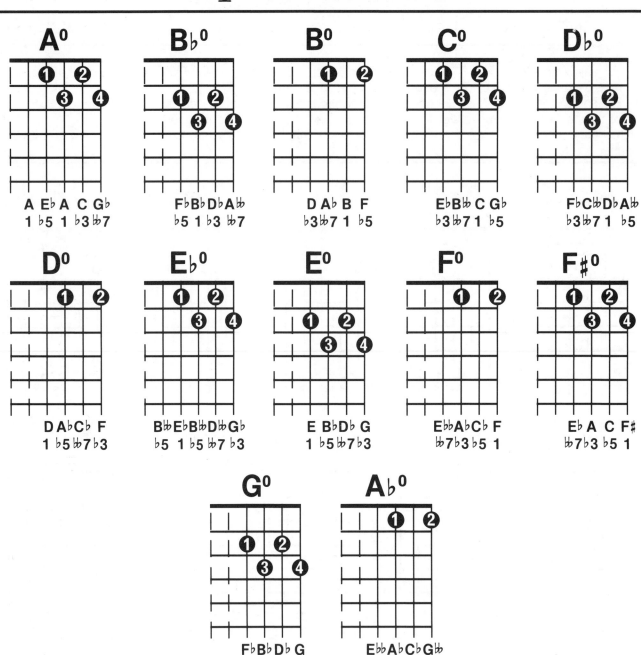

⁰ or ⁰7 — DIMINISHED SEVEN — 1 ♭3 ♭5 ♭♭7
Bar Chord Shapes

In music, the **DIMINISHED SEVEN** chord (1 3♭ 5♭ 7♭♭) is used in place of the **DIMINISHED** chord (1 3♭ 5♭). Each diminished seven chord has 4 different names; the names being taken from each of the 4 notes in the chord.

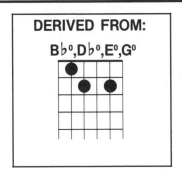

DERIVED FROM: B♭⁰,D♭⁰,E⁰,G⁰

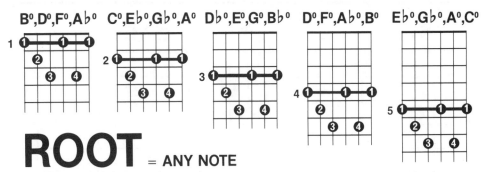

ROOT = ANY NOTE

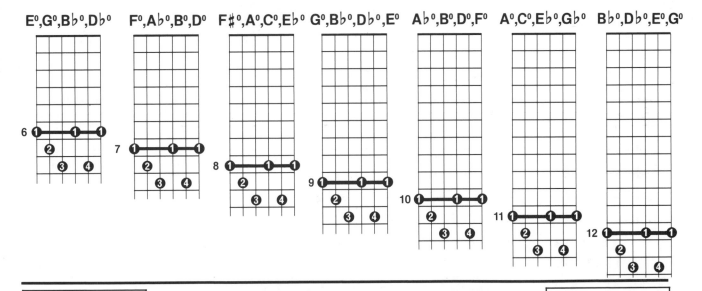

⁰ or ⁰7 — DIMINISHED SEVEN — 1 ♭3 ♭5 ♭♭7
(Or Diminished)
Moveable Shapes

I⁰=VII7♭9 (No Root)
e.g. C⁰=B7♭9 (No B)

For any Diminished Seven chord, a Seven Flat Nine chord (with no Root Note) based upon the Seventh note of the scale may be used e.g. for C⁰ use B7♭9 (No B note) (see page 81).
All moveable chord shapes are shown in first position only but may be moved up the fretboard in the same manner as Bar Chords.

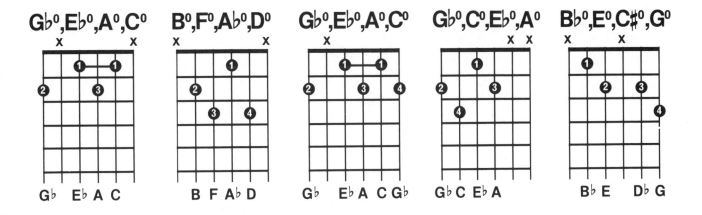

64

7#5 | SEVEN SHARP FIVE | 13#5b7
(Or Seven Augmented Five)

Open Chords

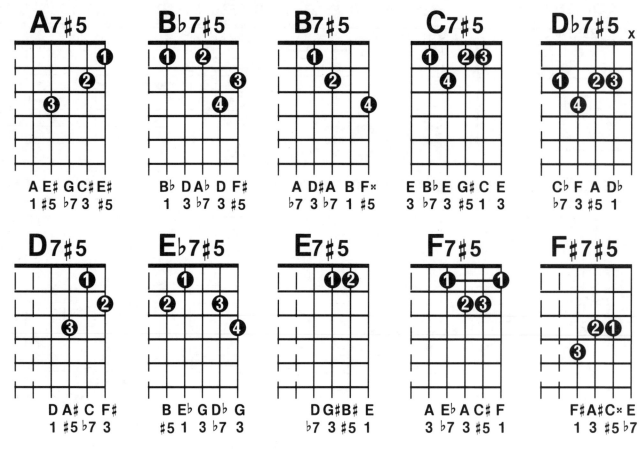

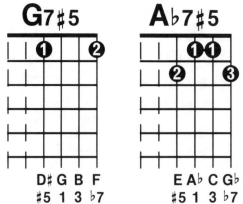

SEVEN SHARP FIVE

7#5

13#5b7

Bar Chord Shapes

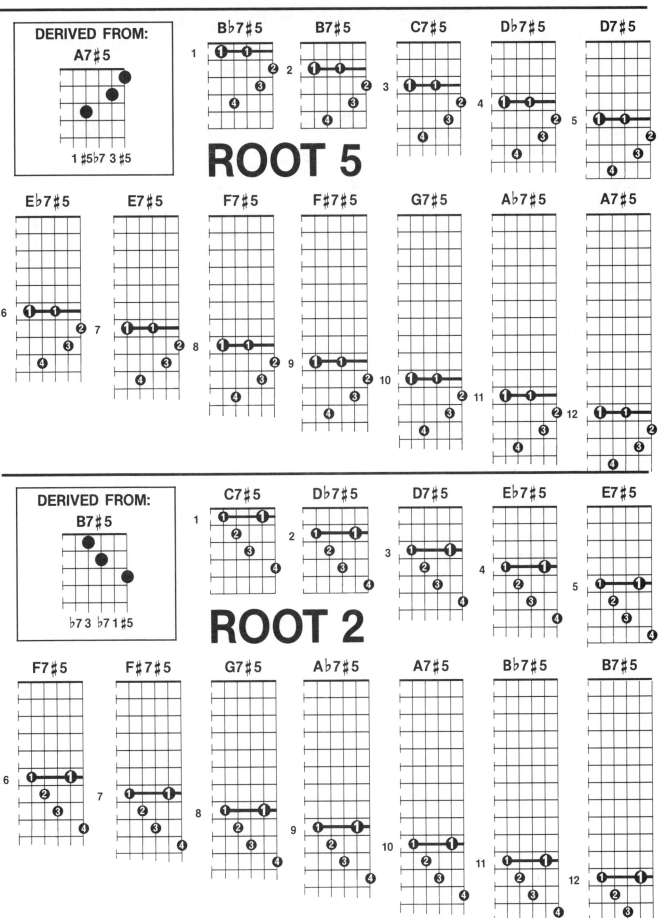

DERIVED FROM:
A7#5
1 #5b7 3 #5

ROOT 5

Bb7#5 · B7#5 · C7#5 · Db7#5 · D7#5
Eb7#5 · E7#5 · F7#5 · F#7#5 · G7#5 · Ab7#5 · A7#5

DERIVED FROM:
B7#5
b73 b71 #5

ROOT 2

C7#5 · Db7#5 · D7#5 · Eb7#5 · E7#5
F7#5 · F#7#5 · G7#5 · Ab7#5 · A7#5 · Bb7#5 · B7#5

7♯5 · SEVEN SHARP FIVE · 1 3 ♯5 ♭7

(Or Seven Augmented Five)

Moveable Shapes

All moveable chord shapes are shown in first position only but may be moved up the fretboard in the same manner as Bar Chords.

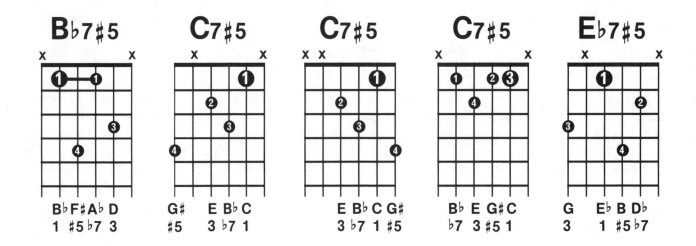

B♭7♯5
B♭ F♯ A♭ D
1 ♯5 ♭7 3

C7♯5
G♯   E B♭ C
♯5   3 ♭7 1

C7♯5
E B♭ C G♯
3 ♭7 1 ♯5

C7♯5
B♭ E G♯ C
♭7 3 ♯5 1

E♭7♯5
G   E♭ B D♭
3   1 ♯5 ♭7

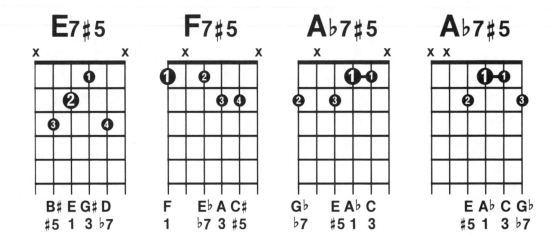

E7♯5
B♯ E G♯ D
♯5 1 3 ♭7

F7♯5
F   E♭ A C♯
1   ♭7 3 ♯5

A♭7♯5
G♭   E A♭ C
♭7   ♯5 1 3

A♭7♯5
E A♭ C G♭
♯5 1 3 ♭7

SEVEN FLAT FIVE

7♭5   1 3 ♭5 ♭7

(Or Seven Diminished Five)

Open Chords

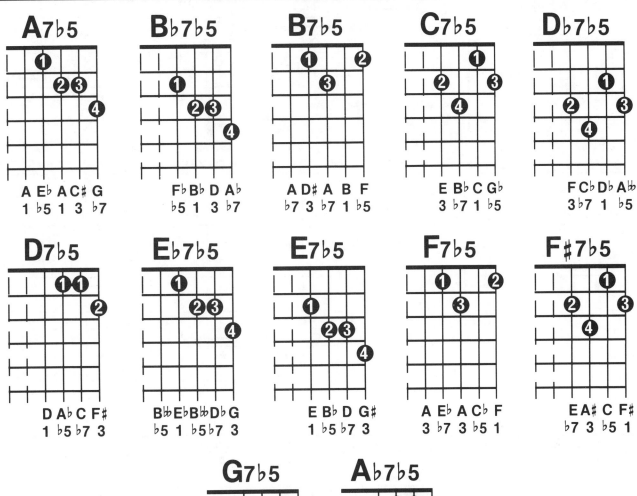

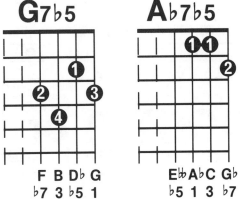

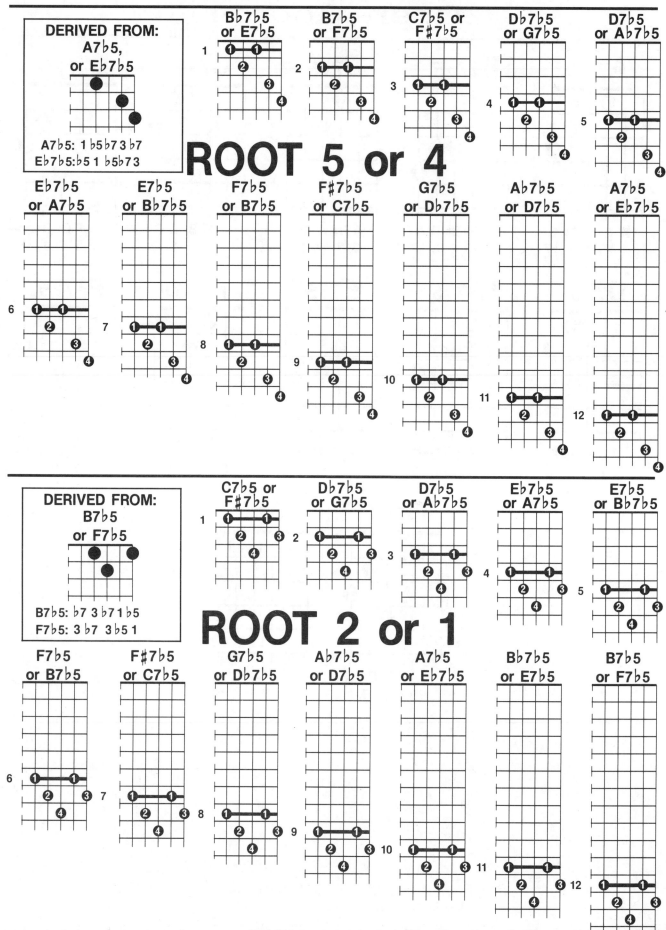

$7\flat5$ SEVEN FLAT FIVE $1\ 3\ \flat5\ \flat7$
(Or Seven Diminished Five)

Moveable Shapes

1.

$I7\flat5 = II9\sharp5$ (No Root)
e.g. $C7\flat5 = D9\sharp5$ (No D)

2.

$I7\flat5 = \flat V7\flat5$
e.g. $C7\flat5 = G\flat7\flat5$

1. For any Seven Flat Five chord, a Nine Sharp Five (without root note) chord based upon the Second note of the scale may be used e.g. for $C7\flat5$ use $D9\sharp5$ (No D note) (see page 94).

2. For any Seven Flat Five chord, a Seven Flat Five chord based upon the flattened fifth note of the scale may be used e.g. for $C7\flat5$ use $G\flat7\flat5$ (see page 67).

All moveable chord shapes are shown in first position only but may be moved up the fretboard in the same manner as Bar Chords.

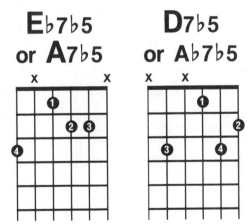

maj7   MAJOR SEVEN   1 3 5 7
Open Chords

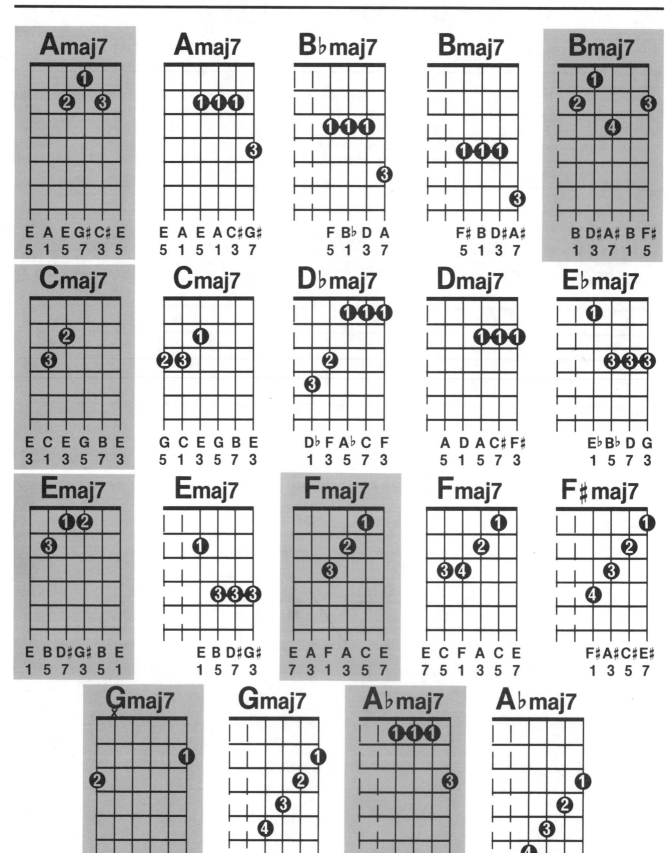

MAJOR SEVEN
Bar Chord Shapes

maj7   1 3 5 7

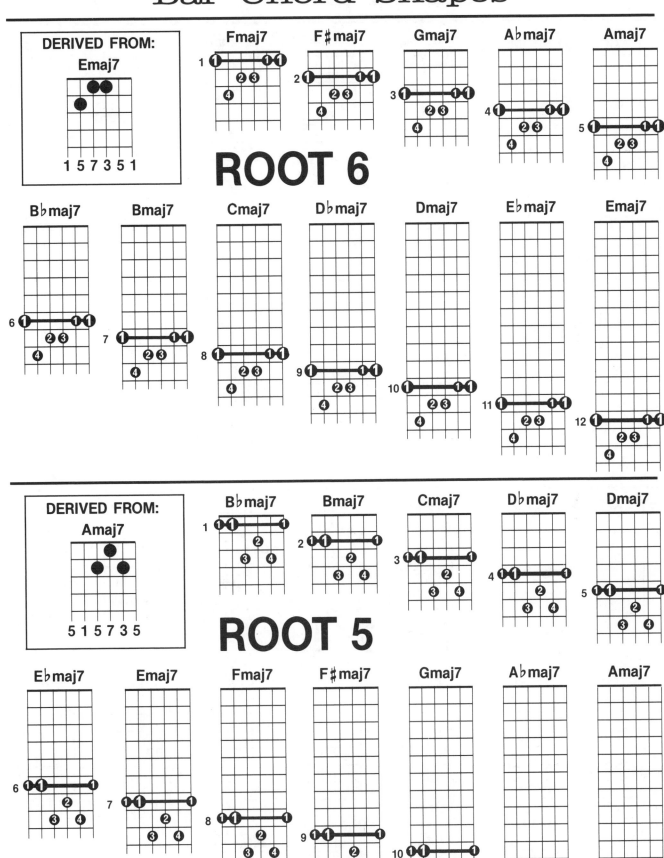

DERIVED FROM: Emaj7 — 1 5 7 3 5 1

ROOT 6

DERIVED FROM: Amaj7 — 5 1 5 7 3 5

ROOT 5

maj7 — MAJOR SEVEN — 1 3 5 7
Bar Chord Shapes(cont.)

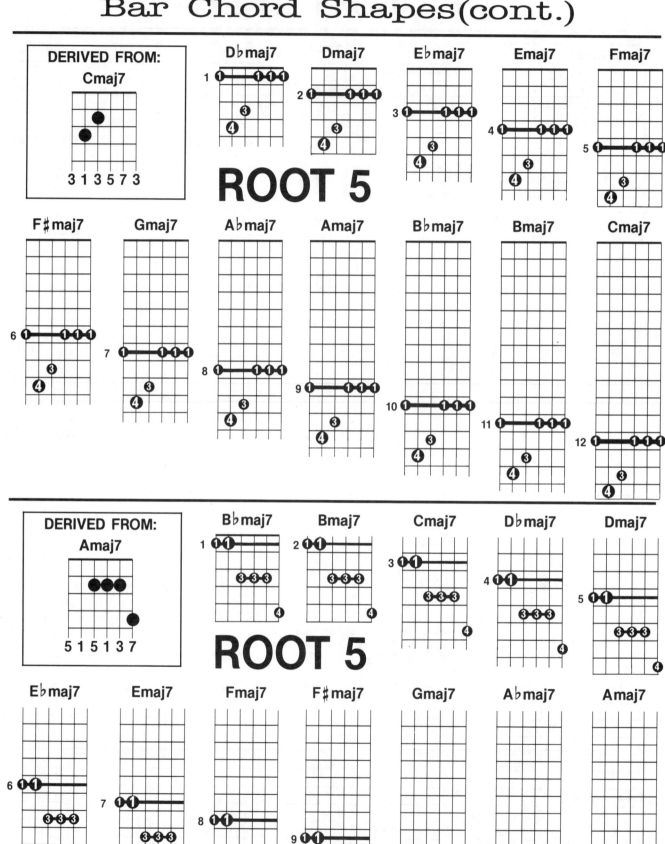

MAJOR SEVEN

maj7   1 3 5 7

Bar Chord Shapes (Cont.)

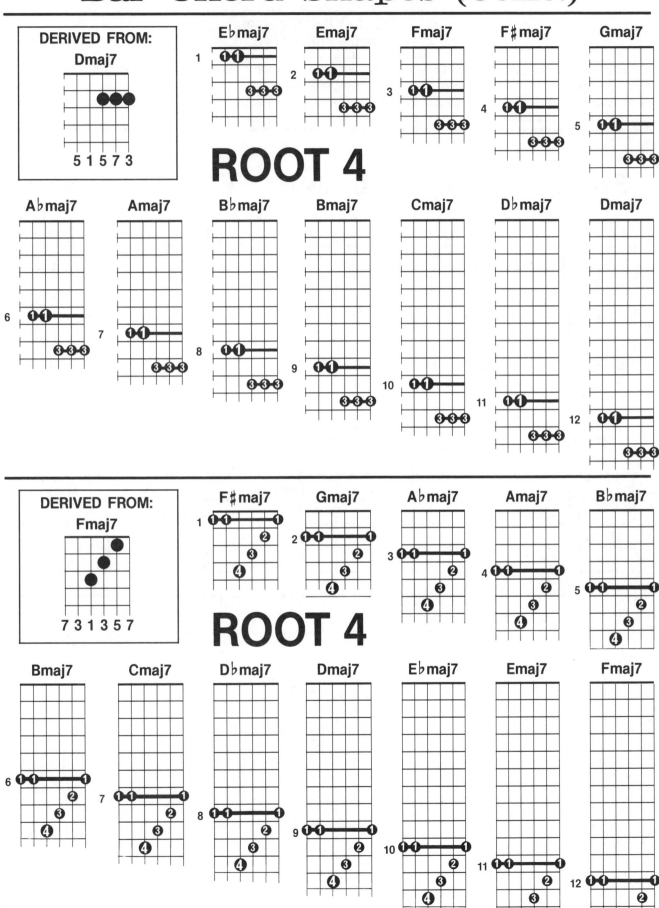

maj7

MAJOR SEVEN
Moveable Shapes

1 3 5 7

Imaj7 = VIm9 (No Root)
e.g. Cmaj7 = Am9 (No A)

For any Major Seven chord, a Minor Nine chord (with no root note) based upon the sixth note of the scale may be used e.g. for Cmaj7 use Am9 (No A note) (see page 91).
All moveable chord shapes are shown in first position only but may be moved up the fretboard in the same manner as Bar Chords.

B♭maj7
```
x           x
● 1
    ● 2
  ● 3   ● 4
```
B♭ F A D
1 5 7 3

D♭maj7
```
x           x
        ● 1
            ● 2
  ● 3 ● 4
```
C F A♭ D♭
7 3 5 1

D♭maj7
```
x           x
    ● 1─● 1
      ● 3
  ● 4
```
D♭ F A♭ C
1 3 5 7

E♭maj7
```
x           x
      ● 1
  ● 2     ● 3 ● 4
```
G   E♭ B♭ D
3   1 5 7

Emaj7
```
x
        ● 1
  ● 2 ● 3
          ● 4─● 4
```
B E G♯ D♯ G♯
5 1 3 7 3

Fmaj7
```
      x
● 1
    ● 2
  ● 3
          ● 4─● 4
```
F C   A E A
1 5   3 7 3

Fmaj7
```
      x           x
● 1         ● 2
      ● 3 ● 4
```
F   E A C
1   7 3 5

Fmaj7
```
x
              ● 1─● 1
      ● 2 ● 3
  ● 4
```
C E A C F
5 7 3 5 1

F♯maj7
```
x x
                ● 1
          ● 2
      ● 3
  ● 4
```
F♯ A♯ C♯ E♯
1 3 5 7

A♭maj7
```
          x
      ● 1─● 1─● 1
  ● 3           ● 4
```
G E♭ A♭ C G
7 5 1 3 7

A♭maj7
```
x   x
        ● 1
    ● 2       ● 3
        ● 4
```
C A♭ E♭ G
3 1 5 7

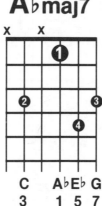

m(maj7) MINOR MAJOR SEVEN 1 ♭3 5 7
(or Minor Sharp Seven)

Open Chords

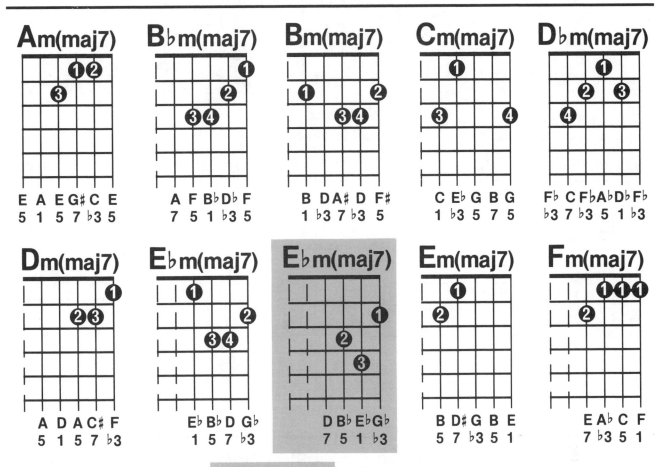

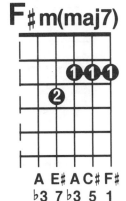 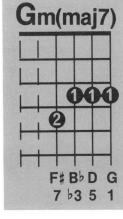 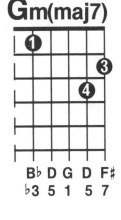 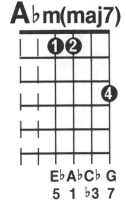

m(maj7) MINOR MAJOR SEVEN 1 ♭3 5 7
(or Minor Sharp Seven)
Bar Chord Shapes

DERIVED FROM:

Em(maj7)

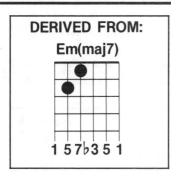

1 5 7 ♭3 5 1

Fm(maj7) · F#m(maj7) · Gm(maj7) · A♭m(maj7) · Am(maj7)

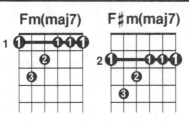 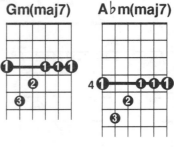 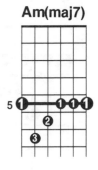

ROOT 6

B♭m(maj7) · Bm(maj7) · Cm(maj7) · D♭m(maj7) · Dm(maj7) · E♭m(maj7) · Em(maj7)

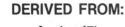

 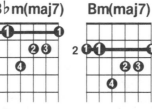 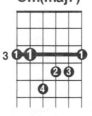 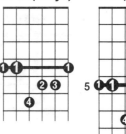 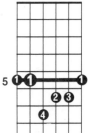

DERIVED FROM:

Am(maj7)

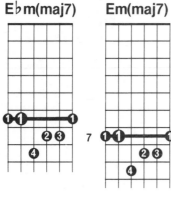

5 1 5 7 ♭3 5

B♭m(maj7) · Bm(maj7) · Cm(maj7) · D♭m(maj7) · Dm(maj7)

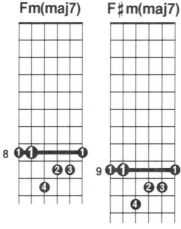 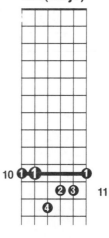 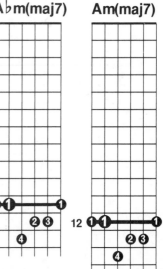

ROOT 5

E♭m(maj7) · Em(maj7) · Fm(maj7) · F#m(maj7) · Gm(maj7) · A♭m(maj7) · Am(maj7)

m(maj7) MINOR MAJOR SEVEN | 1 ♭3 5 7
(or Minor Sharp Seven)
Bar Chord Shapes (Cont.)

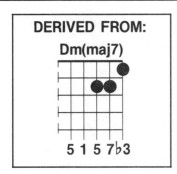

DERIVED FROM:

Dm(maj7)

5 1 5 7♭3

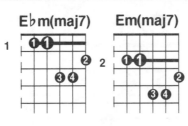

E♭m(maj7)   Em(maj7)

ROOT 4

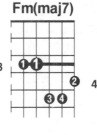

Fm(maj7)

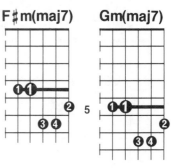

F♯m(maj7)   Gm(maj7)

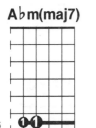

A♭m(maj7)

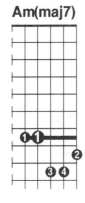

Am(maj7)

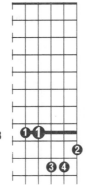

B♭m(maj7)

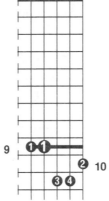

Bm(maj7)

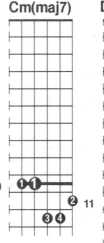

Cm(maj7)

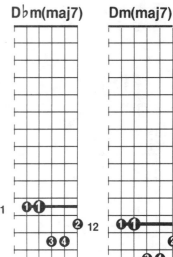

D♭m(maj7)   Dm(maj7)

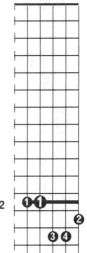

---

m(maj7) MINOR MAJOR SEVEN | 1 ♭3 5 7
(or Minor Sharp Seven)
Moveable Shapes

All moveable chord shapes are shown in first position only but may be moved up the fretboard in the same manner as Bar Chords.

B♭m(maj7)

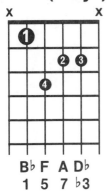

B♭ F A D♭
1 5 7 ♭3

Cm(maj7)

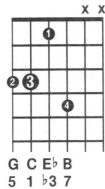

G C E♭ B
5 1 ♭3 7

D♭m(maj7)

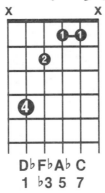

D♭ F♭ A♭ C
1 ♭3 5 7

E♭m(maj7)

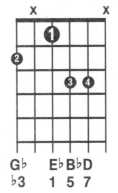

G♭   E♭ B♭ D
♭3   1 5 7

Fm(maj7)

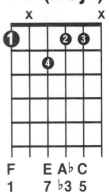

F   E A♭ C
1   7 ♭3 5

78

7♯9 SEVEN SHARP NINE 135♭7♯9
Open Chords

A7♯9

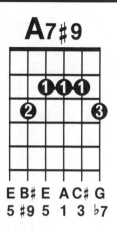

E B♯ E A C♯ G
5 ♯9 5 1 3 ♭7

B♭7♯9

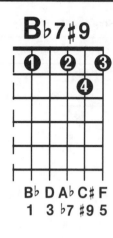

B♭ D A♭ C♯ F
1 3 ♭7 ♯9 5

B7♯9 x

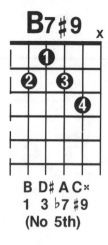

B D♯ A C×
1 3 ♭7 ♯9
(No 5th)

C7♯9 x

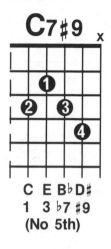

C E B♭ D♯
1 3 ♭7 ♯9
(No 5th)

D♭7♯9

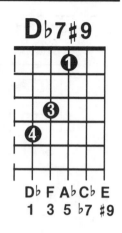

D♭ F A♭ C♭ E
1 3 5 ♭7 ♯9

D7♯9

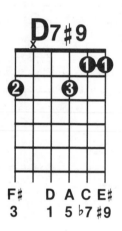

F♯ D A C E♯
3   1 5 ♭7 ♯9

E♭7♯9

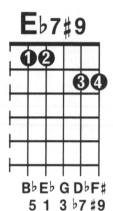

B♭ E♭ G D♭ F♯
5 1 3 ♭7 ♯9

E7♯9

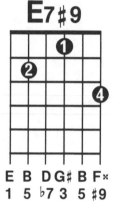

E B D G♯ B F×
1 5 ♭7 3 5 ♯9

F7♯9

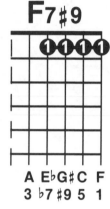

A E♭ G♯ C F
3 ♭7 ♯9 5 1

F♯7♯9

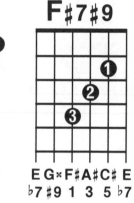

E G× F♯ A♯ C♯ E
♭7 ♯9 1 3 5 ♭7

G7♯9

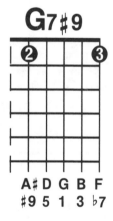

A♯ D G B F
♯9 5 1 3 ♭7

A♭7♯9

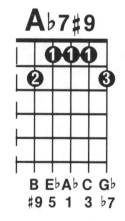

B E♭ A♭ C G♭
♯9 5 1 3 ♭7

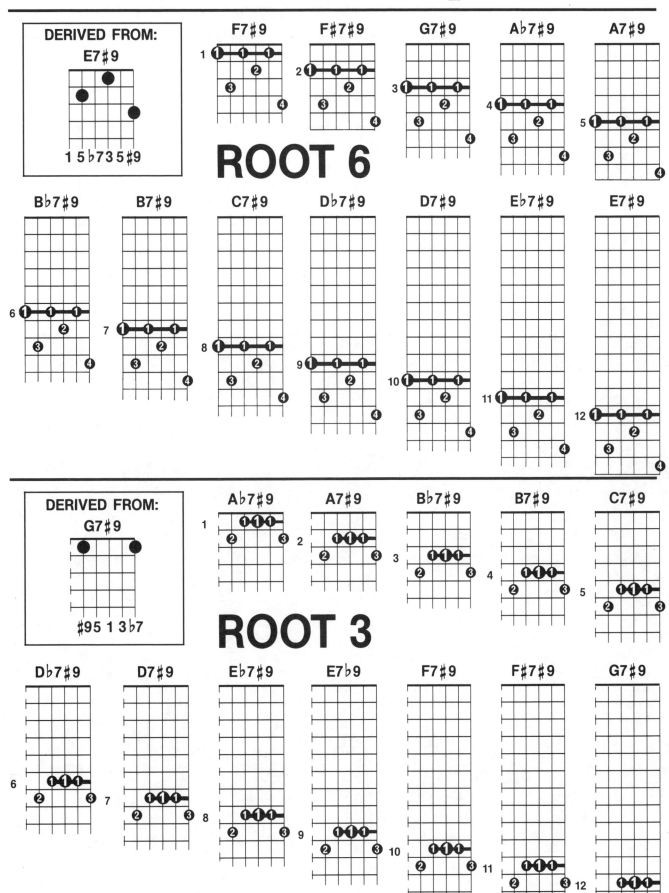

7♯9 | SEVEN SHARP NINE | 1 3 5 ♭7 ♯9
Moveable Shapes

All moveable chord shapes are shown in first position only but may be moved up the fretboard in the same manner as Bar Chords.

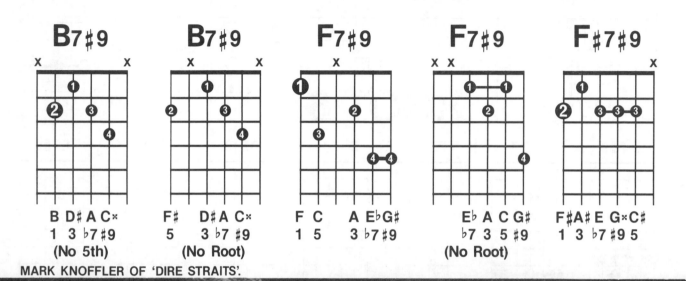

B7♯9

B D♯ A C✕
1 3 ♭7 ♯9
(No 5th)

B7♯9

F♯ D♯ A C✕
5 3 ♭7 ♯9
(No Root)

F7♯9

F C A E♭G♯
1 5 3 ♭7 ♯9

F7♯9

E♭ A C G♯
♭7 3 5 ♯9
(No Root)

F♯7♯9

F♯A♯ E G✕C♯
1 3 ♭7 ♯9 5

MARK KNOFFLER OF 'DIRE STRAITS'.

7♭9 | SEVEN FLAT NINE | 135♭7♭9
Open Chords

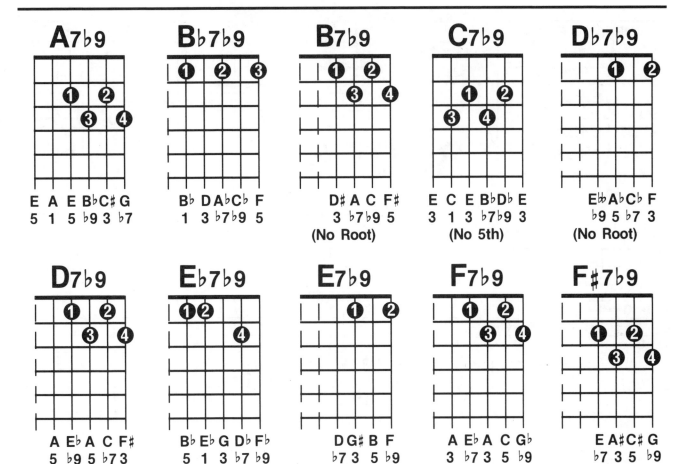

A7♭9

E A E B♭C♯ G
5 1 5 ♭9 3 ♭7

B♭7♭9

B♭ D A♭ C♭ F
1 3 ♭7 ♭9 5

B7♭9

D♯ A C F♯
3 ♭7 ♭9 5
(No Root)

C7♭9

E C E B♭ D♭ E
3 1 3 ♭7 ♭9 3
(No 5th)

D♭7♭9

E♭♭ A♭ C♭ F
♭9 5 ♭7 3
(No Root)

D7♭9

A E♭ A C F♯
5 ♭9 5 ♭7 3
(No Root)

E♭7♭9

B♭ E♭ G D♭ F♭
5 1 3 ♭7 ♭9

E7♭9

D G♯ B F
♭7 3 5 ♭9
(No Root)

F7♭9

A E♭ A C G♭
3 ♭7 3 5 ♭9
(No Root)

F♯7♭9

E A♯ C♯ G
♭7 3 5 ♭9
(No Root)

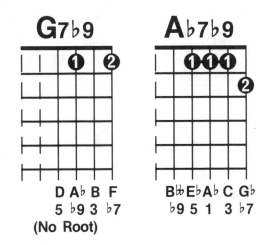

G7♭9

D A♭ B F
5 ♭9 3 ♭7
(No Root)

A♭7♭9

B♭♭ E♭ A♭ C G♭
♭9 5 1 3 ♭7

7♭9   SEVEN FLAT NINE   1 3 5 ♭7 ♭9
Bar Chord Shapes

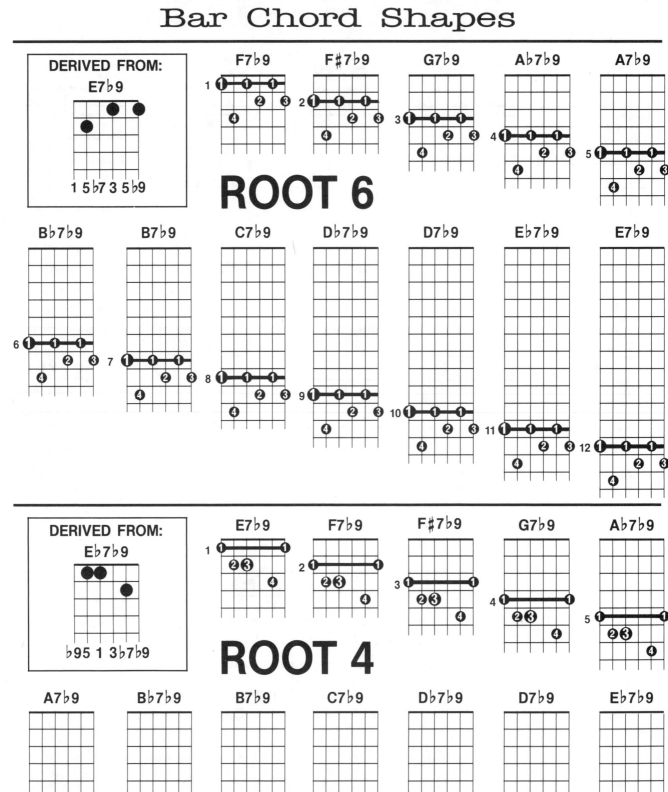

DERIVED FROM:
E7♭9

1 5♭7 3 5♭9

F7♭9 F#7♭9 G7♭9 A♭7♭9 A7♭9

ROOT 6

B♭7♭9 B7♭9 C7♭9 D♭7♭9 D7♭9 E♭7♭9 E7♭9

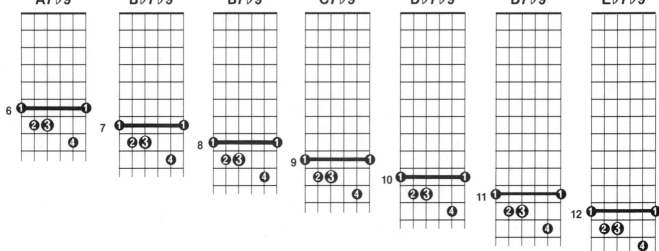

DERIVED FROM:
E♭7♭9

♭9 5 1 3♭7♭9

E7♭9 F7♭9 F#7♭9 G7♭9 A♭7♭9

ROOT 4

A7♭9 B♭7♭9 B7♭9 C7♭9 D♭7♭9 D7♭9 E♭7♭9

| 7♭9 | **SEVEN FLAT NINE** | 135♭7♭9 |

Bar Chord Shapes (Cont.)

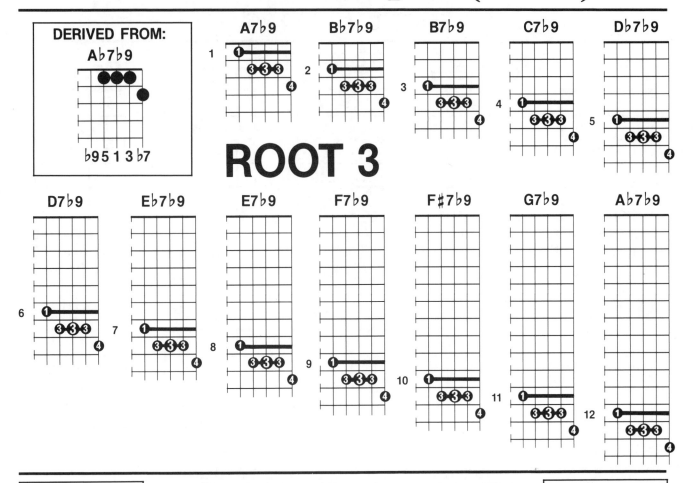

ROOT 3

| 7♭9 | **SEVEN FLAT NINE** | 135♭7♭9 |

Moveable Shapes

1.
I7♭9 (No Root)= ♭II°
e.g. C7♭9 (No C)=D♭°

2.
I7♭9 (No Root)=VI7♭9 (No Root)
e.g. C7♭9 (No C)=A7♭9 (No A)

1. For any Seven Flat Nine chord, (without a root note) a Diminished chord based upon the Flattened Second note of the scale may be used e.g. for C7♭9 (without C note) use D♭° (see page 62).

2. For any Seven Flat Nine chord, (without a root note) a Seven Flat Nine chord (without a root note) based upon the Sixth note of the scale may be used e.g. for C7♭9 (no C note) use A7♭9 (no A note)

All moveable chord shapes are shown in first position only but may be moved up the fretboard in the same manner as Bar Chords.

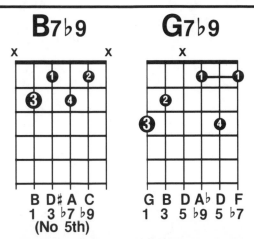

7♯5♭9 SEVEN SHARP FIVE FLAT NINE 13♯5♭7♭9

(Or Seven Augmented Five Flat Nine)

Open Chords

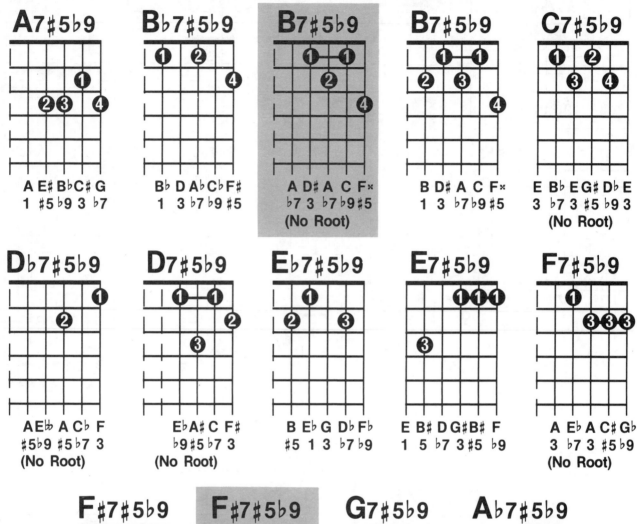

A7♯5♭9

A E♯ B♭ C♯ G
1 ♯5 ♭9 3 ♭7

B♭7♯5♭9

B♭ D A♭ C♭ F♯
1 3 ♭7 ♭9 ♯5

B7♯5♭9

A D♯ A C F𝄪
♭7 3 ♭7 ♭9 ♯5
(No Root)

B7♯5♭9

B D♯ A C F𝄪
1 3 ♭7 ♭9 ♯5

C7♯5♭9

E B♭ E G♯ D♭ E
3 ♭7 3 ♯5 ♭9 3
(No Root)

D♭7♯5♭9

A E♭ A C♭ F
♯5 ♭9 ♯5 ♭7 3
(No Root)

D7♯5♭9

E♭ A♯ C F♯
♭9 ♯5 ♭7 3
(No Root)

E♭7♯5♭9

B E♭ G D♭ F♭
♯5 1 3 ♭7 ♭9

E7♯5♭9

E B♯ D G♯ B♯ F
1 5 ♭7 3 ♯5 ♭9

F7♯5♭9

A E♭ A C♯ G♭
3 ♭7 3 ♯5 ♭9
(No Root)

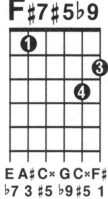

F♯7♯5♭9

E A♯ C𝄪 G C𝄪 F♯
♭7 3 ♯5 ♭9 ♯5 1

F♯7♯5♭9

F♯ A♯ C𝄪 G C𝄪 E
1 3 ♯5 ♭9 ♯5 ♭7

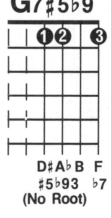

G7♯5♭9

D♯ A♭ B F
♯5 ♭9 3 ♭7
(No Root)

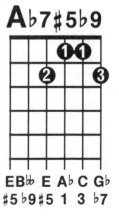

A♭7♯5♭9

E B𝄫 E A♭ C G♭
♯5 ♭9 ♯5 1 3 ♭7

7♯5♭9   SEVEN SHARP FIVE FLAT NINE   13♯5♭7♭9
Bar Chord Shapes

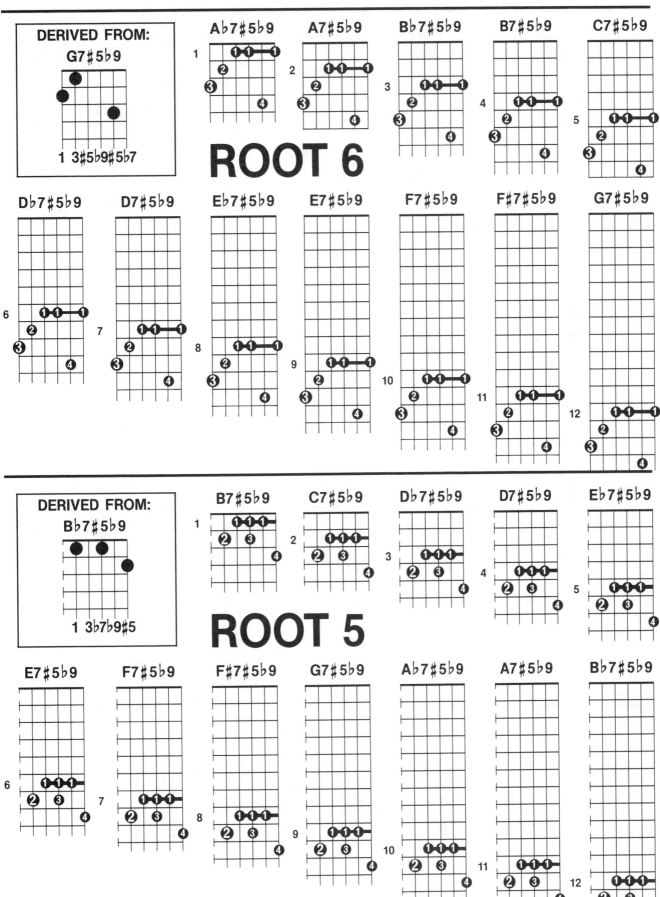

DERIVED FROM:
G7♯5♭9

1 3♯5♭9♯5♭7

A♭7♯5♭9 A7♯5♭9 B♭7♯5♭9 B7♯5♭9 C7♯5♭9

ROOT 6

D♭7♯5♭9 D7♯5♭9 E♭7♯5♭9 E7♯5♭9 F7♯5♭9 F♯7♯5♭9 G7♯5♭9

DERIVED FROM:
B♭7♯5♭9

1 3♭7♭9♯5

B7♯5♭9 C7♯5♭9 D♭7♯5♭9 D7♯5♭9 E♭7♯5♭9

ROOT 5

E7♯5♭9 F7♯5♭9 F♯7♯5♭9 G7♯5♭9 A♭7♯5♭9 A7♯5♭9 B♭7♯5♭9

| 7♯5♭9 | **SEVEN SHARP FIVE FLAT NINE** | 13♯5♭7♭9 |

Bar Chord Shapes (Cont.)

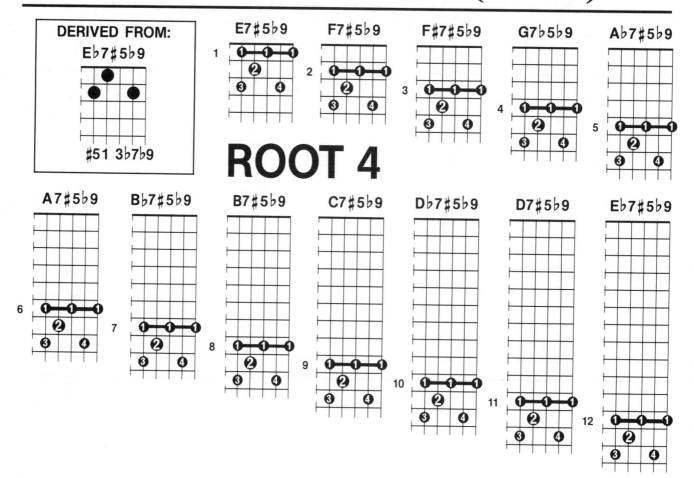

DERIVED FROM:
E♭7♯5♭9

♯51 3♭7♭9

ROOT 4

E7♯5♭9   F7♯5♭9   F♯7♯5♭9   G7♭5♭9   A♭7♯5♭9

A7♯5♭9   B♭7♯5♭9   B7♯5♭9   C7♯5♭9   D♭7♯5♭9   D7♯5♭9   E♭7♯5♭9

| 7♯5♭9 | **SEVEN SHARP FIVE FLAT NINE** | 13♯5♭7♭9 |

Moveable Shapes

I7♯5♭9 (No Root)= ♭IIm6
e.g. C7♯5♭9 (No C)=D♭m6

For any Seven Sharp Five Flat Nine chord, (without a root note) a Minor Six chord based upon the Flattened Second note of the scale may be used e.g. for C7♯5♭9 (No C note) use D♭m6 (see page 39).
All moveable chord shapes are shown in first position only but may be moved up the fretboard in the same manner as Bar Chords.

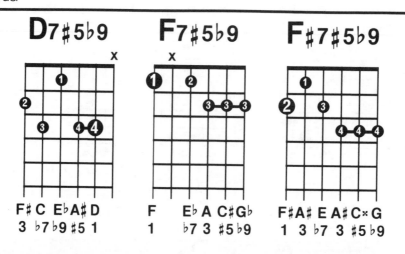

D7♯5♭9

F♯ C E♭A♯ D
3 ♭7♭9♯5 1

F7♯5♭9

F   E♭ A C♯G♭
1   ♭7 3 ♯5♭9

F♯7♯5♭9

F♯A♯ E A♯C✕G
1 3 ♭7 3 ♯5♭9

NINTH
Open Chords

9   135♭79

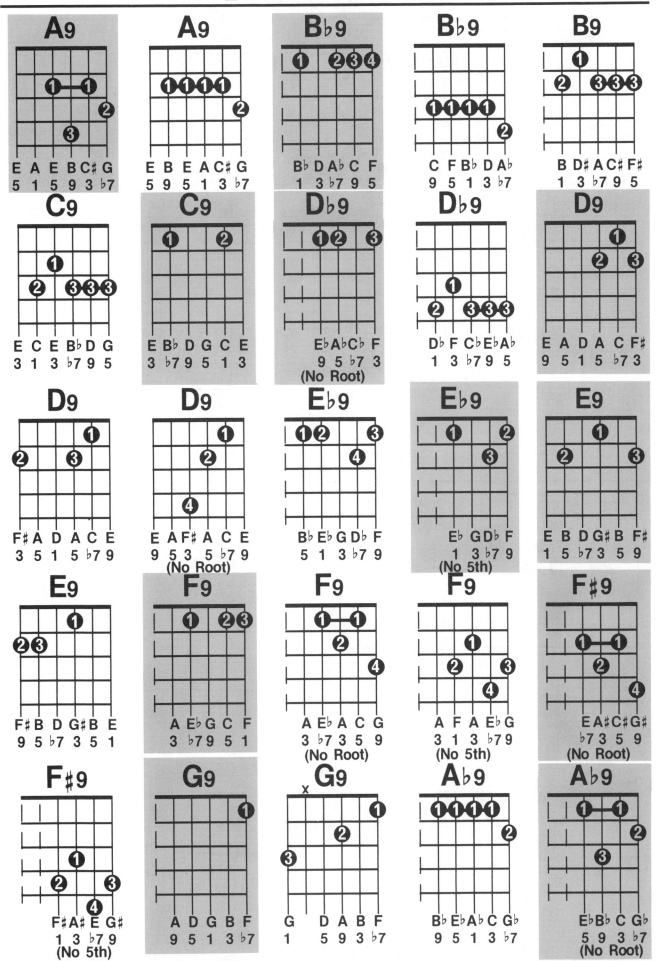

NINTH
Bar Chord Shapes

9   **135♭79**

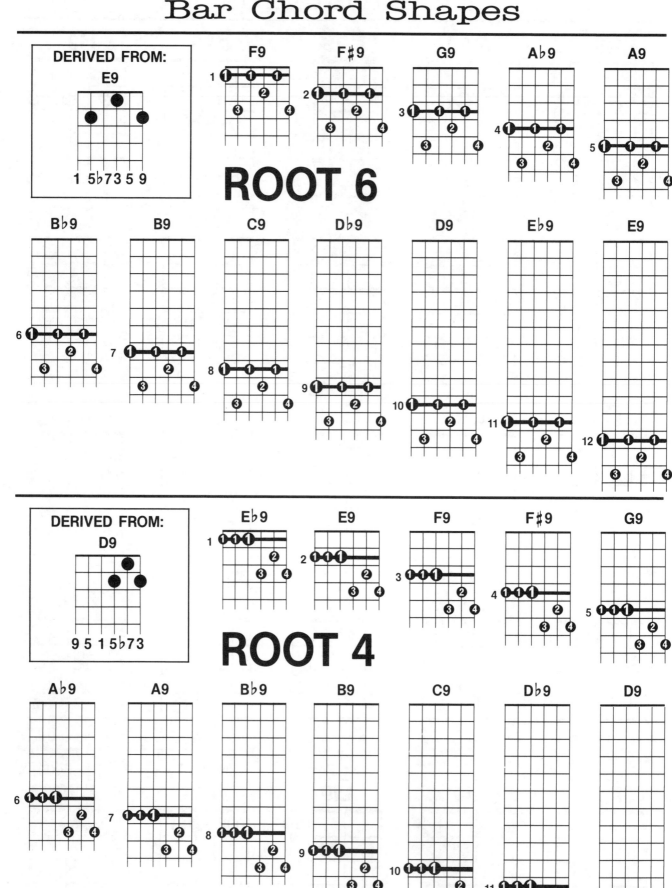

DERIVED FROM: E9

ROOT 6

DERIVED FROM: D9

ROOT 4

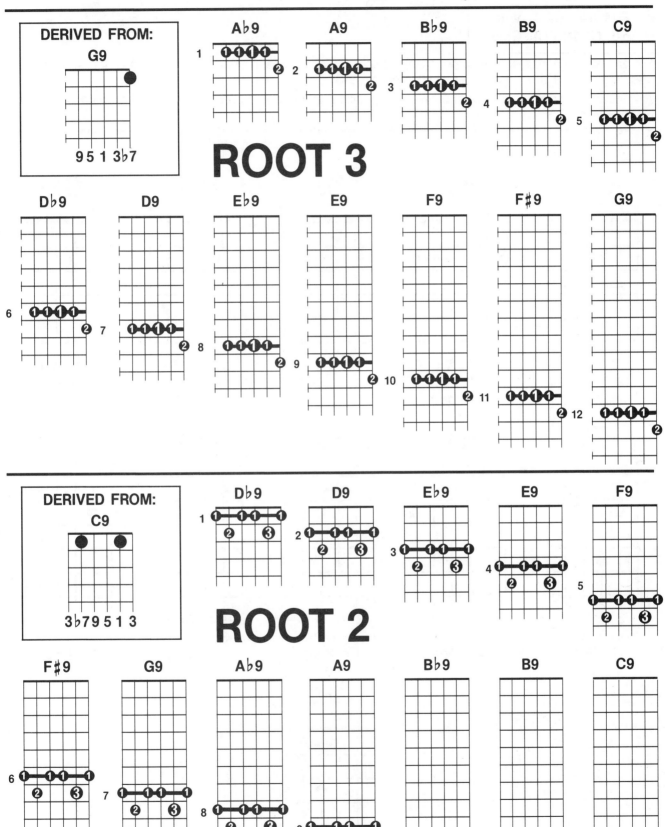

NINTH
Moveable Shapes

9

135♭79

I9 (No Root)=Vm6
e.g. C9 (No C)=Gm6

For any Ninth chord, (without a root note) a Minor Six chord based upon the Fifth note of the scale may be used e.g. for C9 (no C note) use Gm6 (see page 39).

All moveable chord shapes are shown in first position only but may be moved up the fretboard in the same manner as Bar Chords.

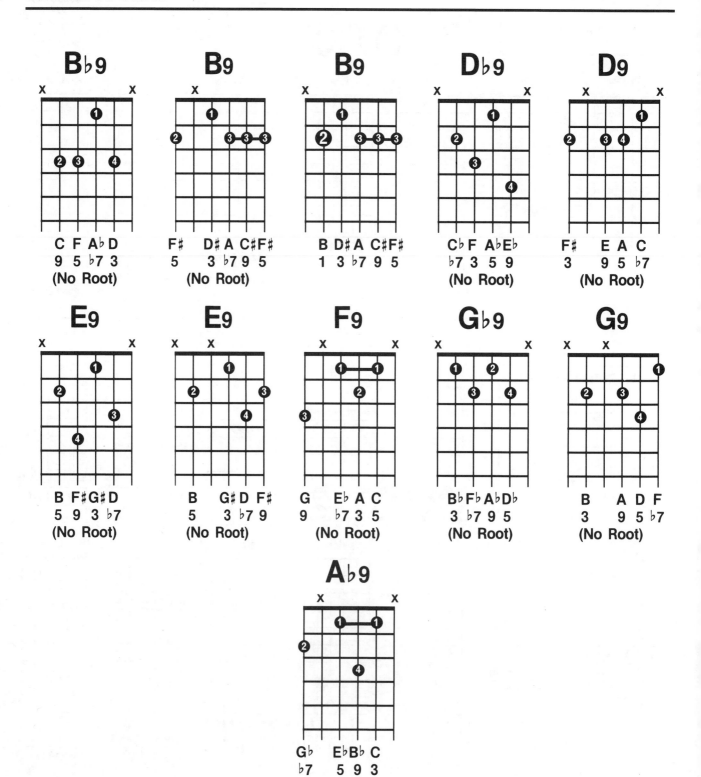

MINOR NINE
Open Chords

m9 | 1♭35♭79

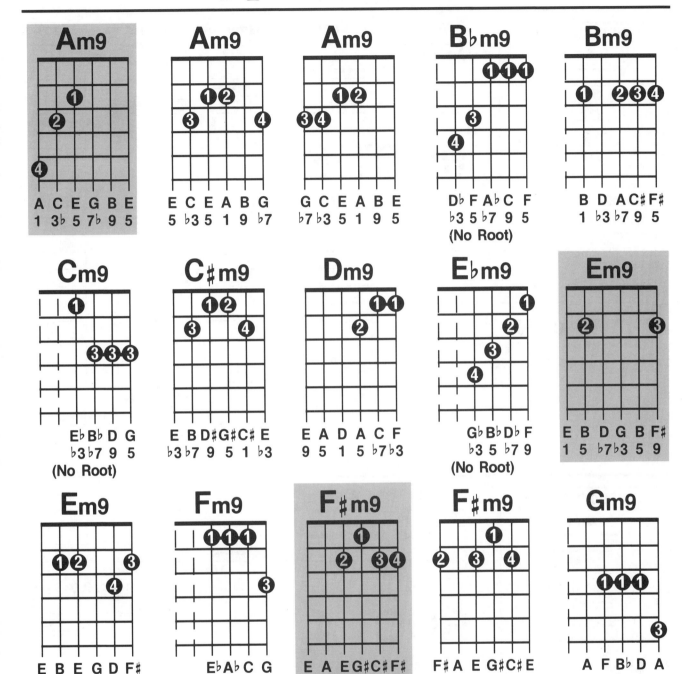

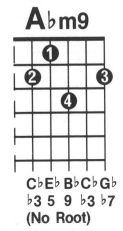

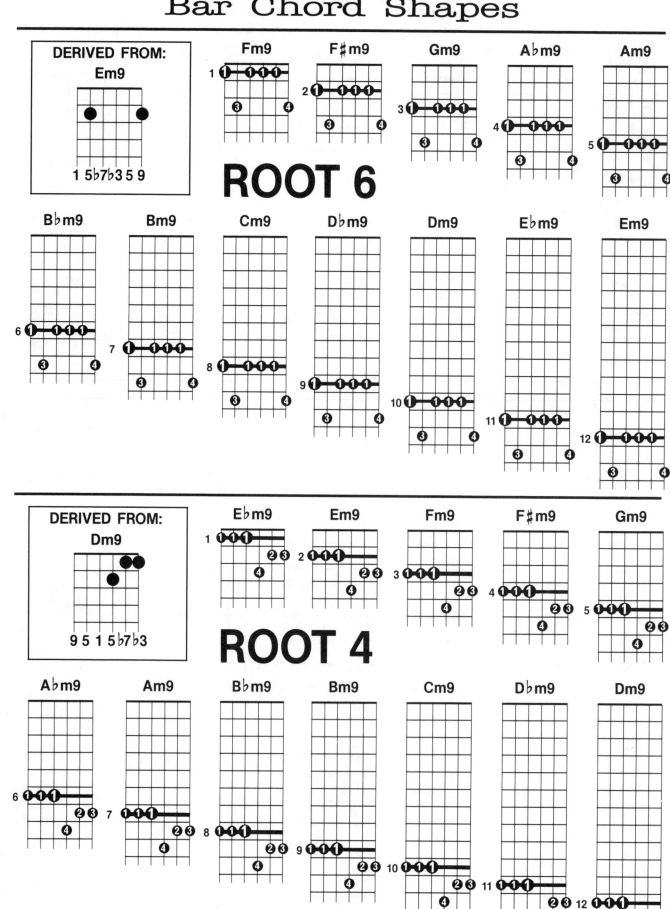

MINOR NINE

m9

1♭3 5♭7 9

Bar Chord Shapes

MINOR NINE
Moveable Shapes

m9

1♭35♭79

Im9 (No Root)= ♭III maj7
e.g. Cm9 (No C)=E♭maj7

For any Minor Nine chord, (without a root note) a Major Seven chord based upon a Flattened third of scale may be used e.g. for Cm9 (No C note) use E♭maj7 (see page 70).

All moveable chord shapes are shown in first position only but may be moved up the fretboard in the same manner as Bar Chords.

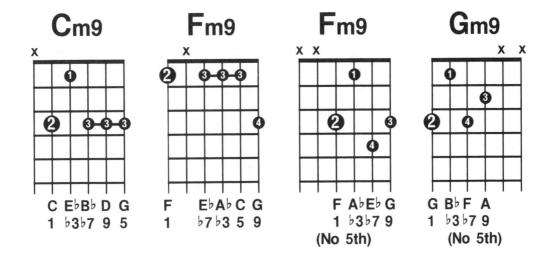

Cm9

C E♭B♭ D G
1 ♭3♭7 9 5

Fm9

F E♭A♭C G
1 ♭7♭3 5 9

Fm9

F A♭E♭G
1 ♭3♭7 9
(No 5th)

Gm9

G B♭F A
1 ♭3♭7 9
(No 5th)

'Z.Z. TOP'.

94

9#5　**NINE SHARP FIVE**　13#5♭79

(Or Nine Augmented Five)

Open Chords

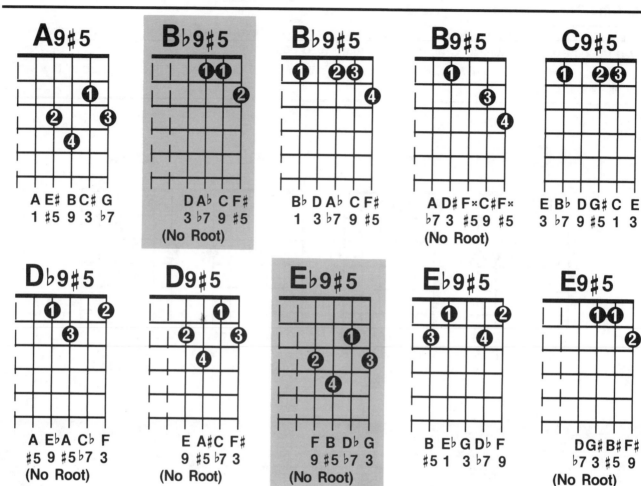

A9#5

A E# B C# G
1 #5 9 3 ♭7

B♭9#5

D A♭ C F#
3 ♭7 9 #5
(No Root)

B♭9#5

B♭ D A♭ C F#
1 3 ♭7 9 #5

B9#5

A D# F× C# F×
♭7 3 #5 9 #5
(No Root)

C9#5

E B♭ D G# C E
3 ♭7 9 #5 1 3

D♭9#5

A E♭ A C♭ F
#5 9 #5 ♭7 3
(No Root)

D9#5

E A# C F#
9 #5 ♭7 3
(No Root)

E♭9#5

F B D♭ G
9 #5 ♭7 3
(No Root)

E♭9#5

B E♭ G D♭ F
#5 1 3 ♭7 9

E9#5

D G# B# F#
♭7 3 #5 9
(No Root)

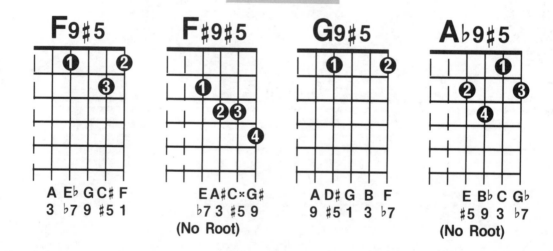

F9#5

A E♭ G C# F
3 ♭7 9 #5 1

F#9#5

E A# C× G#
♭7 3 #5 9
(No Root)

G9#5

A D# G B F
9 #5 1 3 ♭7

A♭9#5

E B♭ C G♭
#5 9 3 ♭7
(No Root)

95

NINE SHARP FIVE
Bar Chord Shapes

9#5   13#5b79

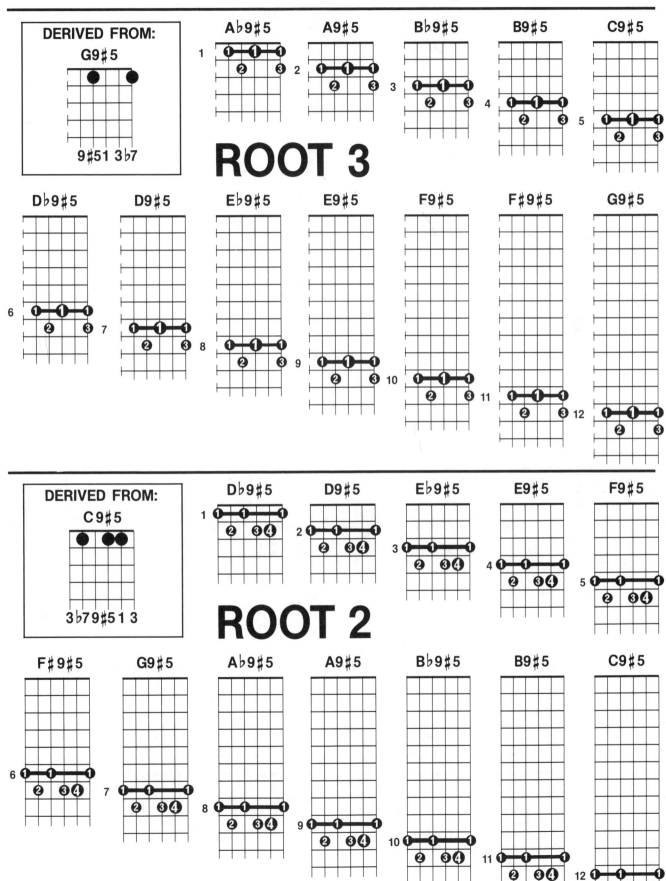

NINE SHARP FIVE

9#5		13#5b79

Bar Chord Shapes (Cont.)

DERIVED FROM:

F9#5

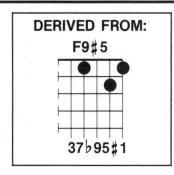

37b95#1

F#9#5 1 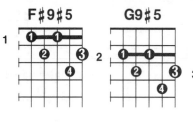 2 **G9#5** 3 **Ab9#5** 4 **A9#5** 5 **Bb9#5**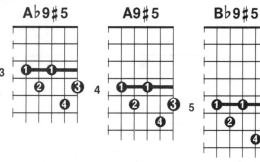

ROOT 1

B9#5 6 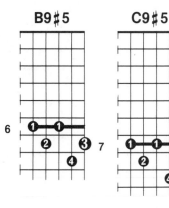 7 **C9#5** 8 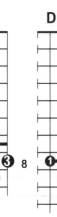 **Db9#5** 9 **D9#5** 10 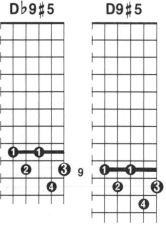 **Eb9#5** 11 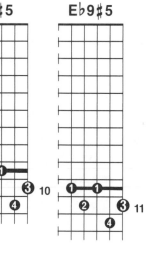 **E9#5** 12 **F9#5**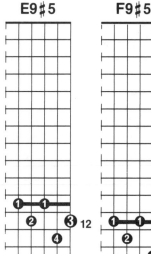

NINE SHARP FIVE

9#5		13#5b79

Moveable Shapes

1.
$$I9\#5 = {}^\flat VII9\flat5$$
e.g. C9#5 = Bb9b5

2.
$$I9\#5 \text{ (No Root)} = III7\flat5$$
e.g. C9#5 (No C) = E7b5

1. For any 9#5 chord, a 9b5 chord based upon the flattened seventh note of the scale may be used e.g. for C9#5 use Bb9b5 (see page 97).

2. For any 9#5 chord, a 7b5 chord based on the third scale note may be used e.g. for C9#5 use E7b5 (see page 67).

All moveable chord shapes are shown in first position only but may be moved up the fretboard in the same manner as Bar Chords.

B9#5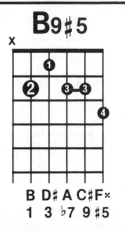

B D# A C# Fx
1 3 b7 9 #5

C#9#5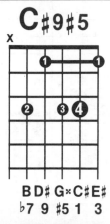

B D# Gx C# E#
b7 9 #5 1 3

F9#5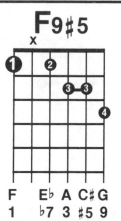

F   Eb A C# G
1   b7 3 #5 9

F#9#5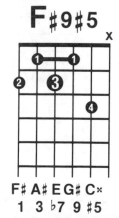

F# A# E G# Cx
1 3 b7 9 #5

NINE FLAT FIVE

9♭5

13♭5♭79

(Or Nine Diminished Five)

Open Chords

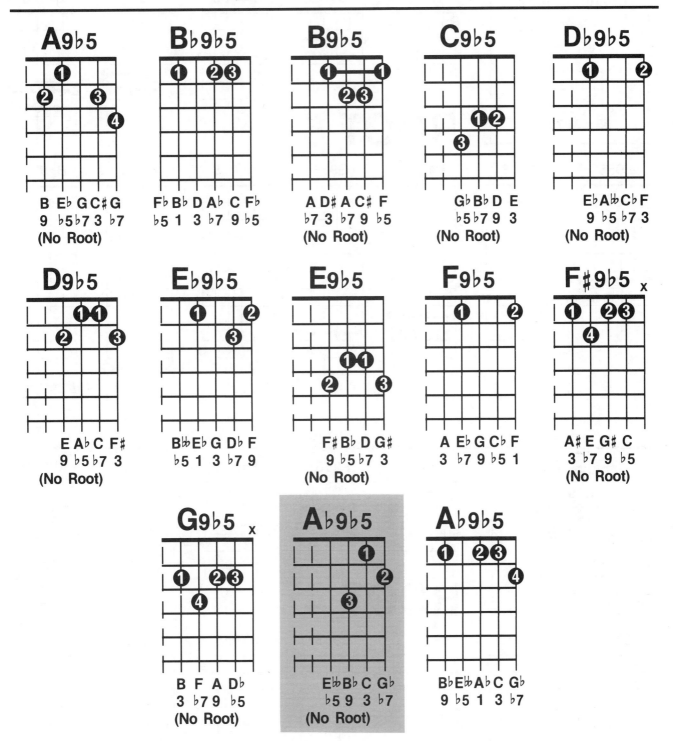

A9♭5

B E♭ G C♯ G
9 ♭5 ♭7 3 ♭7
(No Root)

B♭9♭5

F♭ B♭ D A♭ C F♭
♭5 1 3 ♭7 9 ♭5

B9♭5

A D♯ A C♯ F
♭7 3 ♭7 9 ♭5
(No Root)

C9♭5

G♭ B♭ D E
♭5 ♭7 9 3
(No Root)

D♭9♭5

E♭ A♭ C♭ F
9 ♭5 ♭7 3
(No Root)

D9♭5

E A♭ C F♯
9 ♭5 ♭7 3
(No Root)

E♭9♭5

B♭♭ E♭ G D♭ F
♭5 1 3 ♭7 9

E9♭5

F♯ B♭ D G♯
9 ♭5 ♭7 3
(No Root)

F9♭5

A E♭ G C♭ F
3 ♭7 9 ♭5 1

F♯9♭5 x

A♯ E G♯ C
3 ♭7 9 ♭5
(No Root)

G9♭5 x

B F A D♭
3 ♭7 9 ♭5
(No Root)

A♭9♭5

E♭ B♭ C G♭
♭5 9 3 ♭7
(No Root)

A♭9♭5

B♭ E♭♭ A♭ C G♭
9 ♭5 1 3 ♭7

9♭5   NINE FLAT FIVE   13♭5♭79

Bar Chord Shapes

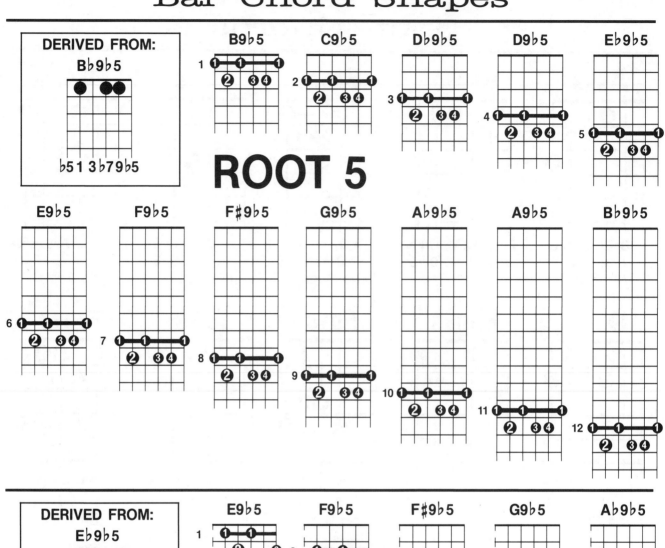

DERIVED FROM: B♭9♭5 — ♭5 1 3 ♭7 9 ♭5

ROOT 5

B9♭5   C9♭5   D♭9♭5   D9♭5   E♭9♭5

E9♭5   F9♭5   F♯9♭5   G9♭5   A♭9♭5   A9♭5   B♭9♭5

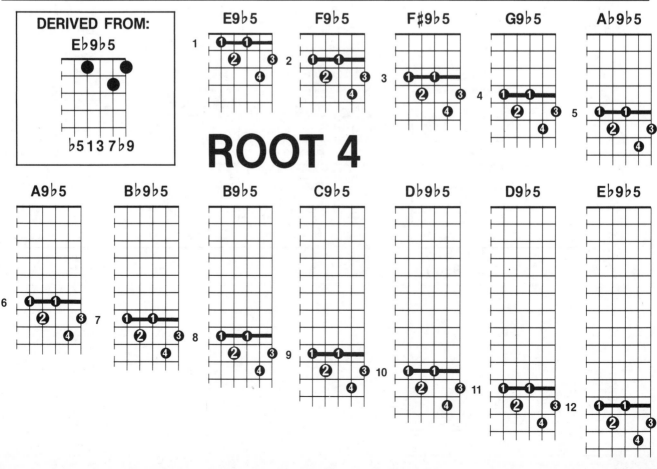

DERIVED FROM: E♭9♭5 — ♭5 1 3 7 ♭9

ROOT 4

E9♭5   F9♭5   F♯9♭5   G9♭5   A♭9♭5

A9♭5   B♭9♭5   B9♭5   C9♭5   D♭9♭5   D9♭5   E♭9♭5

9♭5	# NINE FLAT FIVE	1 3 ♭5 ♭7 9

Bar Chord Shapes (Cont.)

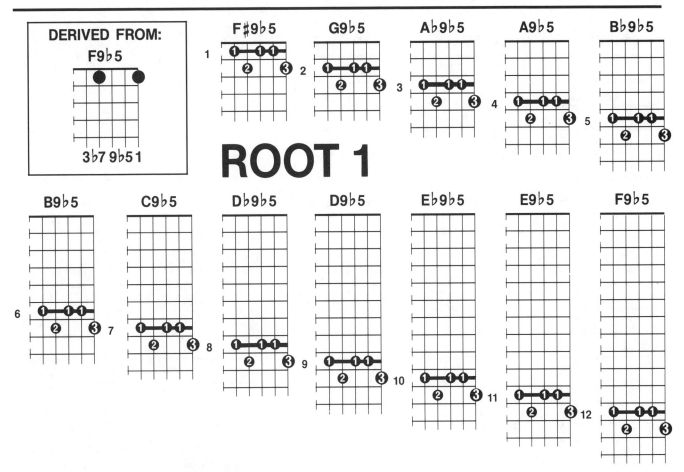

ROOT 1

9♭5	# NINE FLAT FIVE	1 3 ♭5 ♭7 9

Moveable Shapes

1.
I9♭5 (No Root) = ♭V7♯5
e.g. C9♭5 (No C) = G♭7♯5

2.
I9♭5 = II9♯5
e.g. C9♭5 = D9♯5

1. For any 9♭5 chord (without root note), a 7♯5 chord based upon the Flattened fifth note of the scale can be used e.g. for C9♭5 (No C note) use G♭7♯5 (see page 64).
2. For any 9♭5 chord, a 9♯5 chord based upon the second note of the scale may be used e.g. C9♭5 = D9♯5 (see page 94).

All moveable chord shapes are shown in first position only but may be moved up the fretboard in the same manner as Bar Chords.

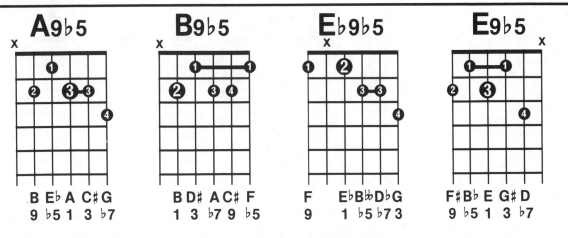

maj9

MAJOR NINE
Open Chords

1 3 5 7 9

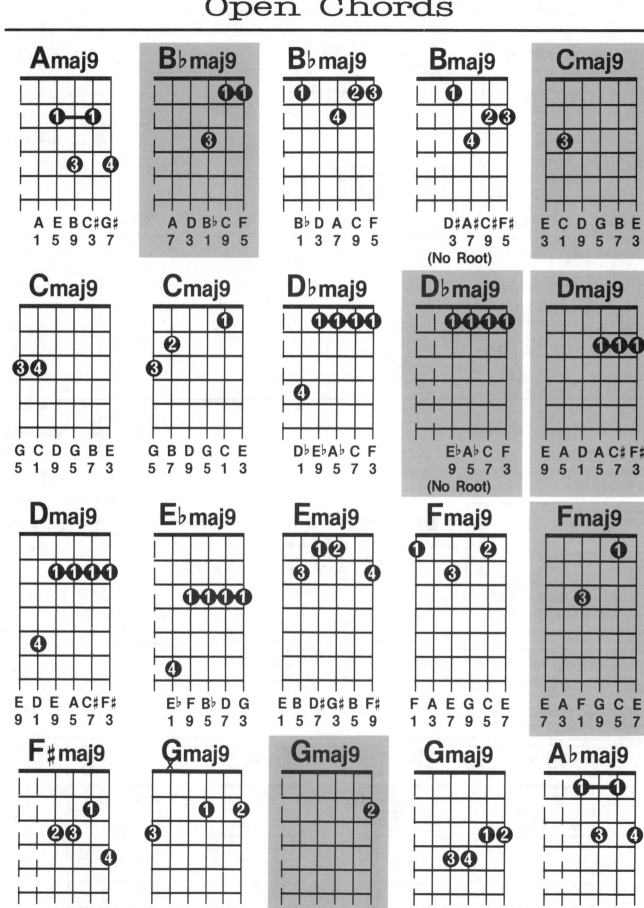

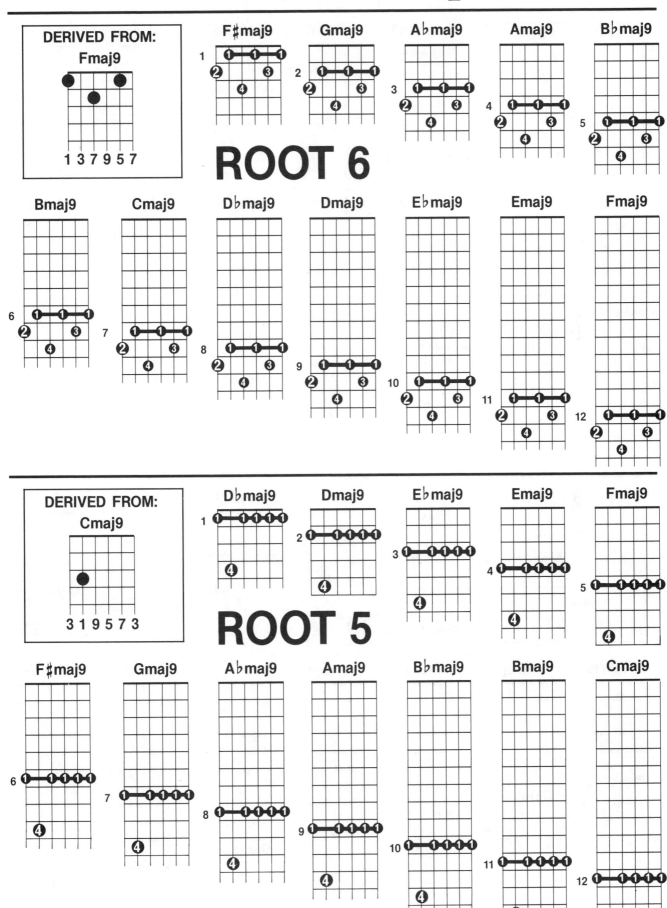

MAJOR NINE

maj9 · 1 3 5 7 9

Bar Chord Shapes (Cont.)

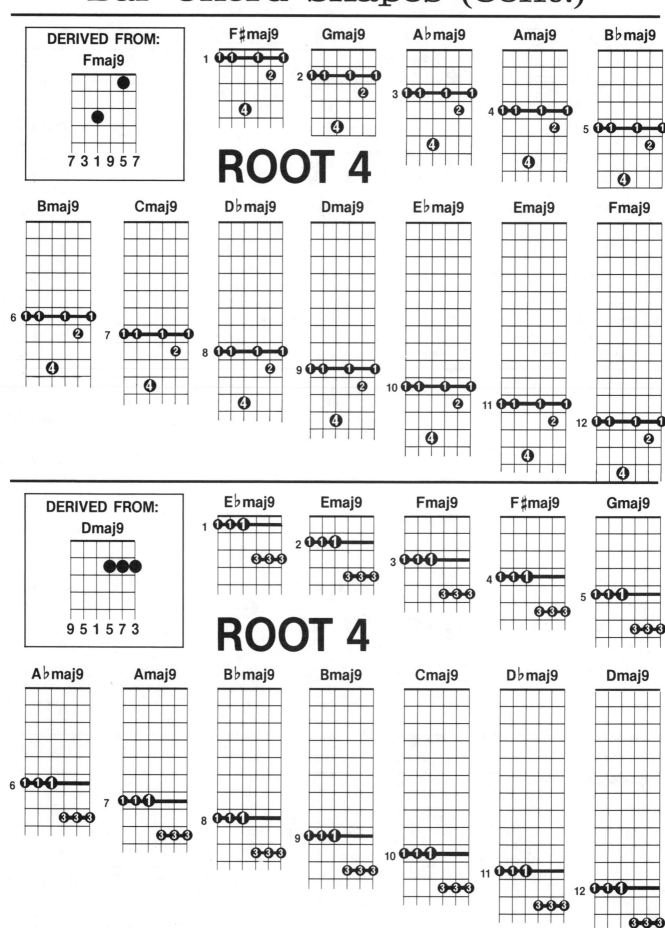

maj9   MAJOR NINE   1 3 5 7 9
Bar Chord Shapes (Cont.)

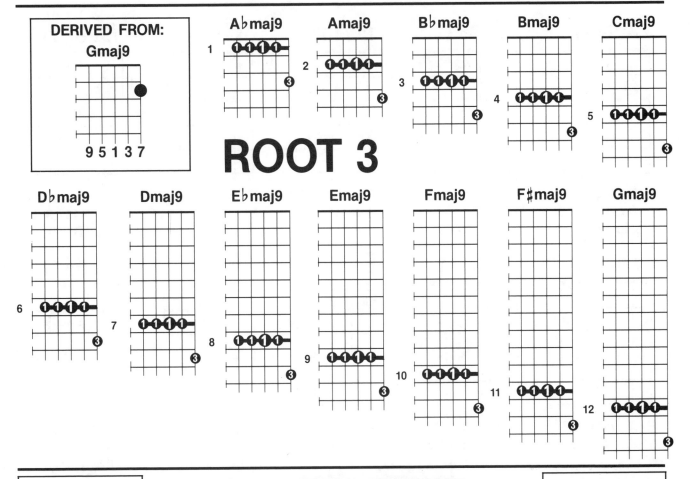

DERIVED FROM:
Gmaj9
9 5 1 3 7

Abmaj9 | Amaj9 | Bbmaj9 | Bmaj9 | Cmaj9

ROOT 3

Dbmaj9 | Dmaj9 | Ebmaj9 | Emaj9 | Fmaj9 | F#maj9 | Gmaj9

---

maj9   MAJOR NINE   1 3 5 7 9
Moveable Shapes

Imaj9 (No Root)=V6
e.g. Cmaj9 (No C)=G6

For any maj9 chord, a 6th chord based upon the fifth note of the scale may be used. e.g. for Cmaj9, use G6 (see page 31).
All moveable chord shapes are shown in first position only but may be moved up the fretboard in the same manner as Bar Chords.

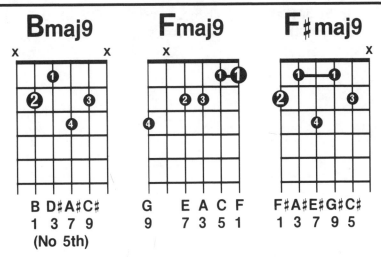

Bmaj9 | Fmaj9 | F#maj9

B D#A#C#
1 3 7 9
(No 5th)

G   E A C F
9   7 3 5 1

F#A#E#G#C#
1 3 7 9 5

9♯11 NINE SHARP ELEVEN 135♭79♯11
Open Chords

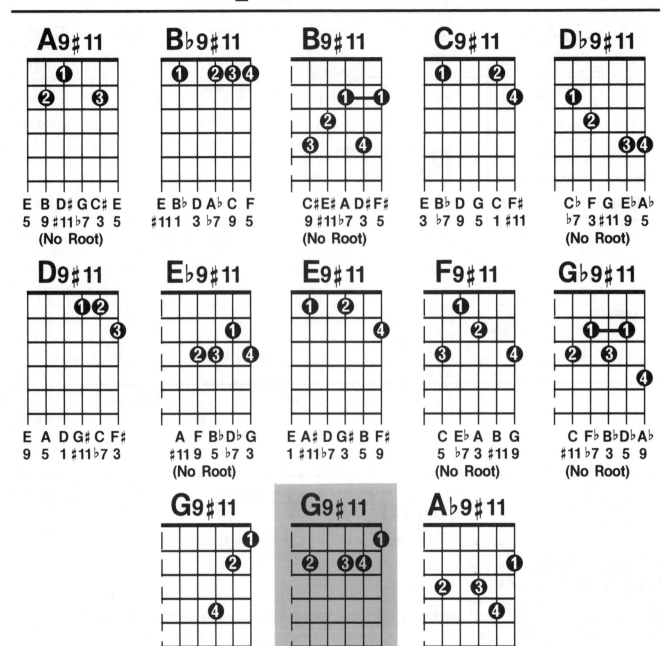

A9♯11

E B D♯ G C♯ E
5 9 ♯11 ♭7 3 5
(No Root)

B♭9♯11

E B♭ D A♭ C F
♯11 1 3 ♭7 9 5

B9♯11

C♯ E♯ A D♯ F♯
9 ♯11 ♭7 3 5
(No Root)

C9♯11

E B♭ D G C F♯
3 ♭7 9 5 1 ♯11

D♭9♯11

C♭ F G E♭ A♭
♭7 3 ♯11 9 5
(No Root)

D9♯11

E A D G♯ C F♯
9 5 1 ♯11 ♭7 3

E♭9♯11

A F B♭ D♭ G
♯11 9 5 ♭7 3
(No Root)

E9♯11

E A♯ D G♯ B F♯
1 ♯11 ♭7 3 5 9

F9♯11

C E♭ A B G
5 ♭7 3 ♯11 9
(No Root)

G♭9♯11

C F♭ B♭ D♭ A♭
♯11 ♭7 3 5 9
(No Root)

G9♯11

A D B C♯ F
9 5 3 ♯11 ♭7
(No Root)

G9♯11

B D A C♯ F
3 5 9 ♯11 7♭
(No Root)

A♭9♯11

C D B♭ E♭ G♭
3 ♯11 9 5 ♭7
(No Root)

9♯11 · NINE SHARP ELEVEN · 135♭79♯11
Bar Chord Shapes

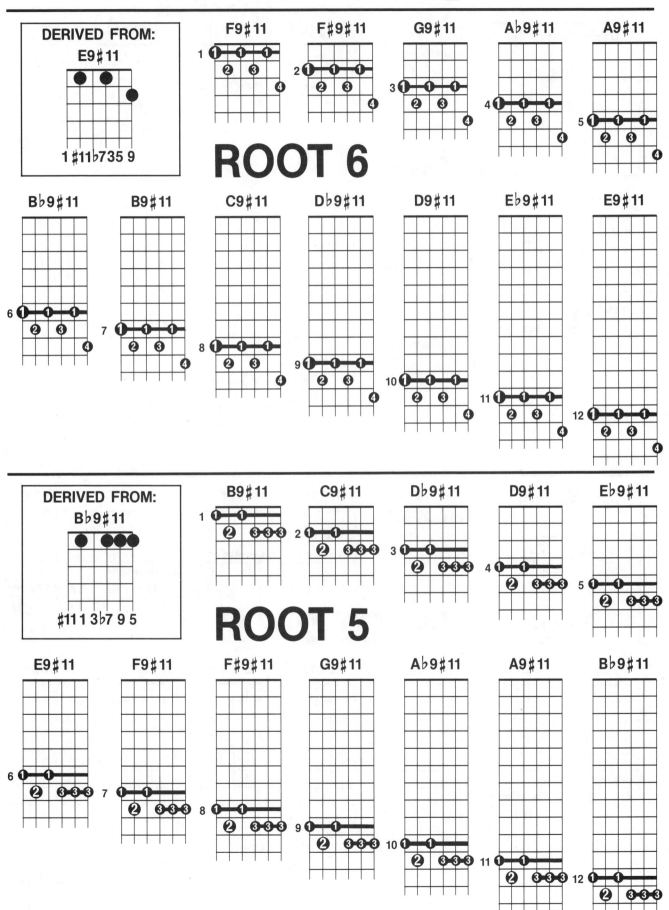

106

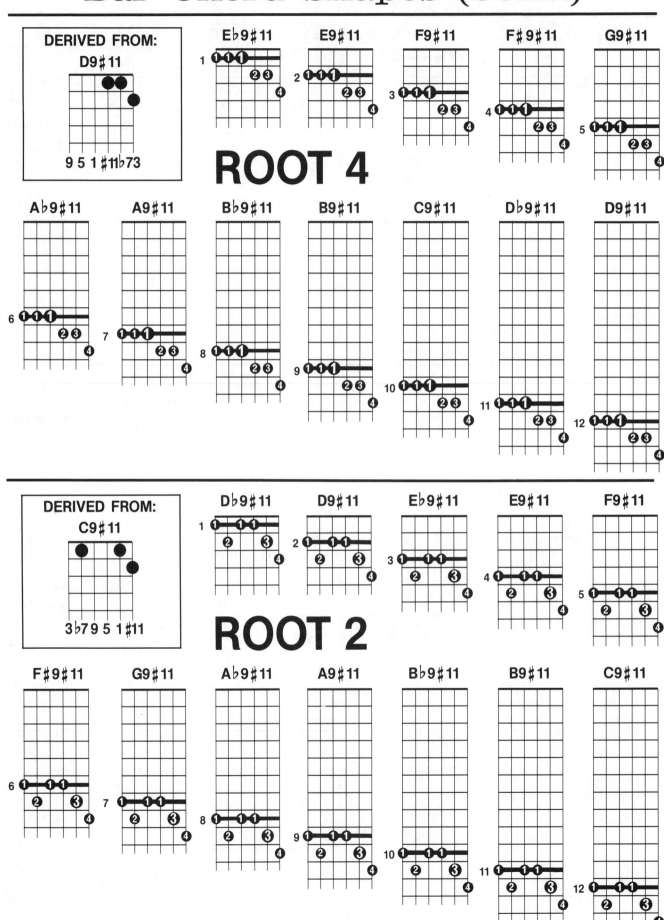

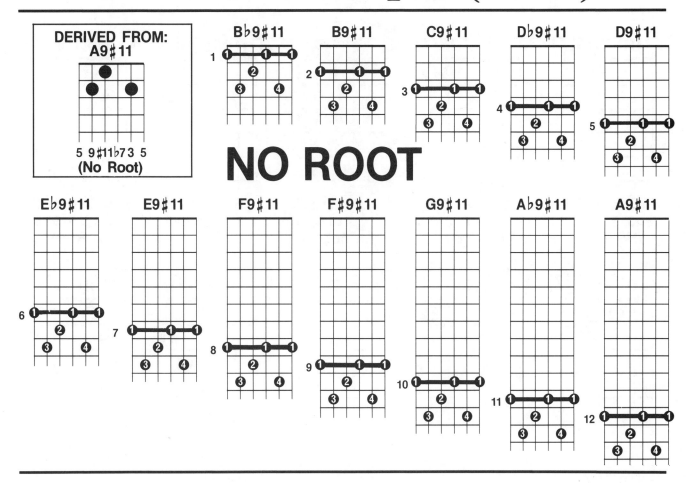

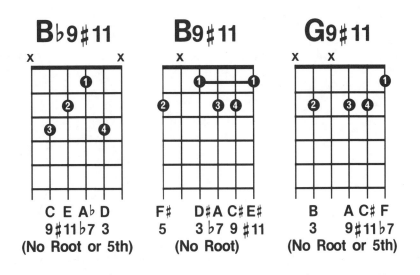

108

m9(maj7) MINOR NINE MAJOR SEVEN 1♭3579
Open Chords

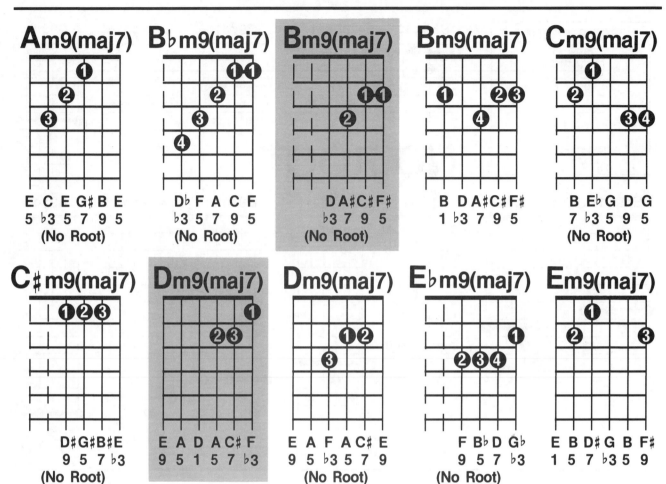

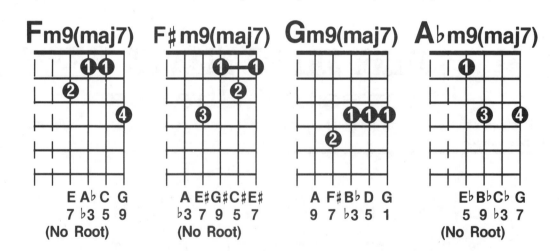

m9(maj7) MINOR NINE MAJOR SEVEN 1♭3 5 7 9
Bar Chord Shapes

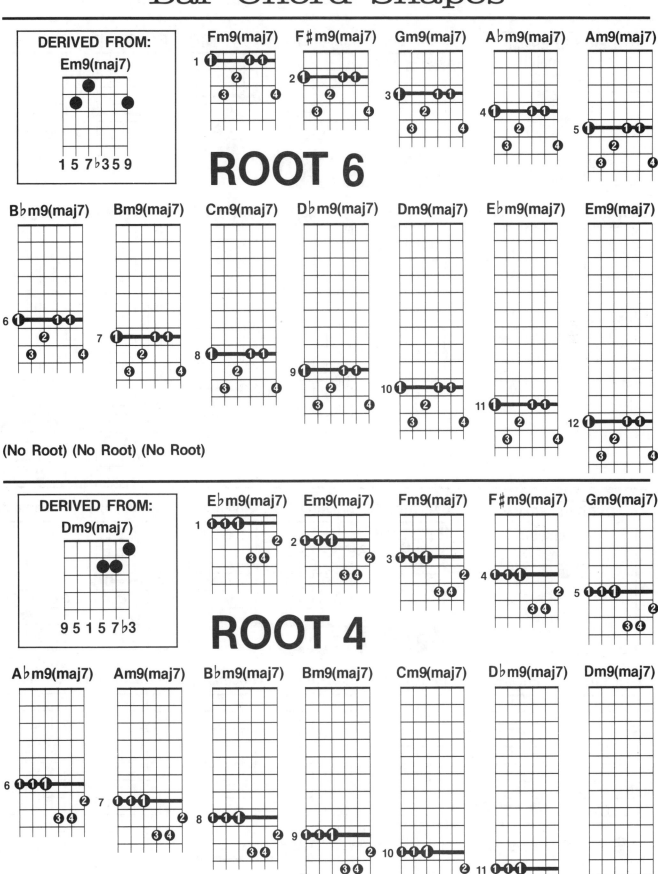

DERIVED FROM:
Em9(maj7)

1 5 7♭3 5 9

Fm9(maj7)   F♯m9(maj7)   Gm9(maj7)   A♭m9(maj7)   Am9(maj7)

ROOT 6

B♭m9(maj7)   Bm9(maj7)   Cm9(maj7)   D♭m9(maj7)   Dm9(maj7)   E♭m9(maj7)   Em9(maj7)

(No Root) (No Root) (No Root)

DERIVED FROM:
Dm9(maj7)

9 5 1 5 7♭3

E♭m9(maj7)   Em9(maj7)   Fm9(maj7)   F♯m9(maj7)   Gm9(maj7)

ROOT 4

A♭m9(maj7)   Am9(maj7)   B♭m9(maj7)   Bm9(maj7)   Cm9(maj7)   D♭m9(maj7)   Dm9(maj7)

m9(maj7) MINOR NINE MAJOR SEVEN 1♭3 5 7 9
Bar Chord Shapes (Cont.)

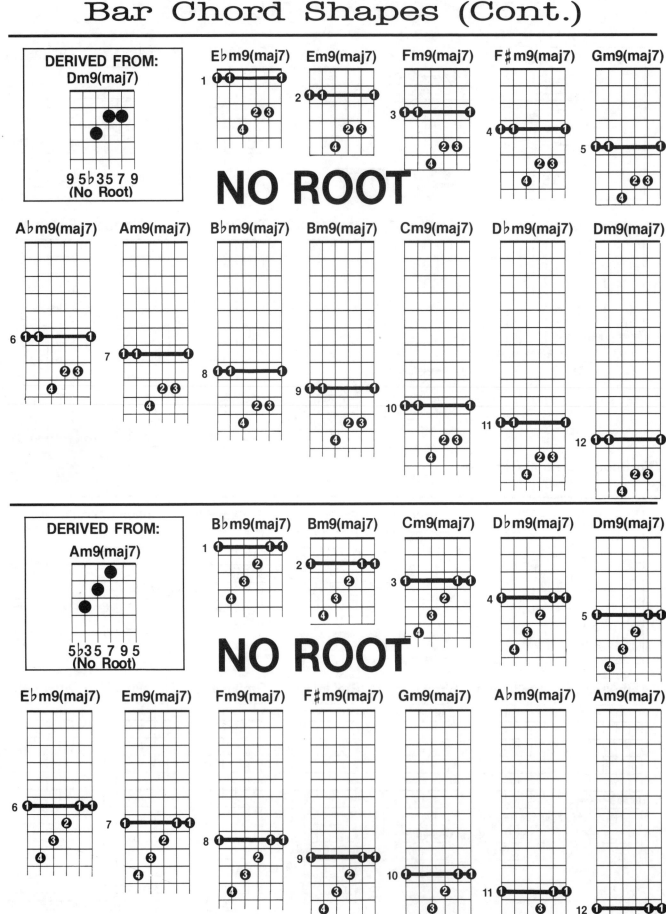

m9(maj7) MINOR NINE MAJOR SEVEN 1♭3 5 7 9
Moveable Shapes

All moveable chord shapes are shown in first position only but may be moved up the fretboard in the same manner as Bar Chords.

B♭m9(maj7)

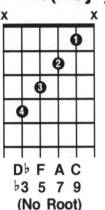

D♭ F A C
♭3 5 7 9
(No Root)

Cm9(maj7)

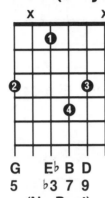

G   E♭ B D
5   ♭3 7 9
(No Root)

Cm9(maj7)

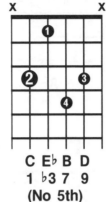

C E♭ B D
1 ♭3 7 9
(No 5th)

D♭m9(maj7)

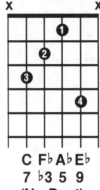

C F♭ A♭ E♭
7 ♭3 5 9
(No Root)

Dm9(maj7)

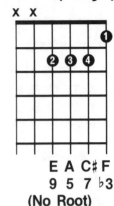

E A C♯ F
9 5 7 ♭3
(No Root)

Dm9(maj7)

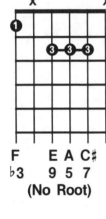

F   E A C♯
♭3 9 5 7
(No Root)

E♭m9(maj7)

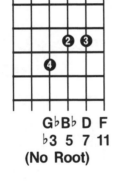

G♭B♭ D F
♭3 5 7 11
(No Root)

Fm9(maj7)

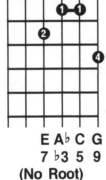

E A♭ C G
7 ♭3 5 9
(No Root)

Gm9(maj7)

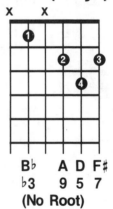

B♭   A D F♯
♭3   9 5 7
(No Root)

112

ELEVENTH
Open Chords

11

1(3)5♭7911
Omitted

Due to the disonance between the 3rd and 11th tones of the 11th chord, the 3rd is usually omitted.

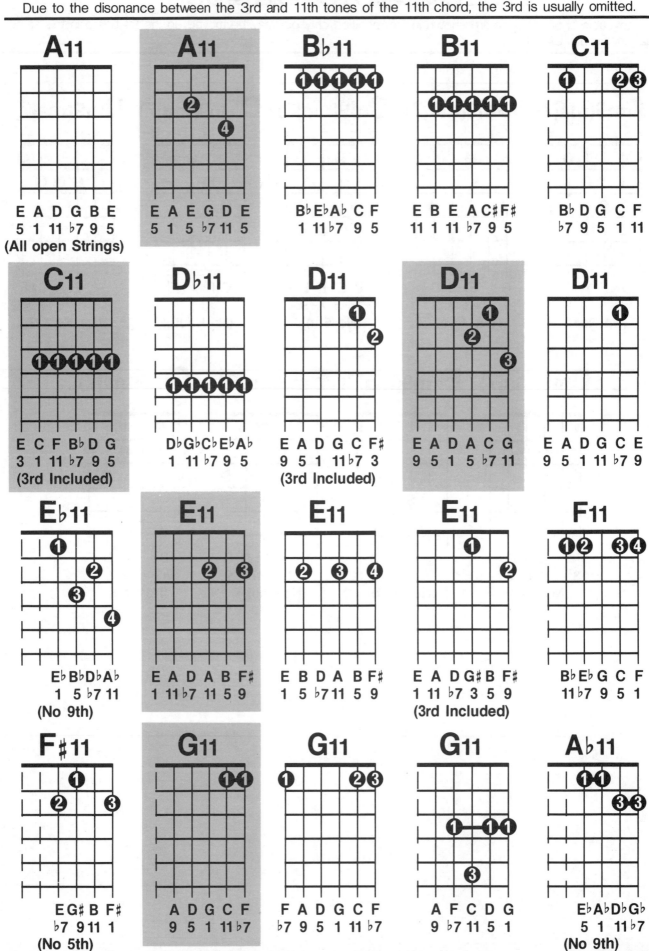

11 ELEVENTH
Bar Chord Shapes

1(3)5♭7 9 11
omitted

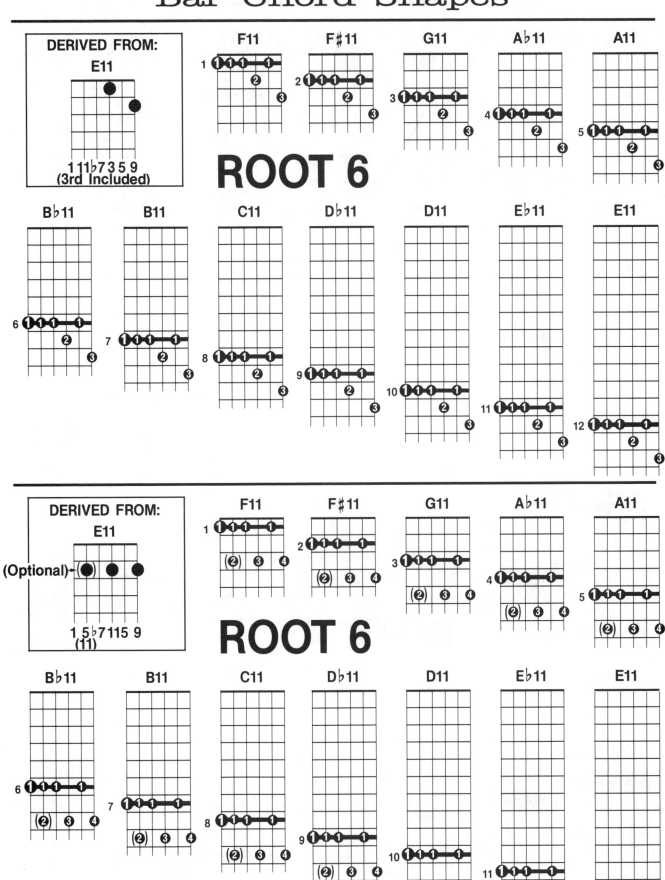

ELEVENTH

11

$1(3)5\flat7\,9\,11$
omitted

Bar Chord Shapes (Cont.)

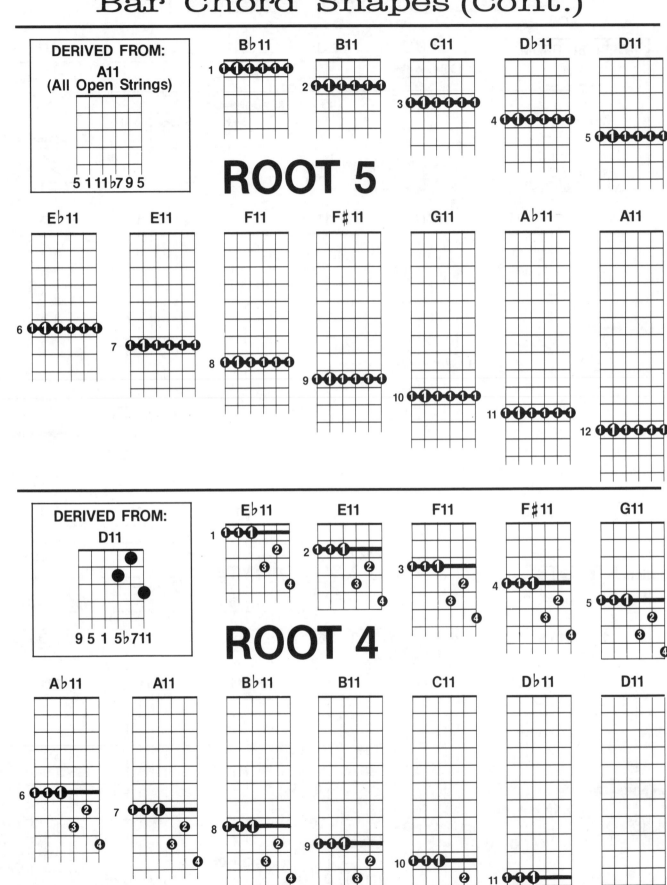

DERIVED FROM:
A11
(All Open Strings)

5 1 11 ♭7 9 5

ROOT 5

Bb11 B11 C11 Db11 D11

Eb11 E11 F11 F#11 G11 Ab11 A11

DERIVED FROM:
D11

9 5 1 5 ♭7 11

ROOT 4

Eb11 E11 F11 F#11 G11

Ab11 A11 Bb11 B11 C11 Db11 D11

ELEVENTH

11

$1(3)5\flat7\,9\,11$

Omitted

Bar Chord Shapes(cont.)

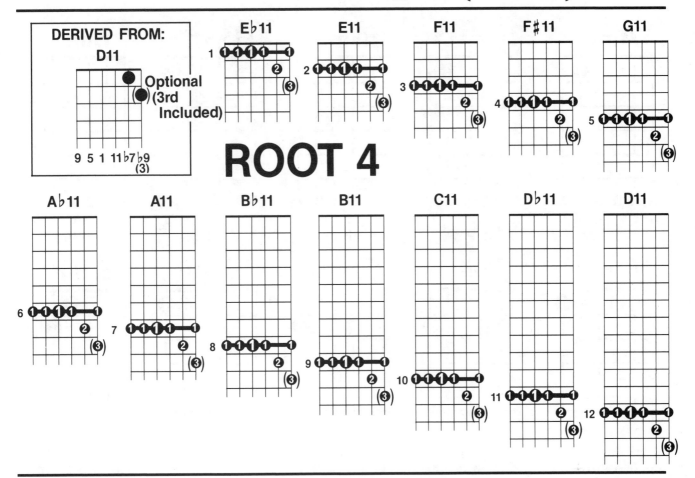

DERIVED FROM:

D11

● Optional
(○) (3rd Included)

9 5 1 11♭7♭9
(3)

E♭11   E11   F11   F♯11   G11

ROOT 4

A♭11   A11   B♭11   B11   C11   D♭11   D11

1.
| I11 (No 3rd)= ♭VII6/9 |
| e.g. C11 (No E)=B♭6/9 |

2.
| I11 (No Root or 3rd)= Vm7 |
| e.g. C11 (No C or E)= Gm7 |

ELEVENTH

Moveable Shapes

All moveable chord shapes are shown in first position only but may be moved up the fretboard in the same manner as Bar Chords.

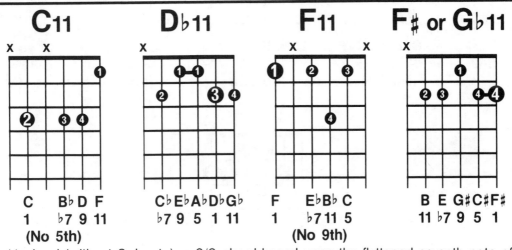

C11   D♭11   F11   F♯ or G♭11

C B♭D F
1 ♭7 9 11
(No 5th)

C♭E♭A♭D♭G♭
♭7 9 5 1 11

F E♭B♭ C
1 ♭7 11 5
(No 9th)

B E G♯C♯F♯
11 ♭7 9 5 1

1. For any 11 chord (without 3rd note), a 6/9 chord based upon the flattened seventh note of the scale may be used e.g. for C11 (no E note) use B♭6/9 (see page 36).

2. For any 11 chord (without a root note or 3rd), a minor seven chord based upon the fifth note of the scale can be used e.g. for C11 (no C or E note) use Gm7 (see page 53).

m11   MINOR ELEVEN   1♭35♭7911
Open Chords

Am11
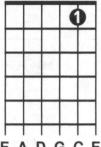

E A D G C E
5 1 11 ♭7 ♭3 5
(No 9th)

Am11
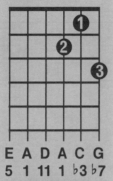

E A D A C G
5 1 11 1 ♭3 ♭7
(No 9th)

B♭m11
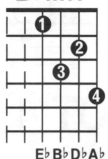

E♭ B♭ D♭ A♭
11 1 ♭3 ♭7
(No 5th or 9th)

Bm11

E A D A B F#
11 ♭7 ♭3 ♭7 1 5
(No 9th)

Bm11
E B D A B F#
11 1 ♭3 ♭7 1 5
(No 9th)

Cm11
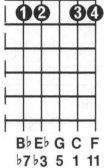

B♭ E♭ G C F
♭7 ♭3 5 1 11
(No 9th)

C#m11
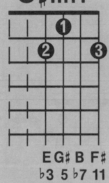

E G# B F#
♭3 5 ♭7 11
(No Root or 9th)

C#m11
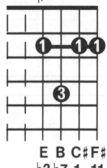

E B C#F#
♭3 ♭7 1 11
(No 5th or 9th)

Dm11
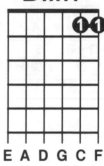

E A D G C F
9 5 1 11 ♭7 ♭3

E♭m11
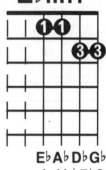

E♭ A♭ D♭ G♭
1 11 ♭7 ♭3
(No 5th or 9th)

Em11
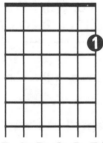

E A D G B F#
1 11 ♭7 ♭3 5 9

Fm11
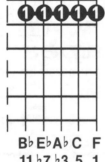

B♭ E♭ A♭ C F
11 ♭7 ♭3 5 1
(No 9th)

F#m11
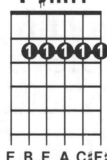

E B E A C#F#
♭7 11 ♭7 ♭3 5 1
(No 9th)

Gm11
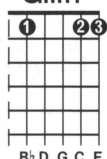

B♭ D G C F
♭3 5 1 11 ♭7
(No 9th)

A♭m11
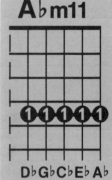

D♭ G♭ C♭ E♭ A♭
11 ♭7 ♭3 5 1
(No 9th)

A♭m11
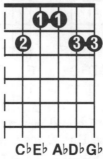

C♭ E♭ A♭ D♭ G♭
♭3 5 1 11 ♭7
(No 9th)

m11 MINOR ELEVEN 1♭35♭7911
Bar Chord Shapes

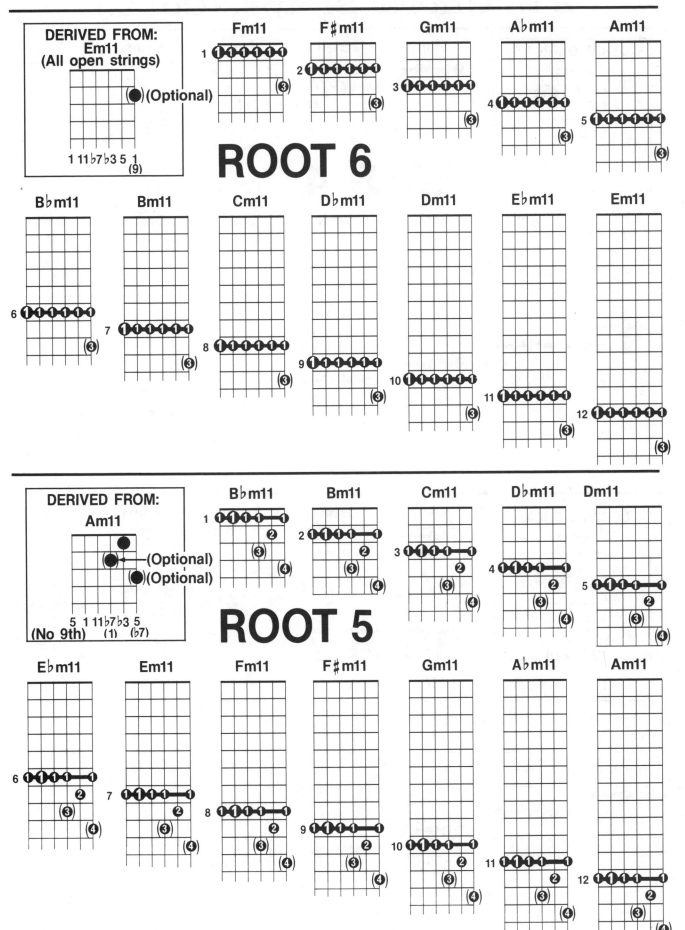

118

m11   MINOR ELEVEN   1♭35♭7 9 11
Bar Chord Shapes(Cont.)

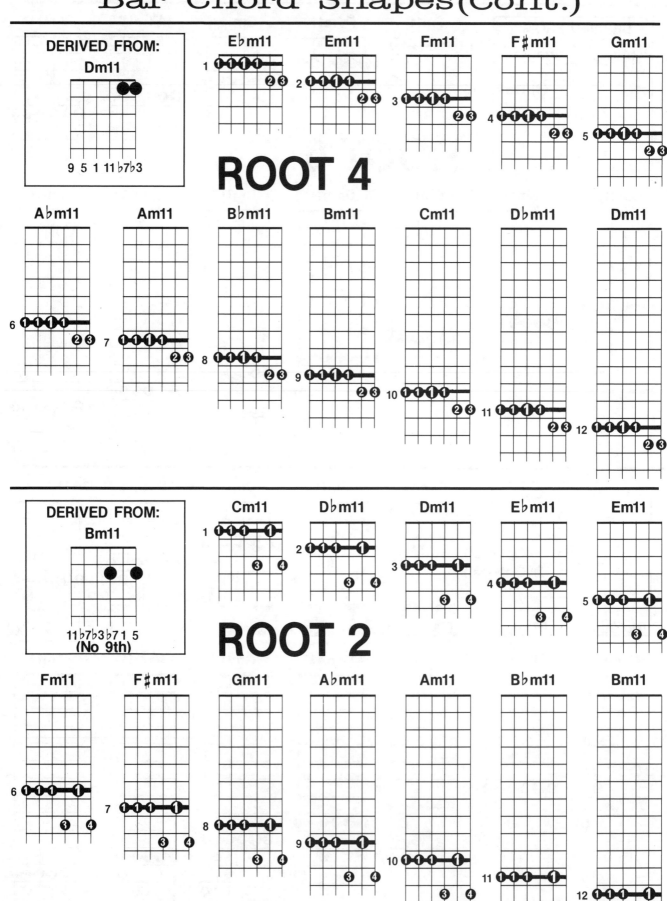

| m11 | # MINOR ELEVEN | 1♭35♭7911 |

Moveable Shapes

1.
| Im11 (No Root)= ♭IIImaj9 |
| e.g. Cm11 (No C)=E♭maj9 |

2.
| Im11 (No 9th)=IV11(No 3rd) |
| e.g.Cm11(No D)=F11 (No A) |

1. For any m11 chord, a maj9 chord based on the flattened third note of the scale may be used. e.g. for Cm11, use E♭maj9 (see pge. 100).

2. For any m11 chord, an 11th chord based upon the fourth note of the scale may be used. e.g. for Cm11, use F11 (see pge. 112).

All moveable chord shapes are shown in first position only but may be moved up the fretboard in the same manner as Bar Chords.

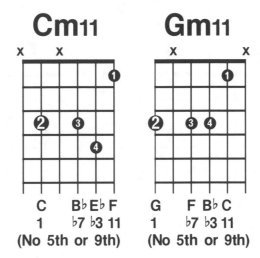

Cm11

x   x

①
② ③
④

C   B♭ E♭ F
1   ♭7 ♭3 11
(No 5th or 9th)

Gm11

x   x

①
② ③ ④

G   F B♭ C
1   ♭7 ♭3 11
(No 5th or 9th)

PAUL SIMON

13

THIRTEENTH
Open Chords

135♭79(11)13
Omitted

Due to the disonance between the 3rd and 11th tones of the 13th chord, the 11th is omitted. This rule will also apply to any altered 13th chord.

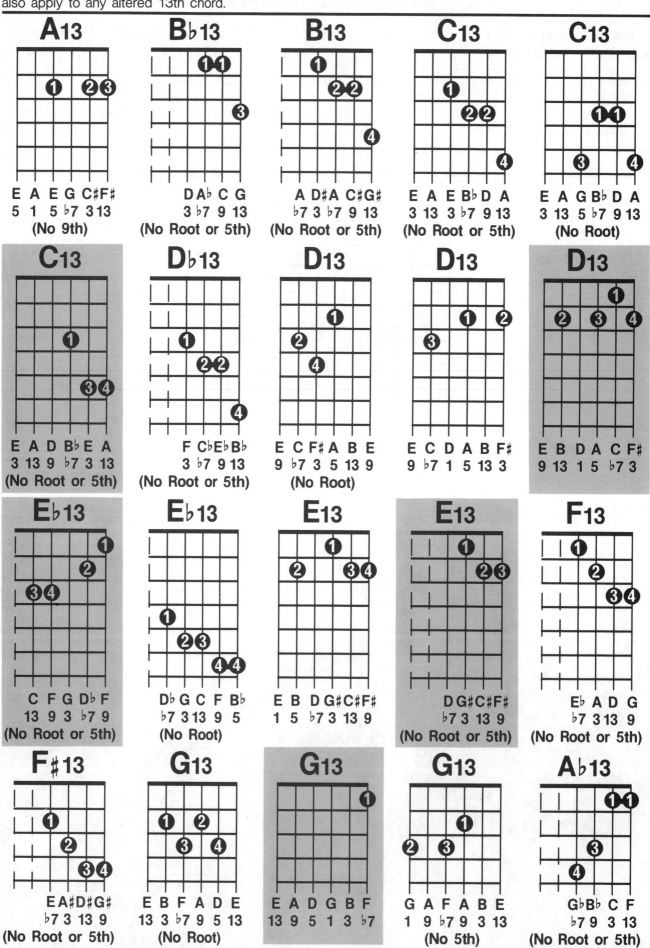

A13
E A E G C#F#
5 1 5 ♭7 3 13
(No 9th)

B♭13
D A♭ C G
3 ♭7 9 13
(No Root or 5th)

B13
A D#A C#G#
♭7 3 ♭7 9 13
(No Root or 5th)

C13
E A E B♭ D A
3 13 3 ♭7 9 13
(No Root or 5th)

C13
E A G B♭ D A
3 13 5 ♭7 9 13
(No Root)

C13
E A D B♭ E A
3 13 9 ♭7 3 13
(No Root or 5th)

D♭13
F C♭E♭ B♭
3 ♭7 9 13
(No Root or 5th)

D13
E C F# A B E
9 ♭7 3 5 13 9
(No Root)

D13
E C D A B F#
9 ♭7 1 5 13 3

D13
E B D A C F#
9 13 1 5 ♭7 3

E♭13
C F G D♭ F
13 9 3 ♭7 9
(No Root or 5th)

E♭13
D♭ G C F B♭
♭7 3 13 9 5
(No Root)

E13
E B D G#C#F#
1 5 ♭7 3 13 9

E13
D G#C#F#
♭7 3 13 9
(No Root or 5th)

F13
E♭ A D G
♭7 3 13 9
(No Root or 5th)

F#13
E A#D#G#
♭7 3 13 9
(No Root or 5th)

G13
E B F A D E
13 3 ♭7 9 5 13
(No Root)

G13
E A D G B F
13 9 5 1 3 ♭7

G13
G A F A B E
1 9 ♭7 9 3 13
(No 5th)

A♭13
G♭B♭ C F
♭7 9 3 13
(No Root or 5th)

13   THIRTEENTH   1 3 5 ♭7 9 (11) 13

Omitted

Bar Chord Shapes

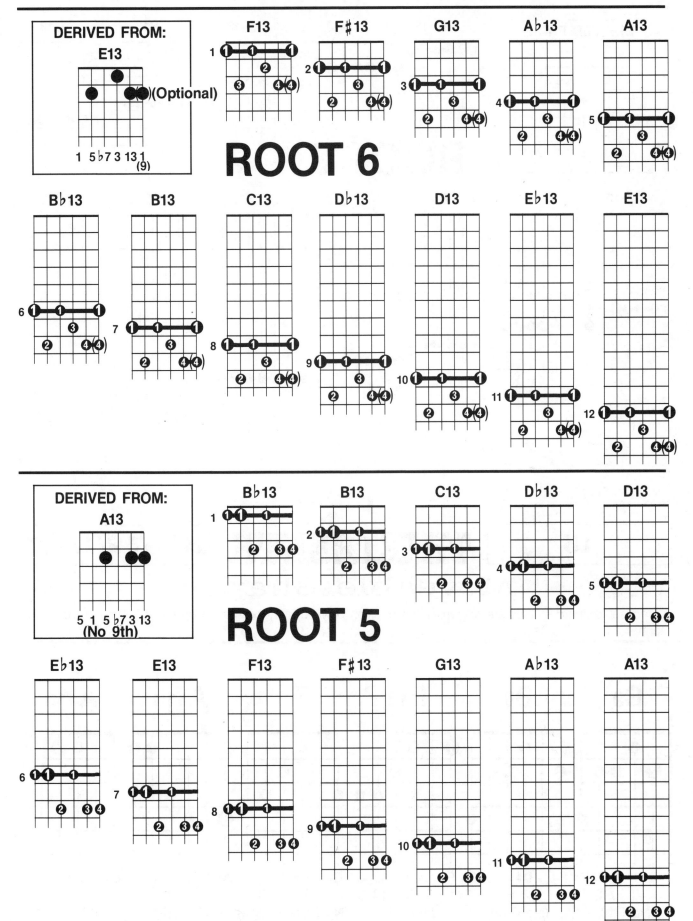

DERIVED FROM: E13 (Optional) — 1 5 ♭7 3 13 1 (9)

F13 · F#13 · G13 · A♭13 · A13

ROOT 6

B♭13 · B13 · C13 · D♭13 · D13 · E♭13 · E13

DERIVED FROM: A13 — 5 1 5 ♭7 3 13 (No 9th)

B♭13 · B13 · C13 · D♭13 · D13

ROOT 5

E♭13 · E13 · F13 · F#13 · G13 · A♭13 · A13

13 THIRTEENTH 1 3 5 ♭7 9 (11) 13

Bar Chord Shapes (Cont.) Omitted

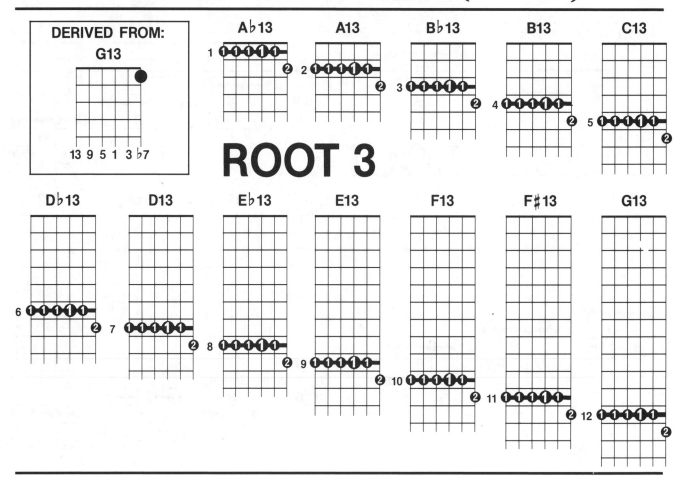

DERIVED FROM:
G13

13 9 5 1 3 ♭7

A♭13   A13   B♭13   B13   C13

ROOT 3

D♭13   D13   E♭13   E13   F13   F♯13   G13

13 THIRTEENTH 1 3 5 ♭7 9 (11) 13

Moveable Shapes Omitted

All moveable chord shapes are shown in first position only but may be moved up the fretboard in the same manner as Bar Chords.

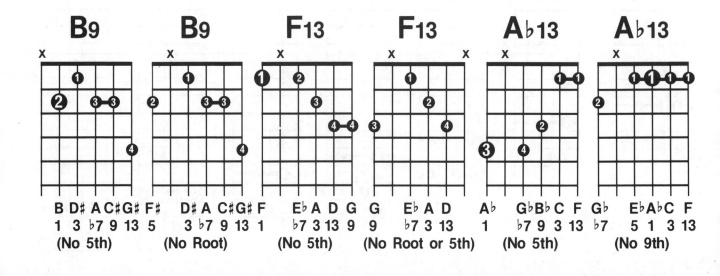

B9	**B9**	**F13**	**F13**	**A♭13**	**A♭13**
B D♯ A C♯ G♯ F♯	D♯ A C♯ G♯ F	E♭ A D G G	G E♭ A D	A♭ G♭ B♭ C F G♭	E♭ A B C F
1 3 ♭7 9 13 5	3 ♭7 9 13 1	♭7 3 13 9 9	9 ♭7 3 13	1 ♭7 9 3 13 ♭7	5 1 3 13
(No 5th)	(No Root)	(No 5th)	(No Root or 5th)	(No 5th)	(No 9th)

13♭9 THIRTEEN FLAT NINE 135♭7♭9(11)13

Omitted

Open Chords

A13♭9
E B♭ E G C♯ F♯
5 ♭9 5 ♭7 3 13
(No Root)

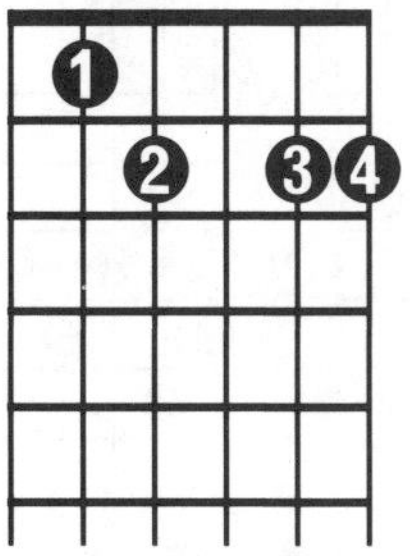

B♭13♭9
B♭ D A♭ C♭ G
1 3 ♭7 ♭9 13
(No 5th)

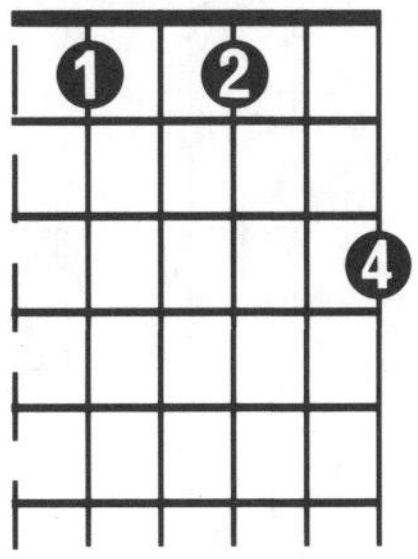

B13♭9
A D♯ G♯ C F♯
♭7 3 13 ♭9 5
(No Root)

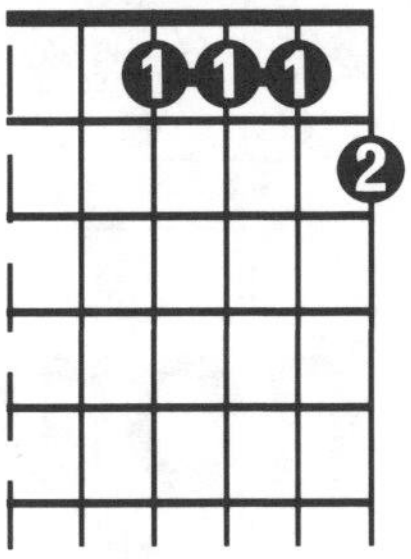

C13♭9
E A E B♭ D♭ G
3 13 3 ♭7 ♭9 5
(No Root)

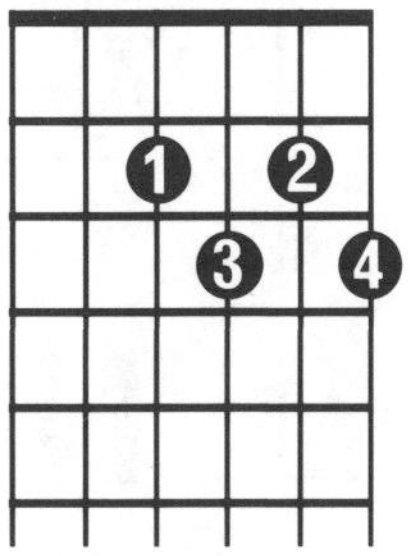

C♯13♭9
B D A♯ C♯ E♯
♭7 ♭9 13 1 3
(No 5th)

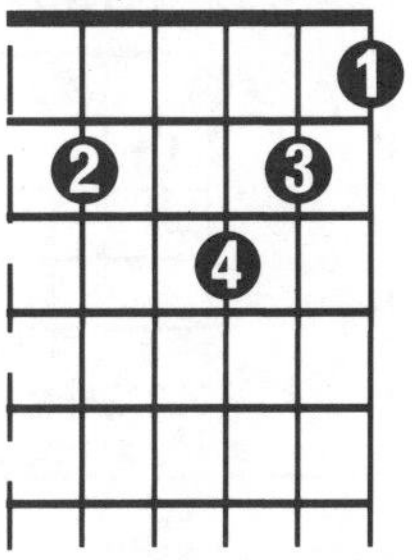

D13♭9
C D B E♭ F♯
♭7 1 13 ♭9 3
(No 5th)

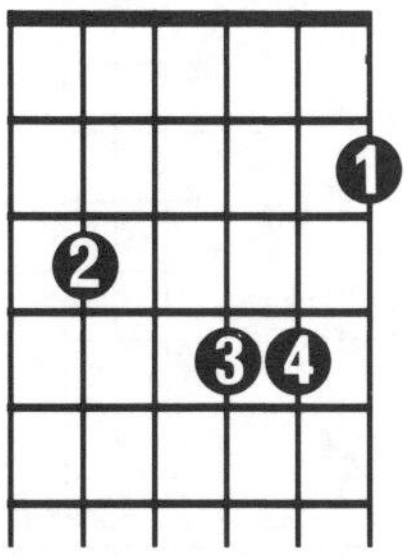

E♭13♭9
C F♭ B♭ D♭ G
13 ♭9 5 ♭7 3
(No Root)

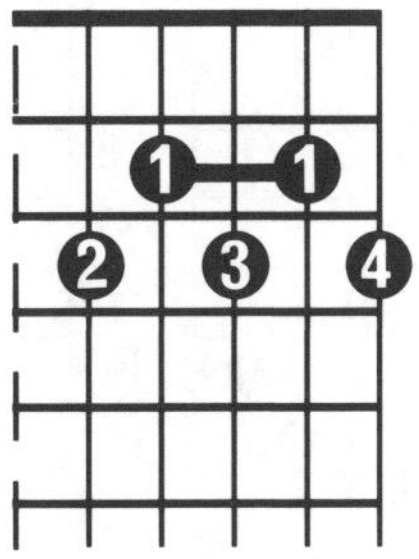

E13♭9
E B D G♯ C♯ F
1 5 ♭7 3 13 ♭9

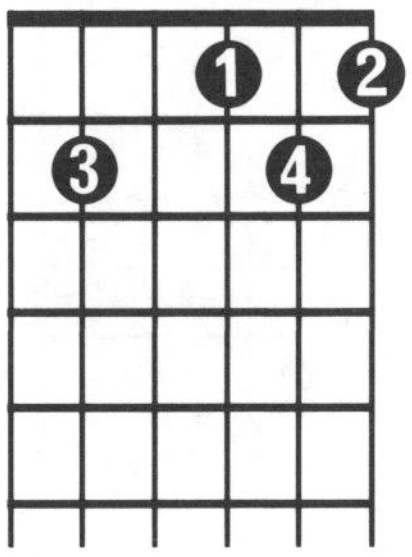

F13♭9
A D C E♭ G♭
3 13 5 ♭7 ♭9
(No Root)

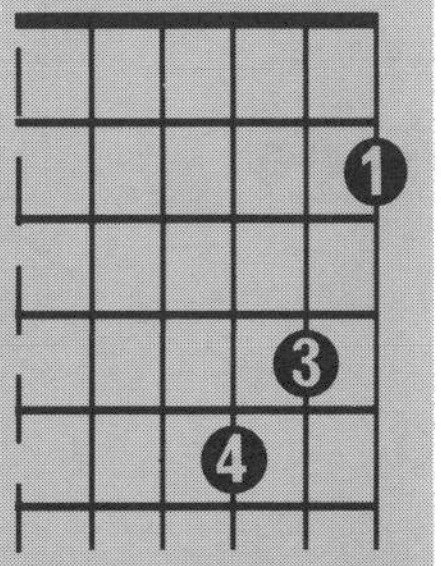

F13♭9
C D A E♭ G♭
5 13 3 ♭7 ♭9
(No Root)

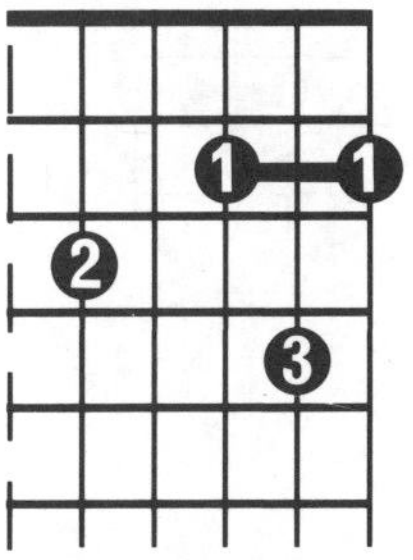

F♯13♭9
E A♯ D♯ G C♯ E
♭7 3 13 ♭9 5 ♭7
(No Root)

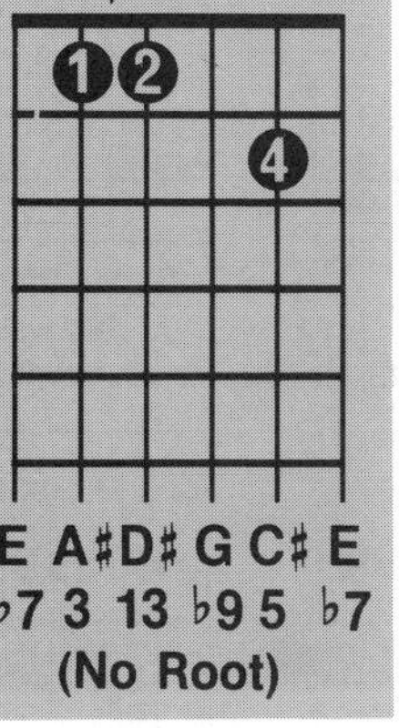

F♯13♭9
E A♯ D♯ G C♯ F♯
♭7 3 13 ♭9 5 1

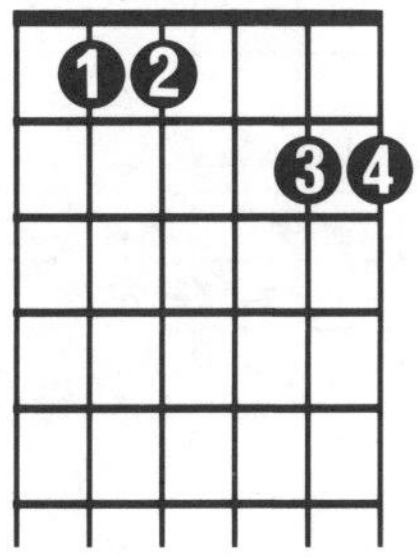

G13♭9
F B D A♭ B E
♭7 3 5 ♭9 3 13
(No Root)

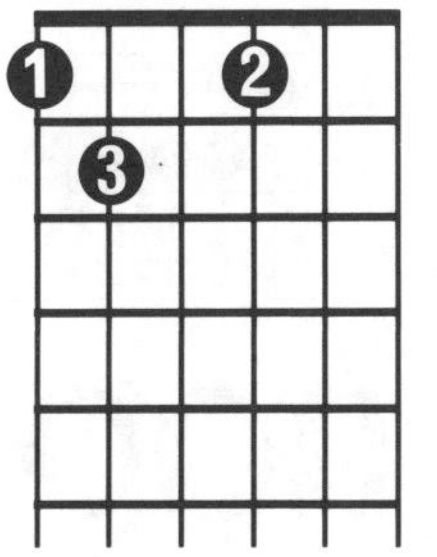

A♭13♭9
G♭ B♭ C F
♭7 ♭9 3 13
(No Root or 5th)

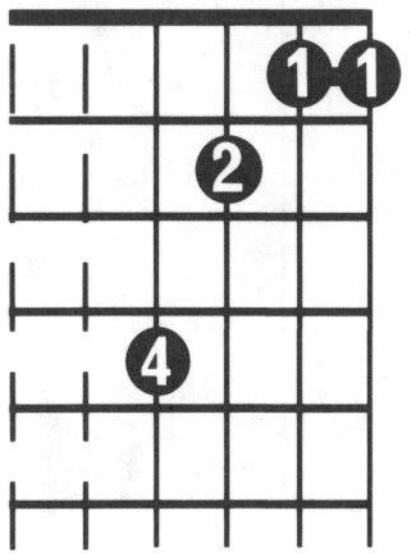

A♭13♭9
C F B♭♭ E♭ G♭
3 13 ♭9 5 ♭7
(No Root)

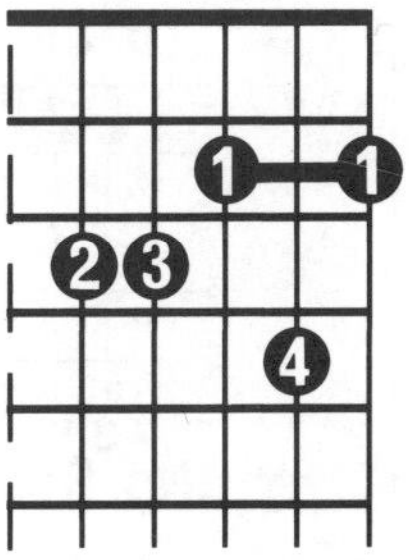

13♭9 | THIRTEEN FLAT NINE | 135♭7♭9(11)13

omitted

Bar Chord Shapes

DERIVED FROM:
G13♭9

♭7 3 5 ♭9 3 13
(No Root)

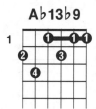 Ab13♭9
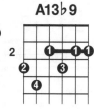 A13♭9
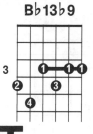 Bb13♭9
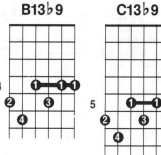 B13♭9
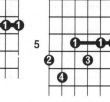 C13♭9

NO ROOT

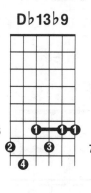 Db13♭9
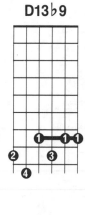 D13♭9
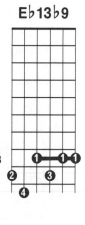 Eb13♭9
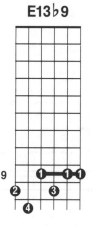 E13♭9
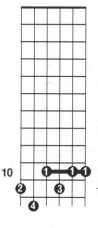 F13♭9
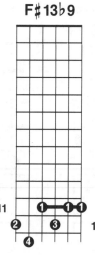 F#13♭9
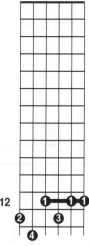 G13♭9

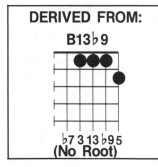

DERIVED FROM:
B13♭9

♭7 3 13 ♭9 5
(No Root)

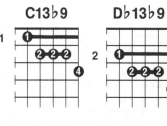 C13♭9 Db13♭9
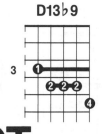 D13♭9
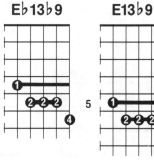 Eb13♭9
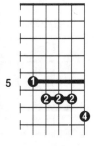 E13♭9

NO ROOT

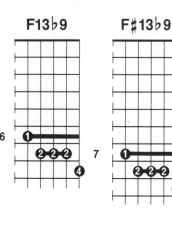 F13♭9 F#13♭9
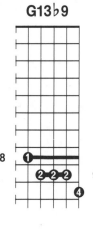 G13♭9
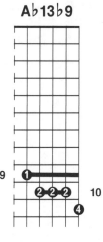 Ab13♭9
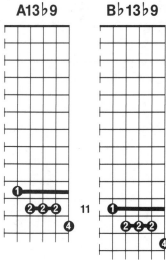 A13♭9 Bb13♭9
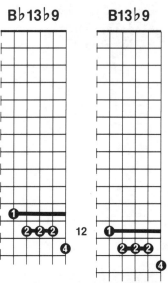 B13♭9

13♭9	**THIRTEEN FLAT NINE**	135♭7♭9(11)13

omitted

Bar Chord Shapes (cont.)

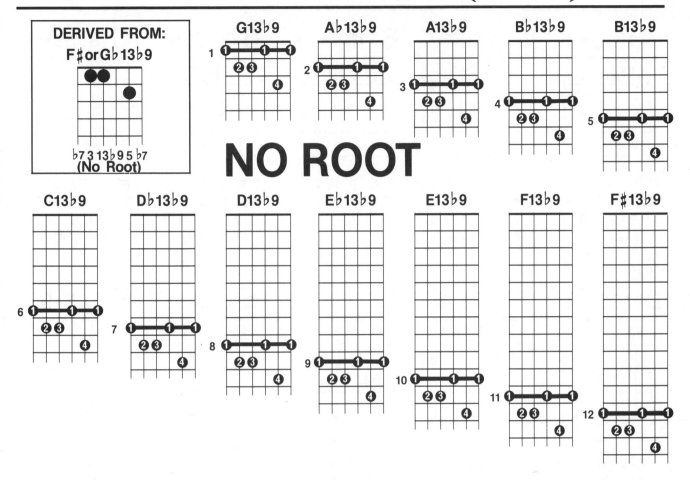

NO ROOT

13♭9	**THIRTEEN FLAT NINE**	135♭7♭9(11)13

omitted

Moveable Shapes

All moveable chord shapes are shown in first position only but may be moved up the fretboard in the same manner as Bar Chords.

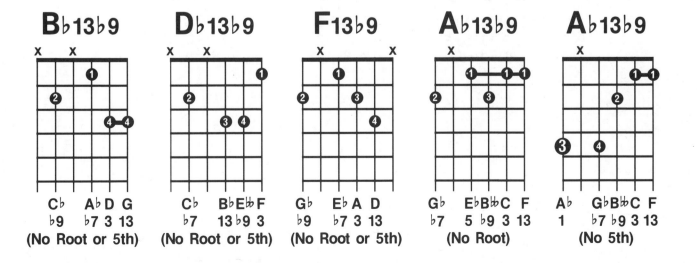

13♭5 ♭9 — THIRTEEN FLAT FIVE FLAT NINE — 1 3 ♭5 ♭7♭9 (11) 13
Omitted
Open Chords

A13♭5♭9

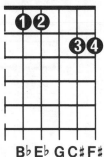

B♭ E♭ G C# F#
♭9 ♭5 ♭7 3 13
(No Root)

B♭13♭5♭9

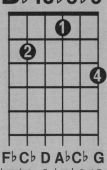

F♭ C♭ D A♭ C♭ G
♭5 ♭9 3 ♭7 ♭9 13
(No Root)

B♭13♭5♭9

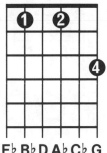

F♭ B♭ D A♭ C♭ G
♭5 1 3 ♭7 ♭9 13

B13♭5♭9

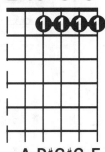

A D#G#C F
♭7 3 13 ♭9 ♭5
(No Root)

C13♭5♭9

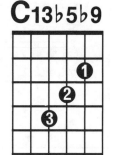

E A G♭ B♭ D♭ E
3 13 ♭5 ♭7 ♭9 3
(No Root)

D♭13♭5♭9

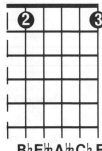

B♭ E♭ A♭♭ C♭ F
13 ♭9 ♭5 ♭7 3
(No Root)

D13♭5♭9

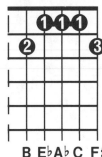

B E♭ A♭ C F#
13 ♭9 ♭5 ♭7 3
(No Root)

E♭13♭5♭9

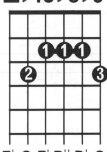

F♭ C F♭ B♭♭ D♭ G
♭9 13 ♭9 ♭5 ♭7 3
(No Root)

E13♭5♭9

E B♭ D G#C# F
1 ♭5 ♭7 3 13 ♭9

F13♭5♭9

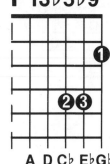

A D C♭ E♭ G♭
3 13 ♭5 ♭7 ♭9
(No Root)

F#13♭5♭9

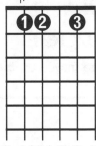

E A#D#G C E
♭7 3 13 ♭9 ♭5 ♭7
(No Root)

G13♭5♭9

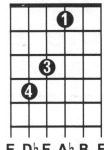

E D♭ F A♭ B E
13 ♭5 ♭7 ♭9 3 13
(No Root)

A♭13♭5♭9

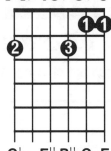

G♭ E♭♭ B♭♭ C F
♭7 ♭5 ♭9 3 13
(No Root)

13♭5♭9 — THIRTEEN FLAT FIVE FLAT NINE — 1 3 ♭5 ♭7 ♭9 (11) 13
omitted

Bar Chord Shapes

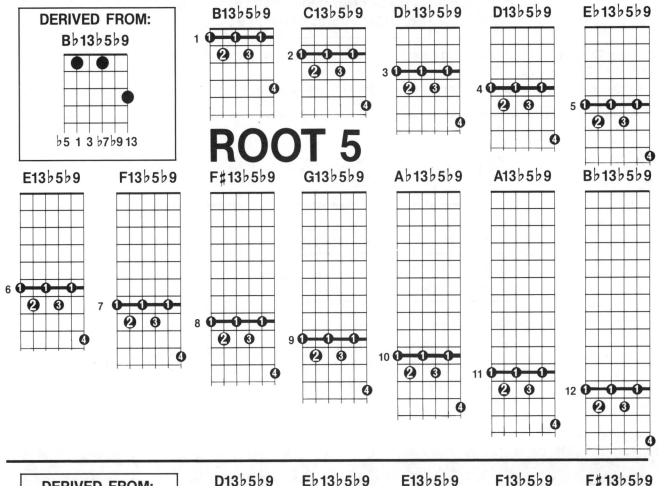

DERIVED FROM: B♭13♭5♭9

♭5 1 3 ♭7♭9 13

ROOT 5

B13♭5♭9 · C13♭5♭9 · D♭13♭5♭9 · D13♭5♭9 · E♭13♭5♭9

E13♭5♭9 · F13♭5♭9 · F#13♭5♭9 · G13♭5♭9 · A♭13♭5♭9 · A13♭5♭9 · B♭13♭5♭9

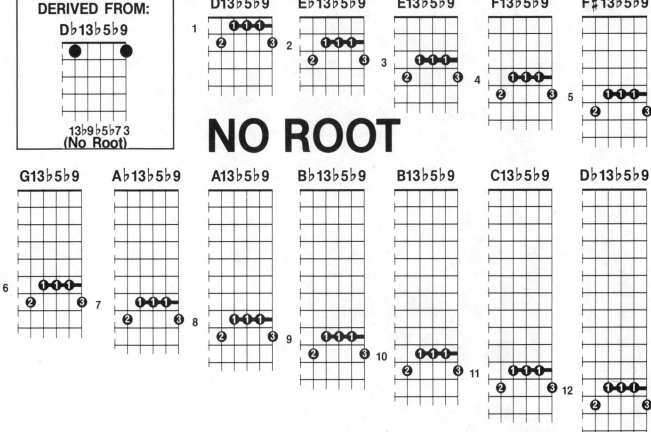

DERIVED FROM: D♭13♭5♭9

13♭9♭5♭7 3
(No Root)

NO ROOT

D13♭5♭9 · E♭13♭5♭9 · E13♭5♭9 · F13♭5♭9 · F#13♭5♭9

G13♭5♭9 · A♭13♭5♭9 · A13♭5♭9 · B♭13♭5♭9 · B13♭5♭9 · C13♭5♭9 · D♭13♭5♭9

13 b5 b9 THIRTEEN FLAT FIVE FLAT NINE   1 3 b5 b7 b9 (11) 13

Moveable Shapes

omitted

> I13b5b9 (No Root) = bV7#9
> e.g. C13b5b9 (No C) = Gb7#9

For any 13b5b9 chord, a 7#9 chord based on the flattened fifth note of the scale may be used. e.g. for C13b5b9, use Gb7#9 (see pge. 78).

All moveable chord shapes are shown in first position only but may be moved up the fretboard in the same manner as Bar Chords.

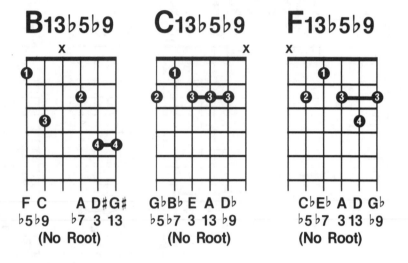

B13b5b9

```
F C   A D#G#
b5 b9  b7 3 13
   (No Root)
```

C13b5b9

```
GbBb E A Db
b5 b7 3 13 b9
   (No Root)
```

F13b5b9

```
Cb Eb A D Gb
b5 b7 3 13 b9
   (No Root)
```

LED ZEPPELIN

m13	# MINOR THIRTEEN	1♭35♭79(11)13

Open Chords

Omitted

Am13
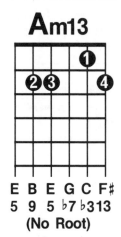

E B E G C F#
5 9 5 ♭7 ♭3 13

B♭m13
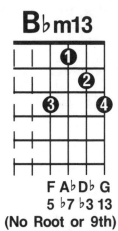

F A♭ D♭ G
5 ♭7 ♭3 13
(No Root or 9th)

Bm13

A F# A D G#
♭7 5 ♭7 ♭3 13
(No Root or 9th)

Cm13

A D B♭ E♭ G
13 9 ♭7 ♭3 5
(No Root)

Cm13
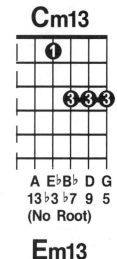

A E♭ B♭ D G
13 ♭3 ♭7 9 5
(No Root)

C#m13
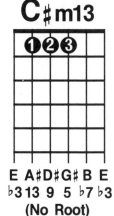

E A# D# G# B E
♭3 13 9 5 ♭7 ♭3
(No Root)

Dm13
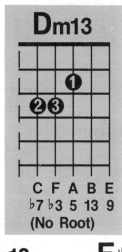

C F A B E
♭7 ♭3 5 13 9
(No Root)

Dm13

E B E A C F
9 13 9 5 ♭7 ♭3
(No Root)

E♭m13
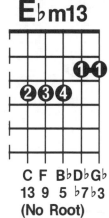

C F B♭ D♭ G♭
13 9 5 ♭7 ♭3
(No Root)

Em13
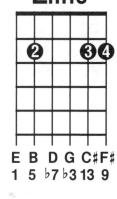

E B D G C# F#
1 5 ♭7 ♭3 13 9

Fm13
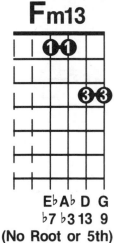

E♭ A♭ D G
♭7 ♭3 13 9
(No Root or 5th)

F#m13
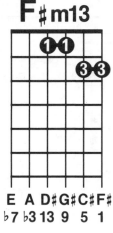

E A D# G# C# F#
♭7 ♭3 13 9 5 1

Gm13
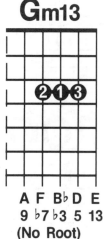

A F B♭ D E
9 ♭7 ♭3 5 13
(No Root)

A♭m13
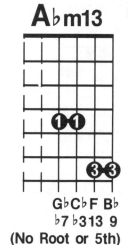

G♭ C♭ F B♭
♭7 ♭3 13 9
(No Root or 5th)

m13   MINOR THIRTEEN   1♭3 5 ♭7 9 (11) 13

omitted

Bar Chord Shapes

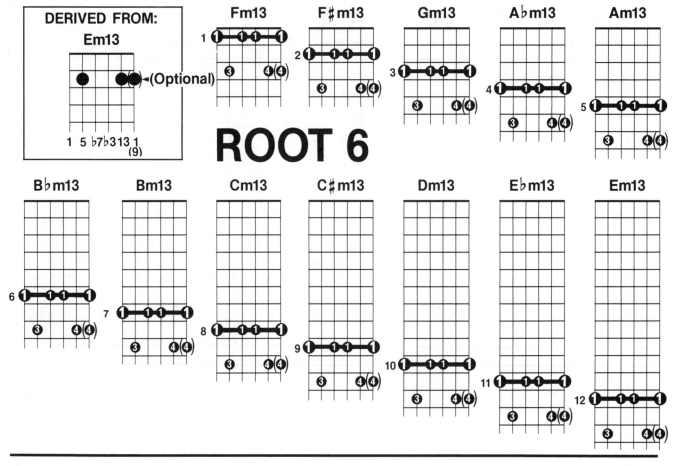

DERIVED FROM: Em13 (Optional)

1 5 ♭7♭3 13 1 (9)

Fm13 · F#m13 · Gm13 · A♭m13 · Am13

ROOT 6

B♭m13 · Bm13 · Cm13 · C#m13 · Dm13 · E♭m13 · Em13

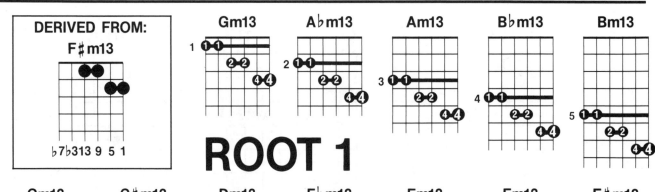

DERIVED FROM: F#m13

♭7♭3 13 9 5 1

Gm13 · A♭m13 · Am13 · B♭m13 · Bm13

ROOT 1

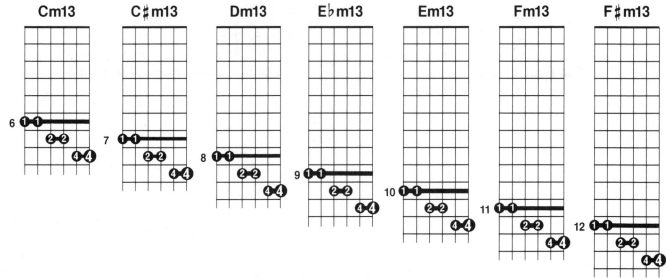

Cm13 · C#m13 · Dm13 · E♭m13 · Em13 · Fm13 · F#m13

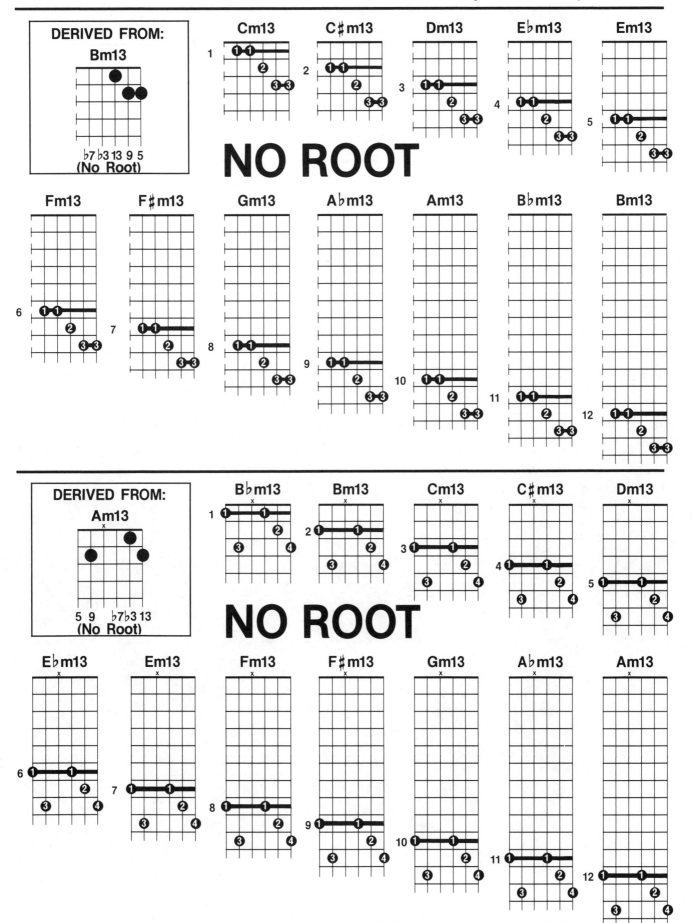

m13 | MINOR THIRTEEN 1 ♭3 5 ♭7 9 (11) 13
↑
omitted

Moveable Shapes

All moveable chord shapes are shown in first position only but may be moved up the fretboard in the same manner as Bar Chords.

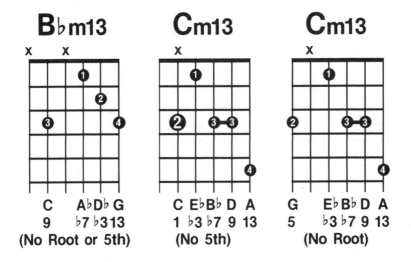

B♭m13

C   A♭ D♭ G
9   ♭7 ♭3 13
(No Root or 5th)

Cm13

C E♭ B♭ D   A
1 ♭3 ♭7 9   13
(No 5th)

Cm13

G   E♭ B♭ D   A
5   ♭3 ♭7 9   13
(No Root)

GEORGE BENSON.

SECTION TWO

MUSIC

THEORY

The information contained in this section need not be memorized immediately, however it is important that it be **THOROUGHLY UNDERSTOOD** and, over a period of time, committed to memory.

1. **Rudiments**
2. **Scales**
3. **Keys and Keysignatures**
4. **Circle of fifths**
5. **"Relative" keys**
6. **Chord construction**
7. **Scale tone chords**
8. **Modulation**
9. **Chord substitution**
10. **Transposing**

1. RUDIMENTS OF MUSIC

The musical alphabet consists of 7 letters: **A   B   C   D   E   F   G**
Music is written on a staff, which consists of 5 parallel lines between which there are 4 spaces.

Music staff

The Treble or "G" clef sign is placed at the beginning of each staff line.

Treble or "G" clef. ——→

This clef indicates the position of the note G. (It is an old fashioned method of writing the letter G, with the centre of the clef being written on the second staff line.)

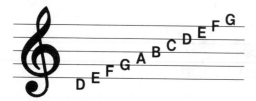

G note

The other lines and spaces on the staff are named as such:

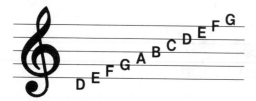

Extra notes can be added by the use of short lines, called ledger lines.

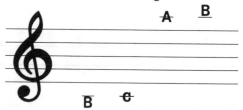

When a note is placed on the staff its head indicates its position. e.g.:

This is a G note.

This is a C note.

When the note head is below the middle staff line the stem points upward and when the head is above the middle line the stem points downward. A note placed on the middle line (B) can have its stem pointing either up or down.

Bar lines are drawn across the staff, which divides the music into sections called Bars or Measures. A double bar line signifies either the end of the music, or the end of an important section of it.

Bar or Measure

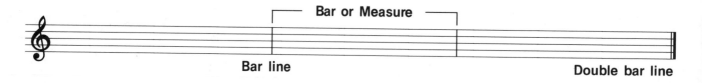

Bar line   **Double bar line**

Two dots placed before a double bar line indicate that the music is to be repeated:

Repeat sign

NOTE VALUES

The tables below set out the most common notes used in music and their respective time values (i.e. length of time held). For each note value there is an equivalent rest, which indicates a period of silence.

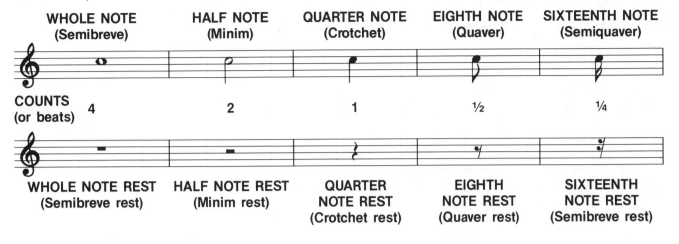

WHOLE NOTE (Semibreve)	HALF NOTE (Minim)	QUARTER NOTE (Crotchet)	EIGHTH NOTE (Quaver)	SIXTEENTH NOTE (Semiquaver)
COUNTS (or beats) 4	2	1	½	¼
WHOLE NOTE REST (Semibreve rest)	HALF NOTE REST (Minim rest)	QUARTER NOTE REST (Crotchet rest)	EIGHTH NOTE REST (Quaver rest)	SIXTEENTH NOTE REST (Semibreve rest)

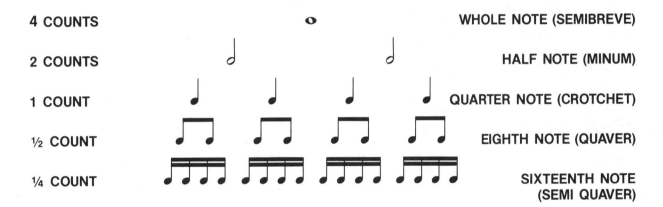

4 COUNTS		WHOLE NOTE (SEMIBREVE)
2 COUNTS		HALF NOTE (MINUM)
1 COUNT		QUARTER NOTE (CROTCHET)
½ COUNT		EIGHTH NOTE (QUAVER)
¼ COUNT		SIXTEENTH NOTE (SEMI QUAVER)

If a dot is placed after a note it increases the value of that note by a half, e.g.

Dotted HALF NOTE (2 + 1) = **3 counts**

Dotted QUARTER NOTE (1 + ½) = **1½ counts**

Dotted WHOLE NOTE (4 + 2) = **6 counts**

A **TIE** is a curved line joining two or more notes of the same pitch. Where the second note(s) is not played, but its time value is added to that of the first note. Here are two examples:

2 + 1 = 3 Counts   4 + 2 + 1 = 7 Counts

In both of these examples only the first note is picked.

TIME SIGNATURES

At the beginning of each piece of music, after the treble clef, is the time signature.

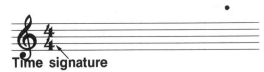

Time signature

The time signature indicates the number of beats per bar (the top number) and the type of note receiving one beat (the bottom number). For example:

4 — this indicates 4 beats per bar.

4 — this indicates that each beat is worth a quarter note (crotchet)

Thus in $\frac{4}{4}$ time there must be the equivalent of 4 quarter note beats per bar, e.g.

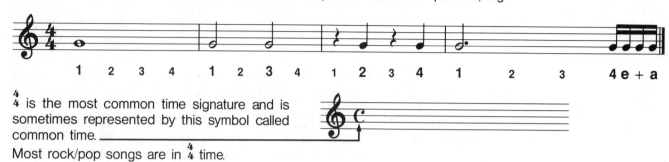

$\frac{4}{4}$ is the most common time signature and is sometimes represented by this symbol called common time.

Most rock/pop songs are in $\frac{4}{4}$ time.

$\frac{4}{4}$ is an example of what is called **SIMPLE TIME**.

Simple time occurs when the beat falls on **UNDOTTED NOTES** (quarter notes, half notes, eighth notes etc) and thus every beat is **DIVISIBLE BY TWO**. In $\frac{4}{4}$ time the basic beat is a quarter note, which can be split into groups of two thus:

QUARTER NOTE

EIGHTH NOTE

SIXTEENTH NOTE

Other common examples of simple time are $\frac{3}{4}$ and $\frac{2}{4}$.

$\frac{3}{4}$ indicates 3 quarter note beats per bar, e.g.

$\frac{2}{4}$ indicates 2 quarter note beats per bar, e.g.:

$\frac{6}{8}$ time indicates 2 dotted quarter note beats per bar, which can be divided into 2 groups of eighth notes as such:

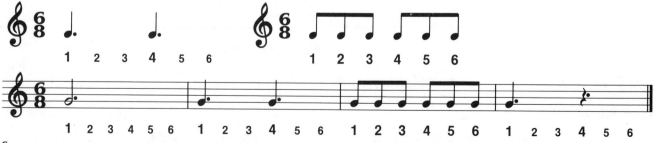

$\frac{6}{8}$ is an example of **COMPOUND TIME** because the beat is a **DOTTED NOTE**.

$\frac{4}{4}$ and $\frac{3}{4}$ are examples of **SIMPLE TIME** because the beat is an **UNDOTTED NOTE**.

NOTES IN THE OPEN POSITION

The open position on the guitar contains the notes of the open strings and the first three frets. Outlined below are the position of these notes on the staff and on the fretboard.

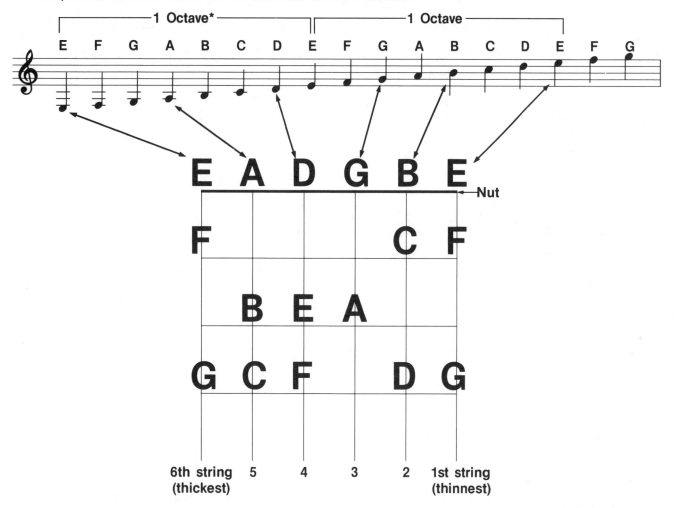

*An octave is the distance between two notes that have the same letter name and are 8 consecutive notes apart. The example above uses E notes, showing 2 octaves.

CHROMATIC NOTES

A sharp (♯) raises the pitch of a note by one semi-tone (1 fret).

A flat (♭) lowers the pitch of a note by one semi-tone.

In music notation the ♯ and ♭ signs (called accidentals) are always placed before the note.

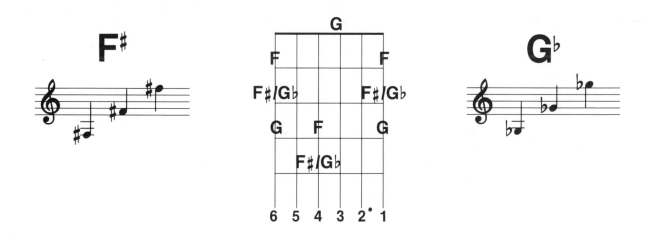

This example illustrates that the same note has two different names (i.e. F♯ and G♭ have the same position on the fretboard). These are referred to as **ENHARMONIC** notes.

Other examples of enharmonic note are: **A♯/B♭ C♯/D♭ D♯/E♭ F♯/G♭ G♯/A♭.** (This principle also applies to the naming of chords e.g. A♯Major = B♭Major, C♯m7 = D♭m7 etc.)

A natural (♮) cancels the effect of a sharp or flat.

A sharp or flat, when placed before a note, effects the same note if it re-occurs in the remainder of that bar.

It does not, however, affect notes in the next bar, e.g.:

E F♯ E F♯ F♯   E F♯ E F♯ F♯   F

With the inclusion of sharps and flats, there are 12 different notes within one octave, e.g.:

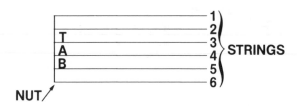

Note that there are no sharps or flats between B and C, and E and F.

TABLATURE

Tablature does not indicate the time values of the notes, only their position on the fretboard. You can read the time values by following the count written beneath the tablature. eg:

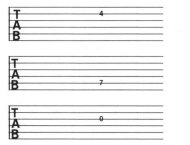

When a number is placed on one of the lines, it indicates the fret location of a note. eg.

This indicates the 4th fret of the second string (an E♭ note)

This indicates the 7th fret of the 5th string (an E note).

This indicates the third string open (a G note).

The tablature, as used in this book, does not indicate the time values of the notes, only their position on the fretboard. You can read the time values by following the count written beneath the tablature. eg,

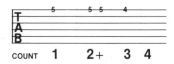

In this example the 1st note is worth 1 count, the 2nd and 3rd notes are worth ½ a count each and the 4th note is worth 2 counts.

COUNT   **1   2+   3   4**

NOTES ON GUITAR FRETBOARD

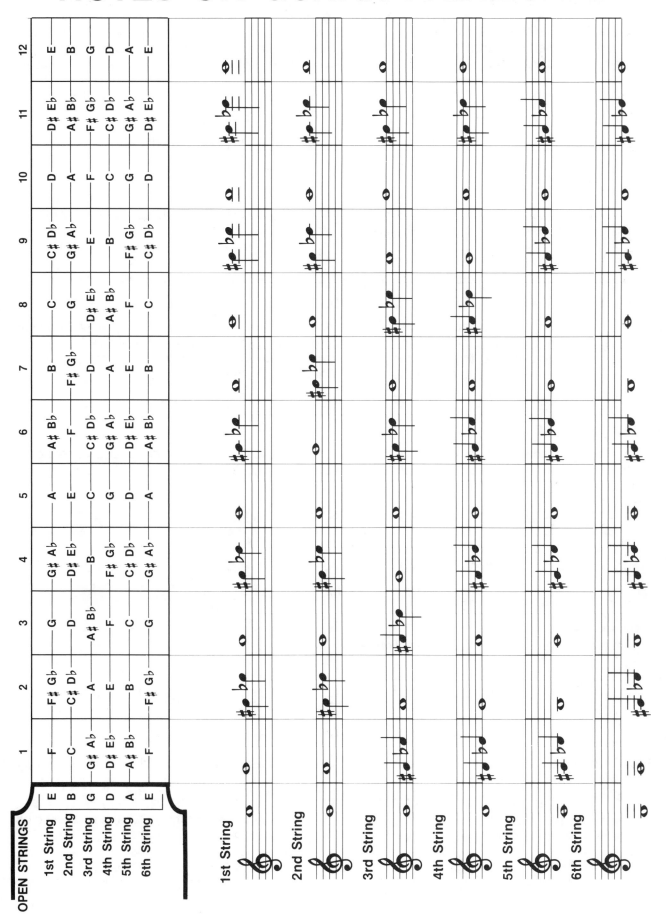

2. SCALES

A scale can be defined as a series of notes, in alphabetical order, going from any given note to its octave and based upon some form of set pattern. The pattern upon which most scales are based involves a set sequence of **TONES** and/or **SEMITONES**. On the guitar, a tone is two frets and a semitone is one fret. As an example, the B note is a tone higher than A, (two frets), whereas the C note is only a semitone higher than B (one fret). Of the other natural notes in music, E and F are a semitone apart, and all the others are a tone apart.

NATURAL NOTES: A   B   C   D   E   F   G   A

In music theory, a tone may be referred to as a **STEP** and a semitone as a **HALF - STEP**.

The 3 main types of scales that you need to become familiar with are the **CHROMATIC**, **MAJOR** and **MINOR** scales.

THE CHROMATIC SCALE

The chromatic scale is based upon a sequence of **SEMITONES** only and thus includes every possible note within one octave. Here is the C chromatic scale:

C   C♯   D   D♯   E   F   F♯   G   G♯   A   A♯   B   C

The same scale could be written out using flats, however it is more common to do this when descending, as such:

C   B   B♭   A   A♭   G   G♭   F   E   E♭   D   D♭   C

Because each chromatic scale contains every possible note within one octave, once you have learnt one you have basically learnt them all. As an example, the A chromatic scale (written below) contains exactly the same notes as the C chromatic scale, the only difference between them being the note upon which they commence. This starting note, in all scales, is referred to as the **TONIC** or **KEY NOTE**.

A Chromatic scale: A   A♯   B   C   C♯   D   D♯   E   F   F♯   G   G♯   A

THE MAJOR SCALE

The most common scale in Western music is called the **MAJOR SCALE**. This scale is based upon a sequence of both tones and semitones, and is thus sometimes referred to as a **DIATONIC** scale. Here is the major scale sequence:

TONE — TONE — SEMITONE — TONE — TONE — TONE — SEMITONE
T   —   T   —   S   —   T   —   T   —   T   —   S

Starting on the C note and following through this sequence gives the C major scale:

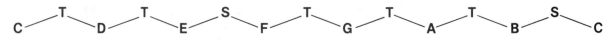

T - tone (2 frets)
S - semitone (1 fret)   and in musical notation:

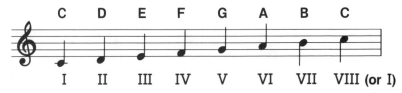

ROMAN NUMERALS are used to number each note of the major scale. Thus F is the 4th note of the C major scale, G is the 5th, and so on.
The major scale will always give the familiar sound of **DO, RA, ME, FA, SO, LA, TE, DO.**

The major scale **ALWAYS** uses the same sequence of tones and semitones, no matter what note is used as the tonic. The table below list the 13 most commonly used major scales.

You will notice that, in order to maintain the correct sequence of tones and semitones, all major scales except C major involve the use of either sharps or flats. You will notice, when playing these scales, that they all maintain the familiar sound of **DO, RA, ME, FA, SO, LA, TE, DO.**

C MAJOR:	C	D	E	F	G	A	B	C
G MAJOR:	G	A	B	C	D	E	F♯	G
D MAJOR:	D	E	F♯	G	A	B	C♯	D
A MAJOR:	A	B	C♯	D	E	F♯	G♯	A
E MAJOR:	E	F♯	G♯	A	B	C♯	D♯	E
B MAJOR:	B	C♯	D♯	E	F♯	G♯	A♯	B
F♯ MAJOR:	F♯	G♯	A♯	B	C♯	D♯	E♯	F♯
F MAJOR:	F	G	A	B♭	C	D	E	F
B♭ MAJOR:	B♭	C	D	E♭	F	G	A	B♭
E♭ MAJOR:	E♭	F	G	A♭	B♭	C	D	E♭
A♭ MAJOR:	A♭	B♭	C	D♭	E♭	F	G	A♭
D♭ MAJOR:	D♭	E♭	F	G♭	A♭	B♭	C	D♭
G♭ MAJOR:	G♭	A♭	B♭	C♭	D♭	E♭	F	G♭
Roman Numerals	I	II	III	IV	V	VI	VII	VIII

MINOR SCALES

In Western music there are three different minor scales. These are the **PURE MINOR**, the **HARMONIC MINOR** and the **MELODIC MINOR**. Each features a slightly different sequence of tones and semitones, as illustrated in the examples below using A as the tonic.

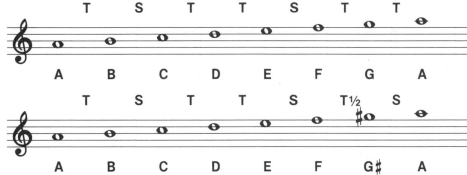

A minor 'pure' scale:

A minor Harmonic—7th note sharpened. (called the LEADING NOTE)

A MINOR MELODIC — 6th and 7th notes sharpened when ascending and returned to natural when descending.

Of these three minor scales outlined above, the **MELODIC MINOR** is the most commonly used. The table below lists the 13 most commonly used minor scales.

A MELODIC MINOR:	A	B	C	D	E	F♯	G♯	A	G♮	F♮	E	D	C	B	A
E MELODIC MINOR:	E	F♯	G	A	B	C♯	D♯	E	D♮	C♮	B	A	G	F♯	E
B MELODIC MINOR:	B	C♯	D	E	F♯	G♯	A♯	B	A♮	G♮	F♯	E	D	C♯	B
F♯ MELODIC MINOR:	F♯	G♯	A	B	C♯	D♯	E♯	F♯	E♮	D♮	C♯	B	A	G♯	F♯
C♯ MELODIC MINOR:	C♯	D♯	E	F♯	G♯	A♯	B♯	C♯	B♮	A♮	G♯	F♯	E	D♯	C♯
G♯ MELODIC MINOR:	G♯	A♯	B	C♯	D♯	E♯	F𝄪	G♯	F♯	E♮	D♯	C♯	B	A♯	G♯
D♯ MELODIC MINOR:	D♯	E♯	F♯	G♯	A♯	B♯	C𝄪	D♯	C♯	B♮	A♯	G♯	F♯	E♯	D♯
D MELODIC MINOR:	D	E	F	G	A	B♮	C♯	D	C♮	B♭	A	G	F	E	D
G MELODIC MINOR:	G	A	B♭	C	D	E♮	F♯	G	F♮	E♭	D	C	B♭	A	G
C MELODIC MINOR:	C	D	E♭	F	G	A♮	B♮	C	B♭	A♭	G	F	E♭	D	C
F MELODIC MINOR:	F	G	A♭	B♭	C	D♮	E♮	F	E♭	D♭	C	B♭	A♭	G	F
B♭ MELODIC MINOR:	B♭	C	D♭	E♭	F	G♮	A♮	B♭	A♭	G♭	F	E♭	D♭	C	B♭
E♭ MELODIC MINOR:	E♭	F	G♭	A♭	B♭	C♮	D♮	E♭	D♭	C♭	B♭	A♭	G♭	F	E♭

MODES

A mode can be described as being a displaced scale. In other words, if you play a C major scale, but starting and finishing on the D note, you are playing a mode:

D	E	F	G	A	B	C	D
II	III	IV	V	VI	VII	I	II

The roman numerals relate to the C scale.

This is called the **DORIAN** mode and it is produced by playing through II-II on the major scale (eg. D—D on the C scale). Each note of the major scale can be used as a tonic (starting note) for a different mode, and the situation can be summarized thus:

Roman numeral representation	Example using C scale								Mode name
I—I	C	D	E	F	G	A	B	C	Ionian (major scale)
II—II	D	E	F	G	A	B	C	D	Dorian
III—III	E	F	G	A	B	C	D	E	Phrygian
IV—IV	F	G	A	B	C	D	E	F	Lydian
V—V	G	A	B	C	D	E	F	G	Mixolydian
VI—VI	A	B	C	D	E	F	G	A	Aeolian (minor "pure" scale)
VII—VII	B	C	D	E	F	G	A	B	Locrian

Modes are commonly used in jazz improvisation.

3. KEYS AND KEY SIGNATURES

When music is talked of as being in a particular key, it means that the melody is based upon notes of the major scale (or minor scale) with the same name e.g. in the key of C, C major scale notes (i.e. C, D, E, F, G, A, and B) will occur much more frequently than notes that do not belong to the C scale (i.e. sharpened and flattened notes).

In the key of G, G scale notes will be most common (i.e. the notes G, A, B, C, D, E and F♯ will occur frequently). You will notice here that F♯ occurs rather than F natural. However, rather than add a sharp to every F note, an easier method is used whereby a sharp sign is placed on the F line (the top one) of the staff at the beginning of each line. This is referred to as the **KEY SIGNATURE**: thus the key signature of G major is F♯.

Written below are the key signatures for all major scales so far discussed.

C MAJOR	G MAJOR	D MAJOR	A MAJOR	E MAJOR	B MAJOR	F♯ MAJOR
No Sharps or Flats	F♯	F♯C♯	F♯C♯G♯	F♯C♯G♯D♯	F♯C♯G♯D♯A♯	F♯C♯G♯D♯A♯E♯

F MAJOR	B♭ MAJOR	E♭ MAJOR	A♭ MAJOR	D♭ MAJOR	G♭ MAJOR
B♭	B♭E♭	B♭E♭A♭	B♭E♭A♭D♭	B♭E♭A♭D♭G♭	B♭E♭A♭D♭G♭C♭

It can be seen, then, that each key signature is a shorthand representation of the scale, showing only the sharps or flats which occur in that scale. Where an additional sharp or flat occurs, it is not included as part of the key signature, but is written in the music, e.g. in the key of G, if a D♯ note occurs, the sharp sign will be written immediately before the D note, **NOT** at the beginning of the line as part of the key signature.

4. CIRCLE OF FIFTHS

The 13 major scales can be summarized in the following diagram, referred to as the "circle of fifths"*.

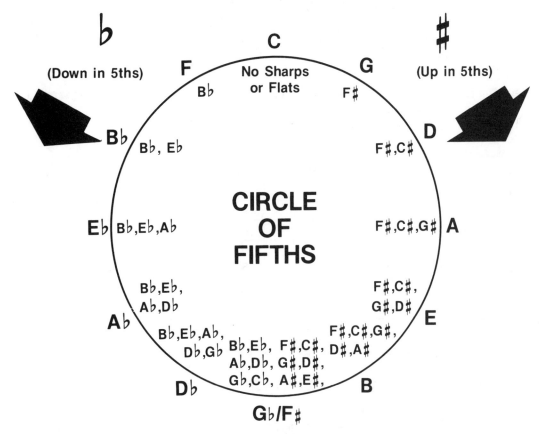

As the number of sharps increase, each new key is a fifth higher than the last.

```
            5th        5th      etc.
KEY          C ⌒  G ⌒  D        A      E      B      F♯
NO. OF SHARPS 0      1      2        3      4      5      6
```

*A FIFTH is calculated by counting up 5 scale notes from a tonic (key note), and INCLUDING the tonic as the first of the five. eg. C to G is a fifth:

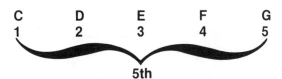

The same progression in fifths applies in each additional sharp:

KEY	NO. OF SHARPS	SHARPS
C	0	—
G	1	F♯
D	2	F♯, C♯
A	3	F♯, C♯, G♯
E	4	F♯, C♯, G♯, D♯
B	5	F♯, C♯, G♯, D♯, A♯
F♯	6	F♯, C♯, G♯, D♯, A♯, E♯

As the number of sharps increases each new key contains all the sharps of the previous keys and the additional sharp is always a **SEMITONE** lower than the root note of the new key. eg. the key of B contains all the sharps of the previous keys (F♯, C♯, G♯, D♯), plus a new sharp, A♯ (a semitone lower than B).

On the flat side of the circle, the same progression in fifths applies, except it works down in fifths rather than up in fifths. Going down a fifth gives a note with the same letter name as going up a fourth eg. a fifth down from C is F (C-B-A-G-F) which is also a fourth up from C (C-D-E-F). It is easier to count up in fourths so that as the number of flats increases each new key is a fourth higher than the previous one.

		4th		4th		etc.			
KEY		C	F	Bb	Eb	Ab	Db	Gb
NO. OF FLATS		0	1	2	3	4	5	6

As the number of flats increases, each new key contains all the flats of the previous keys and the additional flat is always a fourth higher than the last additional flat. eg the key of Db contains all the flats in the key of Ab (Bb Eb Ab Db) plus an additional flat which is a 4th higher than Db — Gb.

KEY	NO. OF FLATS	SHARPS
C	0	—
F	1	Bb
Bb	2	Bb, Eb
Eb	3	Bb, Eb, Ab
Ab	4	Bb, Eb, Ab, Db
Db	5	Bb, Eb, Ab, Db, Gb
Gb	6	Bb, Eb, Ab, Db, Gb, Cb

This process of working through the circle of fifths will enable you to work out the more difficult keys without having to memorize them.

5. "RELATIVE" KEYS

If you compare the A minor "pure" scale with the C major scale you will notice that they contain the same notes (except starting on a different note). Because of this, these two scales are referred to as being "relatives"; A minor is the relative minor of C major and vice versa.

MAJOR SCALE: C MAJOR   **RELATIVE MINOR SCALE: A MINOR (Pure)**

The harmonic and melodic minor scale variations are also relatives of the same major scale. e.g. A harmonic minor and A melodic minor are relatives of C major.

For every major scale (and every major chord) there is a relative minor scale which is based upon the 6th **NOTE** of the major scale. This is outlined in the table below:

MAJOR KEY (I)	C	Db	D	Eb	E	F	F#	Gb	G	Ab	A	Bb	B
RELATIVE MINOR KEY (VI)	Am	Bbm	Bm	Cm	C#m	Dm	D#m	Ebm	Em	Fm	F#m	Gm	G#m

Both the major and the relative minor share the same key signature, as illustrated in the examples below:

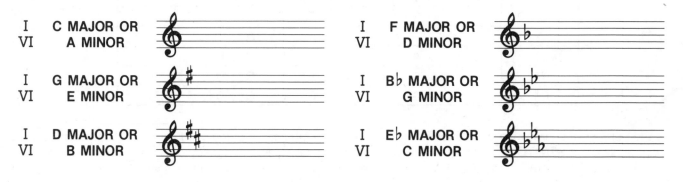

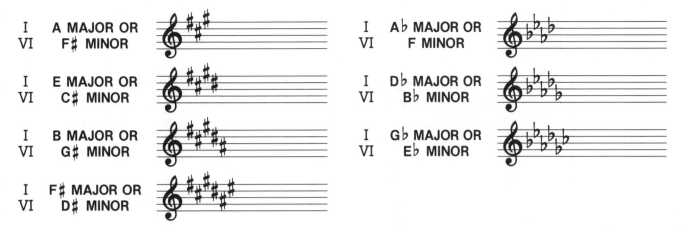

The sharpened 7th note that occurs in the relative minor key is never included as part of the key signature. Because each major and relative minor share the same key signature, you will need to know how to distinguish between the two keys. For example, if given a piece with the key signature of F♯ thus:

it could indicate either the key of G major, or its relative, E minor. The most accurate way of determining the key is to look through the melody for the sharpened 7th note of the E minor scale (D♯). The presence of this note will indicate the minor key. If the 7th note is present, but not sharpened, then the key is more likely to be the relative major (i.e. D natural notes would suggest the key of G major).

Another method is to look at the first and last chords of the progression. These chords usually (but not always) indicate the key of the piece. If the piece starts and/or finishes with Em chords then the key is more likely to be E minor.

6. CHORD CONSTRUCTION

THE MAJOR CHORD

A chord can be defined as a group of 3 or more different notes played together. Every chord is based upon a specific formula which relates back to the major scale after which it is named. The formula for a major chord is 1 3 5 hence the C major chord consists of the first, third and fifth notes of the C major scale, i.e. C-E-G.

C MAJOR SCALE

CHORD FORMULA: 1   3   5
NOTES: C   E   G

A chord must contain at least 3 notes, and any of these three may be repeated. In the open C chord illustrated there are 3 E notes, 2 C notes and 1 G note.

C major

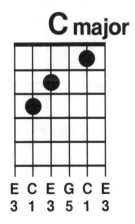

E C E G C E
3 1 3 5 1 3

Now consider the D major chord, which is constructed from the D major scale:

D   E   F♯   G   A   B   C♯   D

The same formula applies, 1 3 5, so the notes of a D major chord will be D-F♯-A. (Play an open D chord and check for yourself).

Applying the 1 3 5 major chord formula to the scales outlined on page 141 gives the following chord notes:

CHORD NAME	NOTES IN THE CHORD		
	1 (Root note)*	3	5
C	C	E	G
G	G	B	D
D	D	F♯	A
A	A	C♯	E
E	E	G♯	B
B	B	D♯	F♯
F♯	F♯	A♯	C♯
F	F	A	C
B♭	B♭	D	F
E♭	E♭	G	B♭
A♭	A♭	C	E♭
D♭	D♭	F	A♭
G♭	G♭	B♭	D♭

*The **ROOT NOTE** is the note after which the chord is named (e.g. C is the root note of C major, Cm, C7 etc.).

THE MINOR CHORD

The formula for minor chords is 1 3♭ 5, where 3♭ indicates that the third note of the scale is flattened. It must be remembered that this formula, although used to construct a minor chord, is still based upon the notes of the **MAJOR SCALE**. Thus the C minor chord consists of the first, flattened third and fifth notes of the **C MAJOR** scale:

C MAJOR SCALE

CHORD FORMULA: 1   3♭   5
NOTES: C   E♭   G

These notes are illustrated in the C minor chord below:

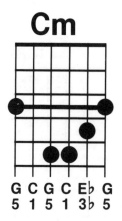

Cm

G C G C E♭ G
5 1 5 1 3♭ 5

The following table lists all of the notes of the minor chords for the scales previously studied:

	NOTES IN THE CHORD		
CHORD NAME	1 (Root note)	3♭	5
Cm	C	E♭	G
Gm	G	B♭	D
Dm	D	F	A
Am	A	C	E
Em	E	G	B .
Bm	B	D	F♯
F♯m	F♯	A	C♯
Fm	F	A♭	C
B♭m	B♭	D♭	F
E♭m	E♭	G♭	B♭
A♭m	A♭	C♭	E♭
D♭m	D♭	F♭	A♭
G♭m	G♭	B♭♭ *	D♭

A DOUBLE FLAT, ♭♭ lowers the note's pitch by **ONE TONE**. B♭♭ = A.

THE DOMINANT SEVENTH CHORD

The dominant seventh chord is formed by adding a flattened 7th note to the major chord.

1 3 5 7♭

Thus the C7 chord consists of the first, third, fifth and flattened seventh notes of the C MAJOR scale:

These notes are illustrated in the C7 chord below:

C7

G C G B♭ E G
5 1 5 7♭ 3 5

The following table lists all of the notes of the dominant 7th chords for the scales previously discussed.

CHORD NAME	NOTES IN THE CHORD			
	1	3	5	7♭
C7	C	E	G	B♭
G7	G	B	D	F
D7	D	F♯	A	C
A7	A	C♯	E	G
E7	E	G♯	B	D
B7	B	D♯	F♯	A
F♯7	F♯	A♯	C♯	E
F7	F	A	C	E♭
B♭7	B♭	D	F	A♭
E♭7	E♭	G	B♭	D♭
A♭7	A♭	C	E♭	G♭
D♭7	D♭	F	A♭	C♭
G♭7	G♭	B♭	D♭	F♭

CHORD FORMULA CHARTS

The following chart gives a comprehensive list of chord formulas, together with an example based on the **C SCALE**:

CHORD NAME	CHORD FORMULA	EXAMPLE
MAJOR	1 3 5	C: C E G
SUSPENDED	1 4 5	Csus: C F G
MAJOR ADD NINE	1 3 5 9	Cadd9: C E G D
MINOR	1 ♭3 5	Cm: C E♭ G
AUGMENTED	1 3 ♯5	Caug: C E G♯
MAJOR SIX	1 3 5 6	C6: C E G A
MAJOR SIX ADD NINE	1 3 5 6 9	C6/9: C E G A D
MINOR SIX	1 ♭3 5 6	Cm6: C E♭ G A
MINOR SIX ADD NINE	1 ♭3 5 6 9	Cm6/9: C E♭ G A D
DOMINANT SEVEN	1 3 5 ♭7	C7: C E G B♭
SEVEN SUSPENDED	1 4 5 ♭7	C7sus: C F G B♭
MINOR SEVEN	1 ♭3 5 ♭7	Cm7: C E♭ G B♭
DIMINISHED SEVEN	1 ♭3 ♭5 ♭♭7	Cdim: C E♭ G♭ B♭♭(A)
MAJOR SEVEN	1 3 5 7	Cmaj7: C E G B
MINOR MAJOR SEVEN	1 ♭3 5 7	Cm(maj7): C E♭ G B
NINTH	1 3 5 ♭7 9	C9: C E G B♭ D
MINOR NINE	1 ♭3 5 ♭7 9	Cm9: C E♭ G B♭ D
MAJOR NINE	1 3 5 7 9	Cmaj9: C E G B D
ELEVENTH	1(3) 5 ♭7 9 11	C11: C(E) G B♭ D F
MINOR ELEVEN	1 ♭3 5 ♭7 9 11	Cm11: C E♭ G B♭ D F
THIRTEENTH	1 3 5 ♭7 9(11) 13	C13: C E G B♭ D(F) A
MINOR THIRTEEN	1 ♭3 5 ♭7 9(11) 13	Cm13: C E♭ G B♭ D(F) A

( ) indicates that a note is optional.

*A **DOUBLE SHARP, ×**, raises the note's pitch by **ONE TONE**.

This next chord chart features chords which have a slight alteration to one of the given formulas, and are therefore called **ALTERED CHORDS**.

CHORD NAME	CHORD FORMULA	EXAMPLE	
MAJOR FLAT FIVE	1 3 ♭5	C♭5:	C E G♭
MINOR SEVEN FLAT FIVE	1 ♭3 ♭5 ♭7	Cm7♭5:	C E♭ G♭ B♭
SEVEN SHARP FIVE	1 3 ♯5 ♭7	C7♯5:	C E G♯ B♭
SEVEN FLAT FIVE	1 3 ♭5 ♭7	C7♭5:	C E G♭ B♭
SEVEN SHARP NINE	1 3 5 ♭7 ♯9	C7♯9:	C E G B♭ D♯
SEVEN FLAT NINE	1 3 5 ♭7 ♭9	C7♭9:	C E G B♭ D♭
SEVEN SHARP FIVE FLAT NINE	1 3 ♯5 ♭7 ♭9	C7♯5♭9:	C E G♯ B♭ D♭
NINE SHARP FIVE	1 3 ♯5 ♭7 9	C9♯5:	C E G♯ B♭ D
NINE FLAT FIVE	1 3 ♭5 ♭7 9	C9♭5:	C E G♭ B♭ D
NINE SHARP ELEVEN	1 3 5 ♭7 9 ♯11	C9♯11:	C E G B♭ D F♯
MINOR NINE MAJOR SEVEN	1 ♭3 5 7 9	Cm9(maj7):	C E♭ G B D
THIRTEEN FLAT NINE	1 3 5 ♭7 ♭9(11) 13	C13:	C E G B♭ D♭(F) A
THIRTEEN FLAT FIVE FLAT NINE	1 3 ♭5 ♭7 ♭9(11) 13	C13♭5♭9:	C E G♭ B♭ D♭(F) A

In altered chords, the notes to be altered are always written as part of the chord name, enabling you to construct the chord. For example, a Cm7♯5♭9 (not listed above) is a Cm7 chord with the fifth sharpened (♯5) and the ninth flattened (♭9). When you are working out a suitable shape for this chord, remember that the root note (C) may be omitted (see pge. 10) leaving the notes E♭(3♭), G♯(5♯), B♭(7♭) and D♭(9♭) to be located. The following shape could be used:

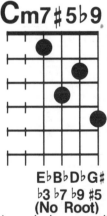

Cm7♯5♭9

E♭ B♭ D♭ G♯
♭3 ♭7 ♭9 ♯5
(No Root)

Another type of alteration occurs when chord symbols are written thus:
    example 1: G/F♯ bass. This indicates that a G chord is played, but using an F♯ note in the bass.
    example 2: C/G bass. This indicates a C chord with a G bass note.
Sometimes the word 'bass' will not be written (i.e. the symbol will be just G/F♯), but the same meaning is implied.

7. SCALE TONE CHORDS

In any given key certain chords are more common than others. For example, in the key of C the chords C, F and G are usually present, and quite often the chords Am, Dm and Em occur. The reason for this is that each key has its own set of chords, which are constructed from notes of its major scale. These chords are referred to as **SCALE TONE** chords.

Consider the C major scale:

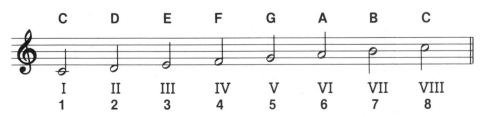

Chords are constructed by combining notes which are a third apart. For example, consider the formula for a major chord:

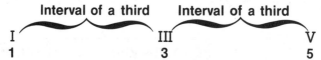

Using the C major scale written above, scale tone chords can be constructed by placing 2 third intervals above each note. This is illustrated in the following table:

5	G	A	B	C	D	E	F	G	) Third Interval
3	E	F	G	A	B	C	D	E	) Third Interval
C Scale: 1	C	D	E	F	G	A	B	C	
Chord Constructed:	C	Dm	Em	F	G	Am	Bdim	C	
	I	IIm	IIIm	IV	V	VI	VIIdim	VIII	

These are all C scale tone chords because they contain only notes of the C major scale (i.e. no sharps or flats). The method used for constructing scale tone chords in the key of C may be applied to ANY major scale. The result will **ALWAYS** produce the following scale tone chords:

Scale note:	I	II	III	IV	V	VI	VII	VIII
Chord Constructed:	Major	Minor	Minor	Major	Major	Minor	Dim.	Major
C Scale	C	Dm	Em	F	G	Am	Bdim	C
G Scale	G	Am	Bm	C	D	Em	F♯dim	G
D Scale	D	Em	F♯m	G	A	Bm	C♯dim	D
A Scale	A	Bm	C♯m	D	E	F♯m	G♯dim	A
E Scale	E	F♯m	G♯m	A	B	C♯m	D♯dim	E
B Scale	B	C♯m	D♯m	E	F♯	G♯m	A♯dim	B
F♯ Scale	F♯	G♯m	A♯m	B	C♯	D♯m	E♯dim	F♯
F Scale	F	Gm	Am	B♭	C	Dm	Edim	F
B♭ Scale	B♭	Cm	Dm	E♭	F	Gm	Adim	B♭
E♭ Scale	E♭	Fm	Gm	A♭	B♭	Cm	Ddim	E♭
A♭ Scale	A♭	Bm	Cm	D♭	E♭	Fm	Gdim	A♭
D♭ Scale	D♭	E♭m	Fm	G♭	A♭	B♭m	Cdim	D♭
G♭ Scale	G♭	A♭m	B♭m	C♭	D♭	E♭m	Fdim	G♭

SCALE TONE CHORD EXTENSIONS

The scale tone chords studied so far involve the placement of two notes (separated by an interval of a third) above a root note. This method of building scale tone chords can be extended by adding another note, illustrated in the following table:

7	B	C	D	E	F	G	A	B	) Third Interval
5	G	A	B	C	D	E	F	G	) Third Interval
3	E	F	G	A	B	C	D	E	) Third Interval
C Scale:	C	D	E	F	G	A	B	C	
Chord Constructed:	Cmaj7	Dm7	Em7	Fmaj7	G7	Am7	Bm7♭5 *	Cmaj7	
	Imaj7	IIm7	IIIm7	IVmaj7	V7	VIm7	VIIm7♭5	Imaj7	

*Another name for a minor seven flat five chord is Half-diminished, indicated thus ᵒ̸.

From this example, the scale tone chords for any key will be:

I	II	III	IV	V	VI	VII	VIII
Major7	Minor7	Minor7	Major7	Dominant7	Minor7	Minor7♭5	Major7
Cmaj7	Dm7	Em7	Fmaj7	G7	Am7	Bm7♭5	Cmaj7
Gmaj7	Am7	Bm7	Cmaj7	D7	Em7	F♯m7♭5	Gmaj7
Dmaj7	Em7	F♯m7	Gmaj7	A7	Bm7	C♯m7♭5	Dmaj7
Amaj7	Bm7	C♯m7	Dmaj7	E7	F♯m7	G♯m7♭5	Amaj7
Emaj7	F♯m7	G♯m7	Amaj7	B7	C♯m7	D♯m7♭5	Emaj7
Bmaj7	C♯m7	D♯m7	Emaj7	F♯7	G♯m7	A♯m7♭5	Bmaj7
F♯maj7	G♯m7	A♯m7	Bmaj7	C♯7	D♯m7	E♯m7♭5	F♯maj7
Fmaj7	Gm7	Am7	B♭maj7	C7	Dm7	Em7♭5	Fmaj7
B♭maj7	Cm7	Dm7	E♭maj7	F7	Gm7	Am7♭5	B♭maj7
E♭maj7	Fm7	Gm7	A♭maj7	B♭7	Cm7	Dm7♭5	E♭maj7
A♭maj7	B♭m7	Cm7	D♭maj7	E♭7	Fm7	Gm7♭5	A♭maj7
D♭maj7	E♭maj7	Fm7	G♭maj7	A♭7	B♭m7	Cm7♭5	D♭maj7
G♭maj7	A♭m7	B♭m7	C♭maj7	D♭7	E♭m7	Fm7♭5	G♭maj7

THE CHORD/KEY RELATIONSHIP

The chords which occur most frequently in any key will be those whose notes are taken from the key's major scale. For example, in the key of C the most likely chord to appear will be those which contain **ALL NATURAL NOTES** (ie notes from the C scale). Here are 25 such chords, which can be said to "belong" to the key of C.

I	C I	C6 I6	Cmaj7 Imaj7	Cmaj9 Imaj9	Csus Isus	
II	Dm IIm	Dm6 IIm6	Dm7 IIm7	Dm9 IIm9		
III	Em IIIm	Em7 IIIm7				
IV	F IV	F6 IV6	Fmaj7 IVmaj7	Fmaj9 IVmaj9		
V	G V	G6 V6	G7 V7	G9 V9	G11 V11	G13 V13
VI	Am VIm	Am7 VIm7	Am9 VIm9			
VII	Bm7♭5 VIIm7♭5					

A thorough knowledge of these chords will help you to decide the key of a piece where no key signature is given (eg for lead guitar improvisation). For example:

Em7	Am7	Em7	Am7	Em7	Am7	F♯m7♭5	Gmaj7

This progression is in the key of G, using the chords:

VIm7	IIm7	VIm7	IIm7	VIm7	IIm7	VIIm7♭5	Imaj7

A knowledge of chords within a given key will also help you to choose the correct backing chords of a melody (or song).

8. MODULATION

Modulation can be defined as the changing of key within a song (or chord progression). It is very important to recognise a modulation.

In sheet music, a modulation is sometimes indicated by changing the key signature. This will usually be done if the modulation occurs between one section of the song and the next (e.g. between one verse and another). Where there is no change of key signature, a modulation may be detected by examining the melody and/or the chords. When examining the melody, remember that each key is recognisable by the notes of its scale. If different notes appear it may indicate a modulation. For example, if a melody in the key of C suddenly features F♯ notes, it could suggest a modulation to the key of G. When examining the chords, a modulation may be determined by following the chord/key relationship, i.e. looking for chords that "fit in" to a certain key. Consider the following progression:

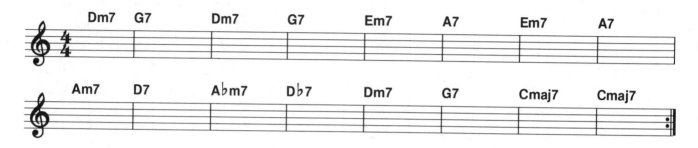

which can be analysed as such:

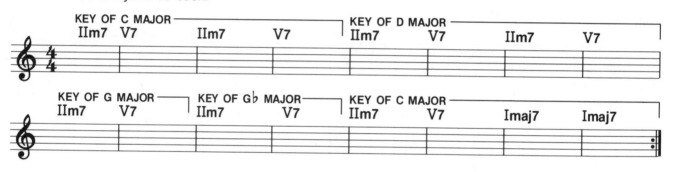

The use of Roman numerals makes the lay-out of this progression very clear, it is based on the IIm7—V7 chords, modulating through four different keys. This type of modulation is most common in jazz songs. You will find that many rock songs, although featuring modulation, will not do so to such a great extent.

One of the most common modulations in songs is from the major key to its relative minor:

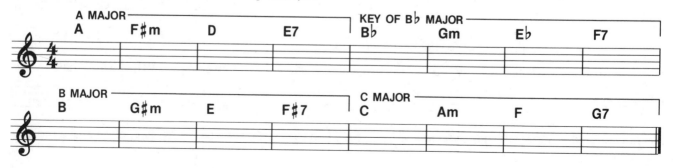

Another common form of modulation is to change up to the key one semitone or one tone higher. This can be done successively, as in the following example:

9. CHORD SUSBSTITUTION

Chord substitution involves playing a different set of chords for a given chord progression. This is useful for both beginners and advanced players. Beginners will be able to substitute easier chords for a given chord line (e.g. working from sheet music); and advanced players will be able to embellish a chord progression, often creating a "jazz" flavour.

The table below summarises common substitutions for beginners. These substitutions can be used because the chords contain similar notes and hence have a similar sound.

GIVEN CHORD	USE	GIVEN CHORD	USE	GIVEN CHORD	USE
6 6/9 add9 maj7 maj9 maj11 maj13 maj7♯11 sus	MAJOR	m6 m7 m6/9 m9 m11 m13 m(maj7) m7♭5 m9♭5	MINOR	7♯5 7♭5 7♯9 7♭9 9 11 13 7♯5♯9 7♯5♭9 7♭5♯9 7♭5♭9 7♯11 9♯5 9♭5	DOM7th

Here is an example of simplifying a chord progression, by using the substitutions outlined above.

Given Chords: Cmaj7   C6   Dm7   Dm6   Em7   Em6   G9   **Finish on** G7♭9 Cmaj7

Substitute: C   Dm   Em   G7   **Finish on Cmaj**

More advanced players can use a **REVERSE** of the above table. eg for Am, play Am7, Am6 or perhaps use a combination of the two. This type of substitution is called **DIRECT SUBSTITUTION**, and here are two examples:

TURNAROUND IN A

Given Chords: A   F♯m   D   E7   **Finish on Amaj**

Substitute: Amaj7   F♯m7   Dmaj7   E9   E13 **Finish on Amaj7**

JAZZ BLUES IN B♭

Given Chords: B♭7   E♭7   B♭7   B♭

Substitute: B♭7   E♭9   B♭9   B♭6

E♭7   E♭7   B♭7   B♭7

E♭9   E♭9   B♭7   B♭9

F7   E♭7   B♭7   F7   **Finish on B♭**

F9   E♭9   B♭7   F9   **Finish on B♭**

Further examples of direct substitution can be found in Section III, where each basic scale tone chord progression is repeated using scale tone chord extensions.

With all substitutions you should **EXPERIMENT** and let your **EAR** be the final judge.

10. TRANSPOSING

The term 'Transposing' is used to describe the process whereby a progression (or song) is changed from one key to another. This is done for two main reasons:

1. Singing — to sing the whole song at a lower or higher pitch (depending on the singer's vocal range).

2. Ease of playing — because of the musical structure of the guitar, some keys are easier to play in than others (e.g. Beginning students may not be able to play a song in the key of say E♭, but could perhaps play it in the key of C.)

Consider the following turnaround in the key of C:

If you needed to transpose this progression into the key of G, the following method may be used:

1. Write out the C chromatic scale.

2. Write out the G chromatic scale, with each note directly below its counterpart in the C chromatic scale, as such:

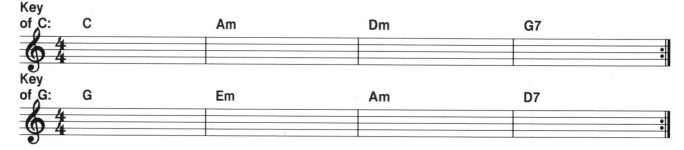

3. When the given progression is transposed to the key of G, the first chord, C major, will become G major. This can be seen by relating the two chromatic scales via arrow one.

4. The second chord of the progression, Am, will become Em (arrow two). Although the chord **NAME** will change when transposing, its **TYPE** (i.e. major, minor, seventh etc) will remain the same.

5. The complete transposition will be:

Key of C: C   Am   Dm   G7

Key of G: G   Em   Am   D7

Play both progressions and notice the similarity in sound.

Beginners will mainly transpose for ease of playing, and thus the easiest keys for a song to be transposed into are C, G and D (for major keys) and Am, Em and Bm (for minor keys). Remember to write the second chromatic scale directly under the first, note for note, in order to transpose correctly. Try transposing the previous progression into the key of D major.

THE CAPO

The capo is a device which is place across the neck of the guitar (acting as a moveable nut). It has 2 uses:

1. To enable the use of easier chord shapes, without changing the key of a song.

2. To change the key of a song, without changing the chord shapes.

Expanding upon point 1, if a song is in a key which is within your singing range, but involves playing difficult chords (e.g. in the key of E♭), a capo may be used.

 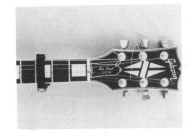

(Capos come in various shapes and sizes.)

The capo allows you to play the song in the same key, yet at the same time use easier (open) chords. Consider a turnaround in E♭:

If you place the capo on the third fret, the following chords can be played without changing the song's key.

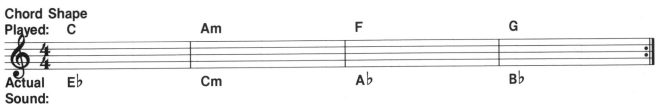

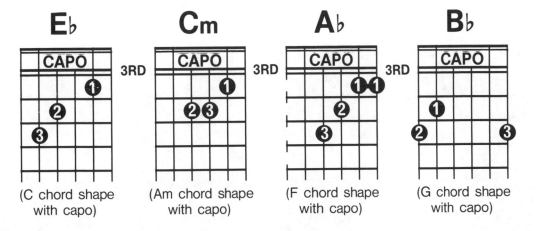

(C chord shape with capo)   (Am chord shape with capo)   (F chord shape with capo)   (G chord shape with capo)

If you have studied bar chords, you will notice that the capo is acting as a bar.

To work out which fret the capo must be placed on, simply count the number of semitones between the "capo" key you have selected to change to* (e.g. C, as used in the above example) and the original key (i.e. E♭ as above). Hence C to E♭ = 3 semitones, and therefore the capo must be placed on the third fret.

Expanding upon point 2, consider a song in the key of C, using the turnaround progression:

A singer may decide that this key is unsuitable for his or her voice range and may wish to use the key of, say, E♭. The progression, transposed to E♭, will become:

*Remember you are not actually changing key but merely changing the chord shapes, for ease of playing.

156

Instead of changing to these new chord shapes (i.e. having to use bar chords), the guitarist may still play the C, Am, F and G chords, but **MUST PLACE THE CAPO AT THE 3RD FRET** to do so.

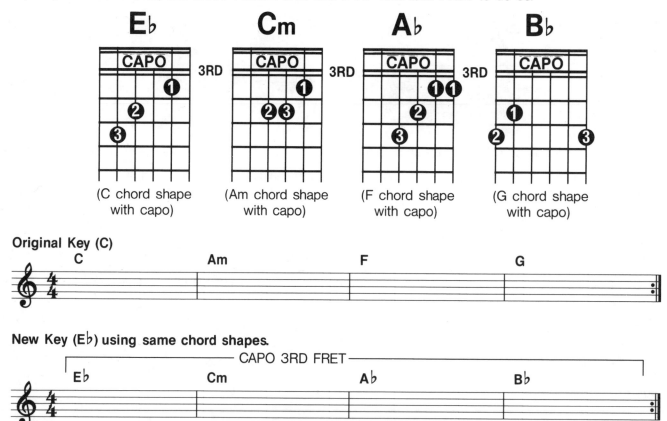

(C chord shape with capo)   (Am chord shape with capo)   (F chord shape with capo)   (G chord shape with capo)

Original Key (C)

C   Am   F   G

New Key (E♭) using same chord shapes.

CAPO 3RD FRET

E♭   Cm   A♭   B♭

'PRINCE'.

SECTION III

CHORD/KEY RELATIONSHIPS

This section introduces the most common chords in each major and relative minor key; together with example progressions based upon **SCALE TONE** chords (see pge. 149). The chord shapes illustrated are those most likely to be used by rock guitarists (i.e. mainly bar chords), however beginners should use open chords and advanced players should experiment with moveable shapes.

KEY OF A MAJOR

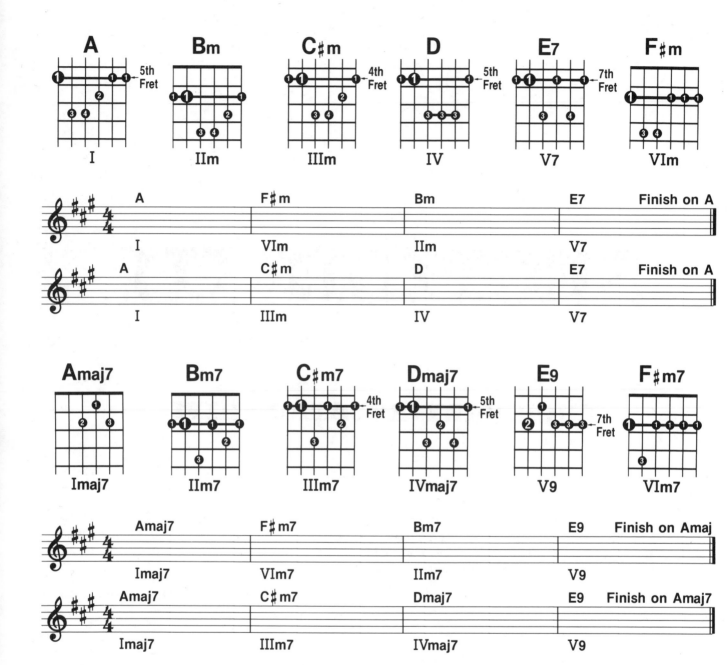

RELATIVE MINOR: F# minor

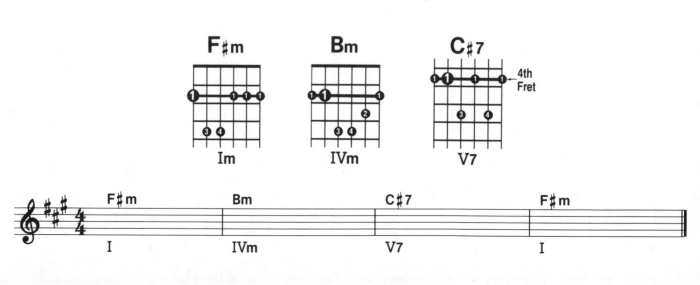

KEY OF B♭ MAJOR

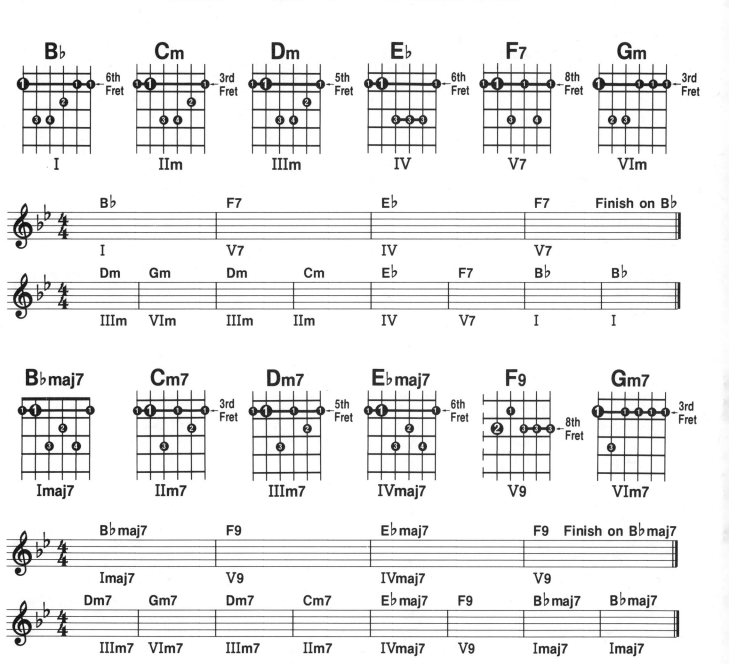

RELATIVE MINOR: G minor

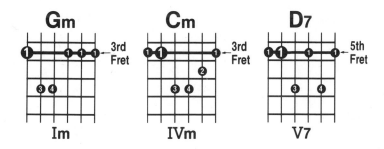

KEY OF B MAJOR

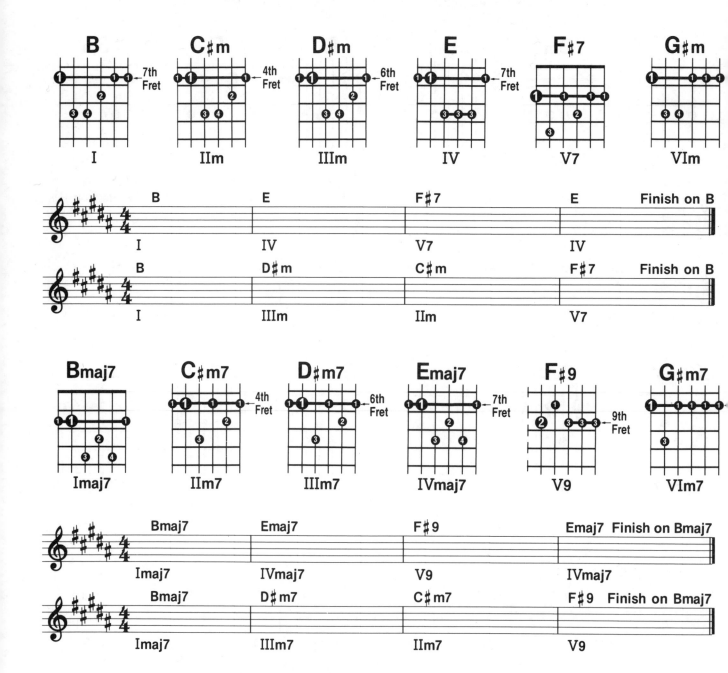

RELATIVE MINOR: G♯ minor

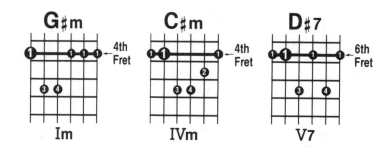

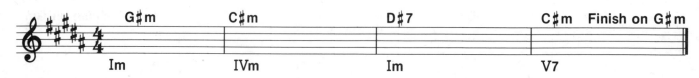

KEY OF C MAJOR

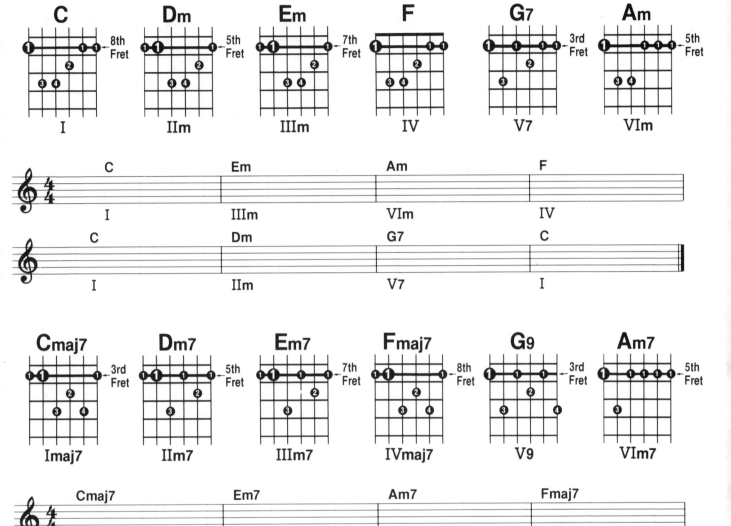

RELATIVE MINOR: A minor

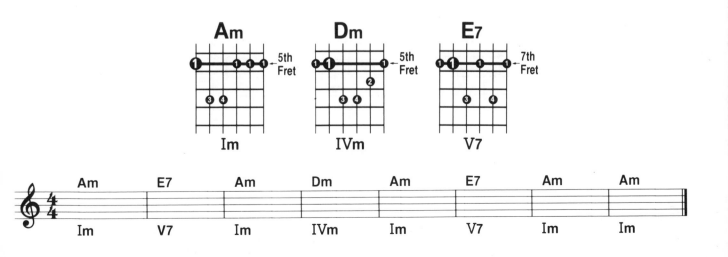

KEY OF D♭ MAJOR

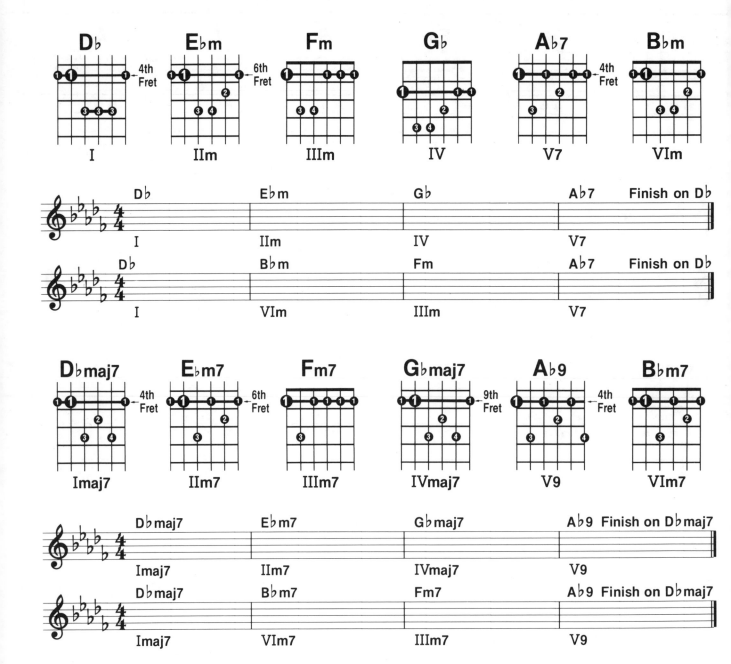

RELATIVE MINOR: B♭ minor

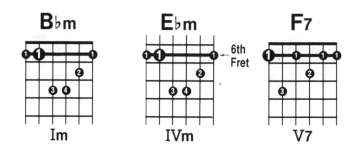

KEY OF D MAJOR

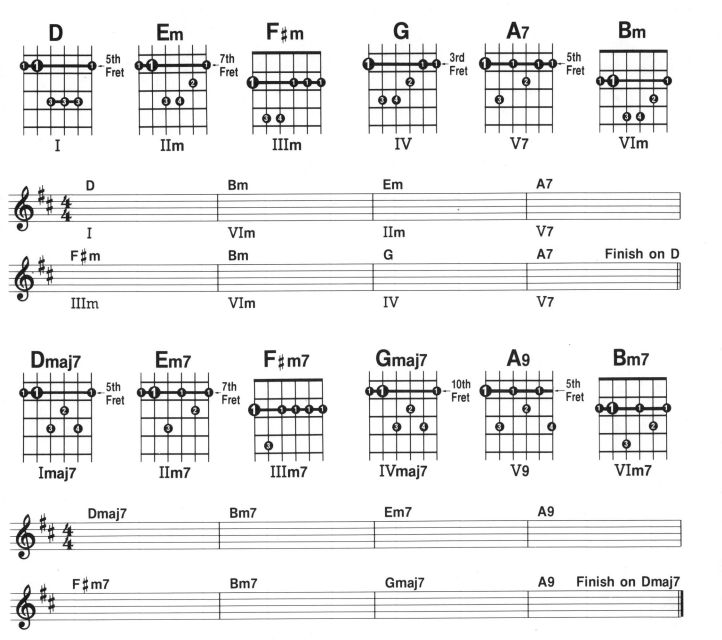

RELATIVE MINOR: B minor

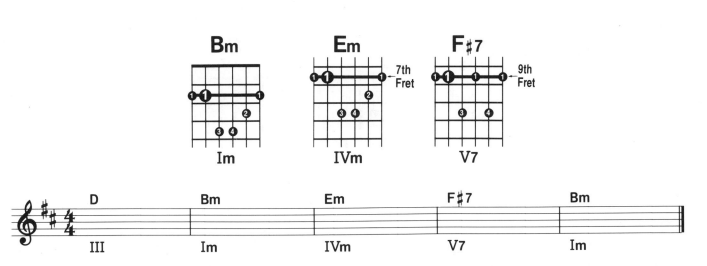

KEY OF E♭ MAJOR

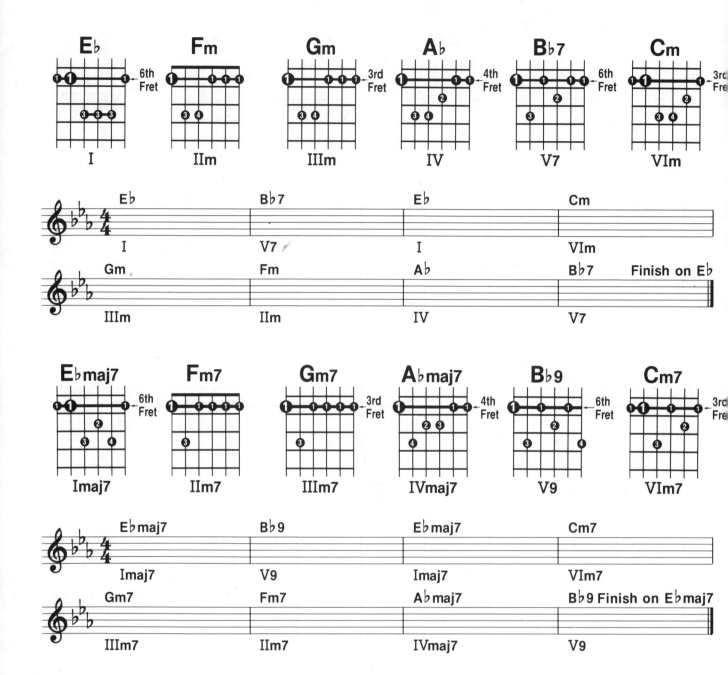

RELATIVE MINOR: C minor

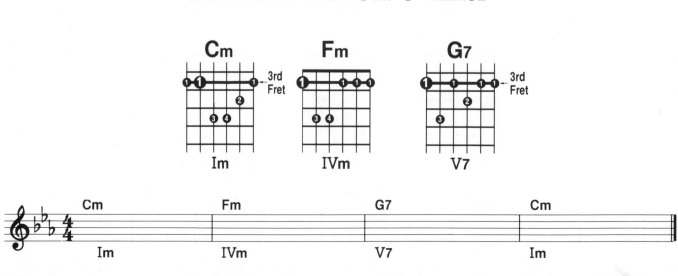

KEY OF E MAJOR

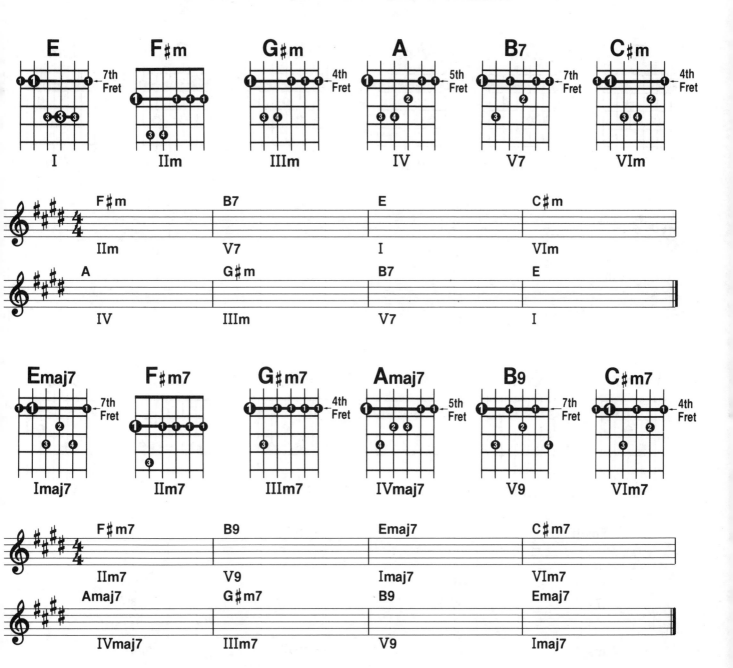

RELATIVE MINOR: C♯ minor

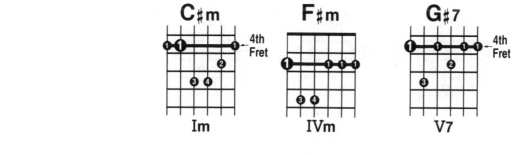

KEY OF F MAJOR

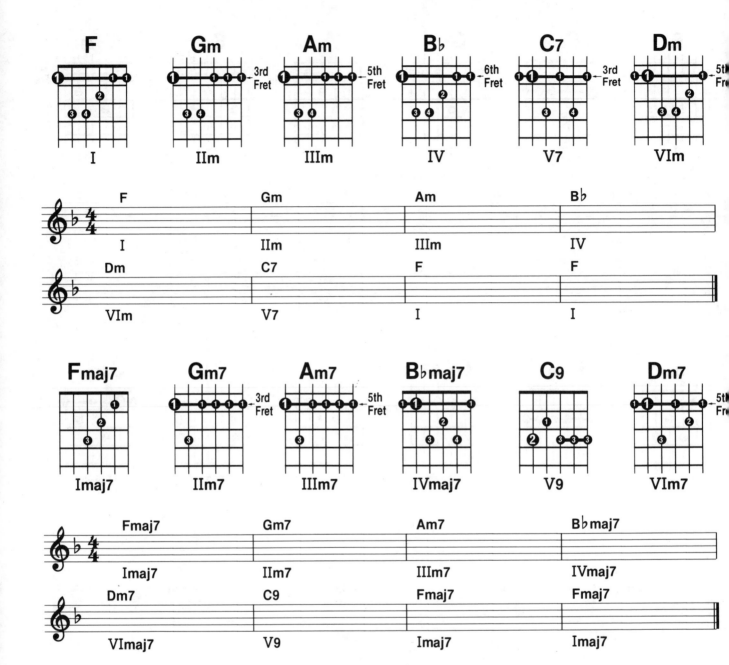

RELATIVE MINOR: D minor

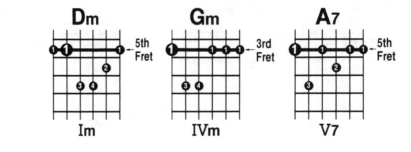

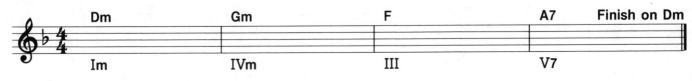

KEY OF F♯ MAJOR

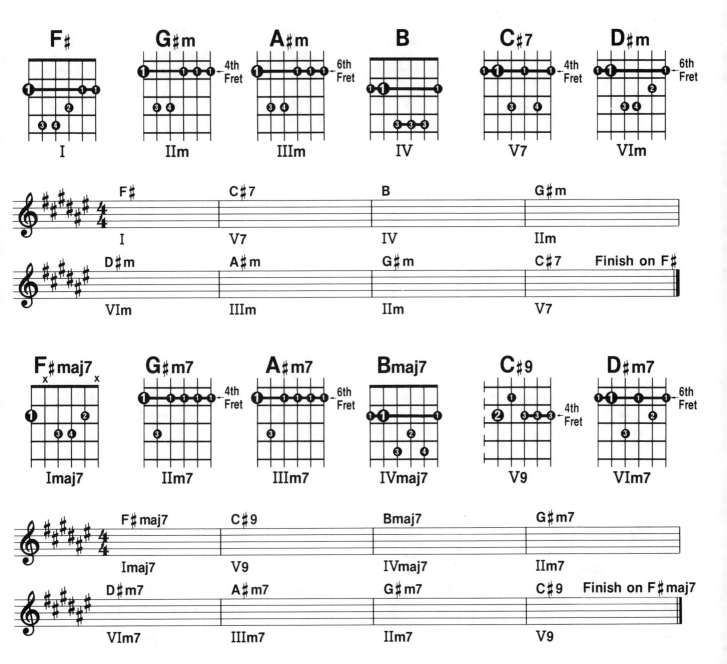

RELATIVE MINOR: D♯ minor

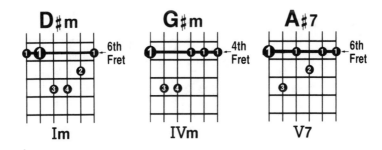

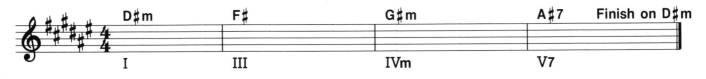

KEY OF G MAJOR

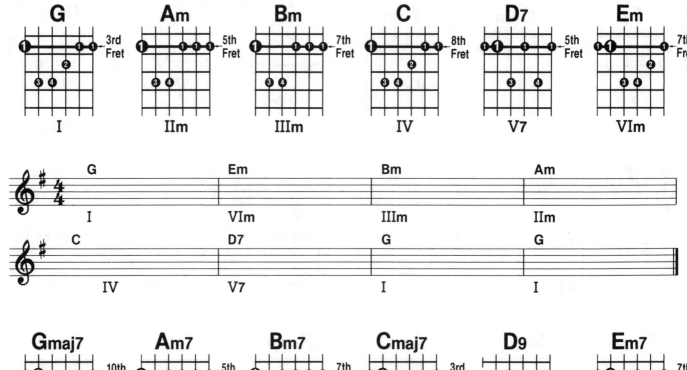

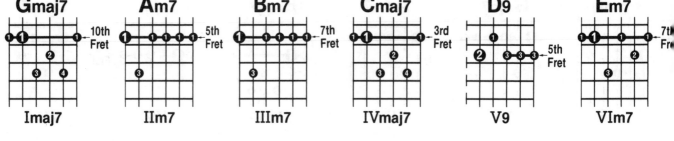

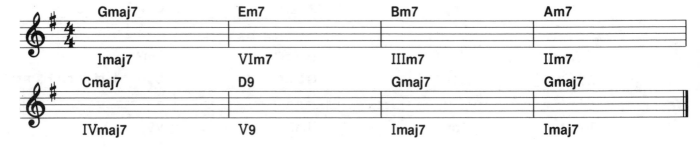

RELATIVE MINOR: E minor

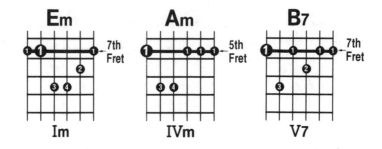

KEY OF A♭ MAJOR

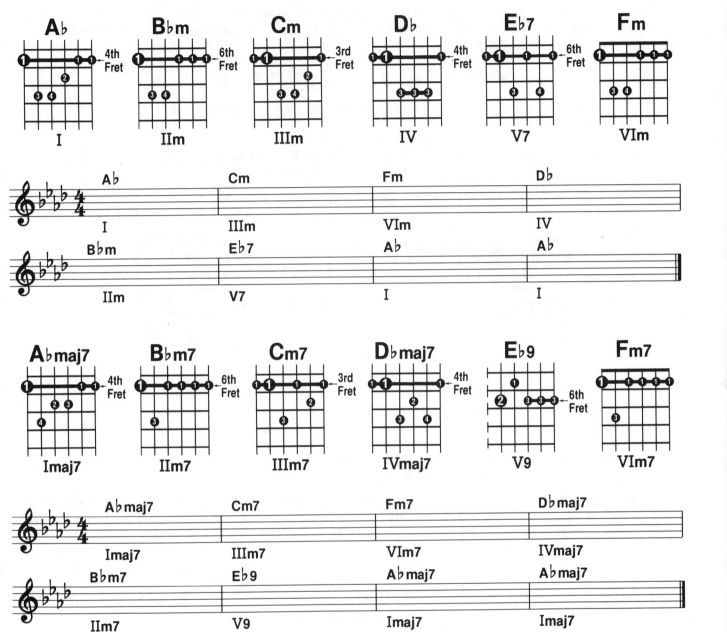

RELATIVE MINOR: F minor

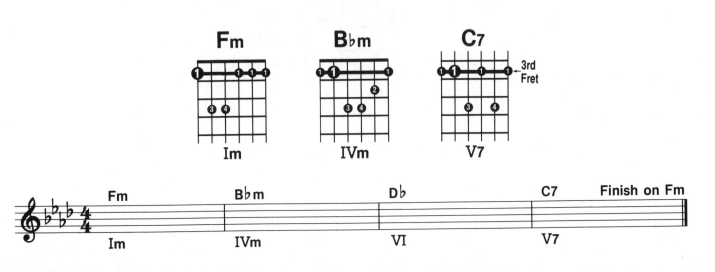

APPENDIX ONE

MOVING LINES

Many chords feature identical notes, which are called **COMMON TONES**. As a result of this, many chord shapes are similar in that they only have one note different from each other. For example, the only difference between major and minor chords is the third:

MAJOR: 1   3   5   **MINOR: 1   3♭   5**

Thus a major chord can be converted to a minor chord by lowering the third note one fret, as illustrated in the diagrams below:

Lift off 2nd finger to change from major to minor.

Move the 2nd finger down one fret to change from major to minor.

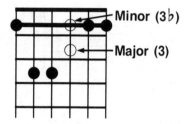
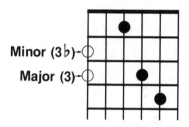

These examples illustrate what is called a **MOVING LINE**. The most common examples of moving lines occur with either the **ROOT** or **FIFTH** notes of the chord.

In the next example, a moving line starting from the root note on the 4th string is used. By changing the position of this one note, four different chords are created. The notes on the 2nd, 3rd and 6th strings do not change, however your fingering of them will.

MAJOR
Root Note Movement

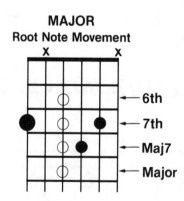

The following examples feature moving lines based on the root or 5th notes of major and minor chord shapes:

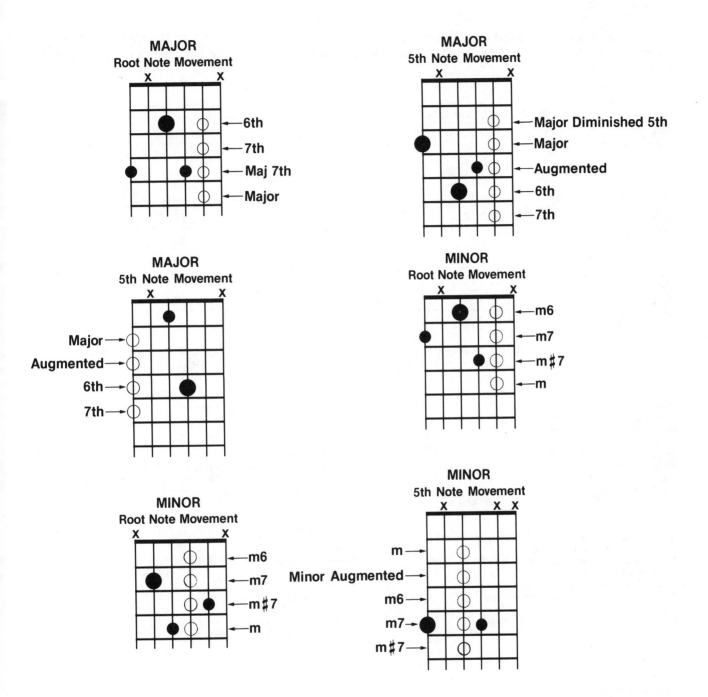

Moving lines are one example of what is called **VOICE LEADING**, which is the process of connecting each note of a given chord with each note of the preceding and following chords.

APPENDIX TWO

SONG LIST

12 BAR BLUES

12 bar blues is a very common chord progression used in many songs. It involves a set pattern, over 12 bars, of the I, IV and V chords in either major or minor keys. The most common 12 bar pattern is outlined below, in the key of E:

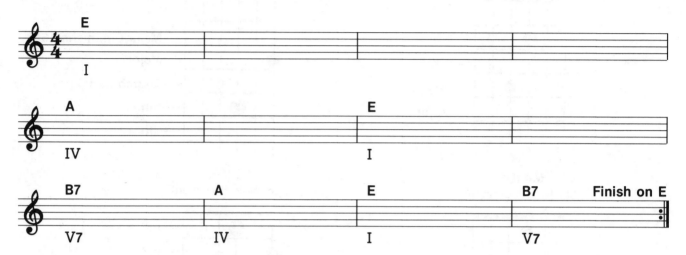

Written below is a list of songs which are based upon the 12 bar blues progression.

Be-bop-a-lula — Gene Vincent/John Lennon
Hound Dog — Elvis Presley
Johnny B. Goode — Chuck Berry
Boppin' the Blues — Blackfeather
The Wanderer — Dion
Going up the Country — Canned Head
Makin' your mind up — Bucks Fizz
Green Door — Shakin' Stevens
In the Summertime — Mungo Jerry
Rock Around the Clock — Bill Haley & The Comets
Barbara Ann — Beach Boys
Let's Stick Together — Brian Ferry
Long Tall Glasses (I Know I can Dance) — Leo Sayer
Blue Suede Shoes — Elvis Presley
School Days (Ring Ring Goes The Bell) — Chuck Berry
Roll Over Beethoven — Chuck Berry
Spirit in the Sky — Norman Greenbaum
Turn up your Radio — Masters Apprentices
Tutti Frutti — Little Richard
Dizzy Miss Lizzy — Larry Williams/Beetles
Peggy Sue — Buddy Holly
Jailhouse Rock — Elvis Presley

Get Down and Get With It — Slade
Good Golly Miss Molly — Little Richard
Lucille — Little Richard
In the Mood — Glen Miller
Sufin' Safari — Beach Boys
Peppermint Twist — Sweet
Boogie Woogie Bugle Boy — Andrew Sisters/Bette Midler
I hear you Knocking — Dave Edmunds
Boy from New York City — Darts/Manhattan Transfer
Mountain of Love — Johnny Rivers
I Love to Boogie — T-Rex
Shake, Rattle & Roll — Bill Haley
Lady Rose — Mungo Jerry
Theme to Batman
Theme to Spiderman
Stuck in the Middle with you — Stealers Wheel
Hot Love — T-Rex
The Huckle Buck — Brendan Bower
Way Down — Elvis Presley
I Can Help — Billy Swan
Rockin' Robin — Michael Jackson

TURNAROUNDS

The turnaround is another very common chord progression, occuring in many rock, pop (top 40) and folk songs. There are two variations of the turnaround; namely, **TURNAROUND ONE**, which is based upon the I-VIm-IV-V7 chords, and **TURNAROUND TWO**, based upon the I-IIIm-IV-V7 chords. In the key of C, these two turnarounds are:

TURNAROUND ONE:

TURNAROUND TWO:

Unlike 12 bar blues, where the progression occurs over a fixed number of bars, the turnaround progression may vary in length. In the following example, turnaround one occurs over two bars:

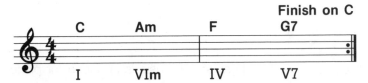

It is the **CHORD SEQUENCE**, not the length of bars, that makes a progression a turnaround. Here the songs which are based, entirely or in part, upon turnarounds one and two.

TURNAROUND ONE*

The night has a 1,000 Eyes — Bobby Vee
It's Raining Again — Supertramp
More — Various Artists
Ti Amo — Umberto Tozzi
Crocodile Roc (chorus) — Elton John
One Last Kiss — Various Artists
Stand by Me — John Lennon
Dream — Everly Brothers
Return to Sender — Elvis Presley
Telstar — Tornadoes
Always Look on the Bright Side of Life — Monty Python
Why do fools fall in love — Frankie Lyman/Diana Ross
Sarah — Fleetwood Mac
Take Good Care of my Baby — Bobby Vee/Smokie
Where have all the Flowers Gone — Various Artists
Runaround Sue — Dion & The Belmonts
Tell me Why — Beatles
Let's Twist Again — Chubby Checker
Stay (Just a Little Bit Longer) — Four Seasons/Jackson Brown
Cool for Cats — U.K. Squeeze
Y.M.C.A. — Village People
Tired of toein' the Line — Rocky Burnett
You Drive Me Crazy — Shakin' Stevens
Should I do it — Pointer Sisters
Poor Little Fool — Rick Nelson
You Don't have to say you Love Me — Dusty Springfield/Elvis Presley
Breaking up is hard to do — Neil Sedaka/Partridge Family
Oh Carol — Neil Sedaka
Two Faces Have I — Lou Christie
Every Day — Buddy Holly
Poetry in Motion — Johnny Tillotson
Sweet Little 16 — Neil Sedaka
Big Girls Don't Cry — Four Seasons
Sherry — Four Seasons
How Do you do it — Jerry & The Pacemakers
Shout, Shout — Rocky Sharp and The Replays
Aces With You — Moon Martin
Houses of the Holy — Led Zeppelin
Uptown Girl — Billy Joel
Build me up Buttercup — Foundations
'Happy Days' — Theme
Should I Do It — Pointer Sisters

Joane — Michael Nesmith
Goodnight Sweetheart — Various Artists
Looking for an Echo — Ol' 55
Summer Holiday — Cliff Richard
Be My Baby — The Ronettes/Rachel Sweet
Everlasting Love — Rachel Sweet/Love Affair
I Go To Pieces (verse) — Peter & Gordon
Love Hurst — Everly Brothers/Jim Capaldi/Nazareth
Gee Baby — Peter Shelley
Classic — Adrian Gurvitz
Teenage Dream — T-Rex
Blue Moon — Various Artists
The Tide is High — Blondie
Dennis — Blondie
It Ain't Easy — Normie Rowe
My World — Bee Gees
Hey Paula — Various Artists
It's Only Make Believe — Glen Campbell
Can't Smile Without You — Barry Manilow
Take Good Care of My Baby — Bobby Vee/Smokie
Crossfire — Bellamy Brothers
Bobby's Girl — Marcie Blane
Do that to me one more time — Captain and Tenile
Please Mr Postman — Carpenters/Beatles
Sharin' the Night Together — Dr Hook
9 to 5 (Morning Train) — Sheena Easton
Diana — Paul Anka
Telstar — Tornadoes
Enola Gay — Orchestral Manoeuvres in the Dark
Some Guys have all the Luck — Robert Palmer
So Lonely — Get Wet
Hungry Heart — Bruce Springsteen
Land of Make Believe (chorus) — Bucks Fizz
Daddys Home — Cliff Richard
The Wonder of You — Elvis Presley
So You Win Again — Hot Chocolate
Hang Five — Rolling Stones
Paper Tiger — Sue Thompson
Venus — Frankie Avalon
Costafine Town — Splinter
If You Leave — OMD
True Blue — Madonna

TURNAROUND TWO

Crocodile Rock (verse) — Elton John
I Started a Joke — Bee Gees
Different Drum — Linda Ronstadt
Key Largo — Bertie Higgins
Black Berry Way — The Move
Georgy Girl — Seekers
Where Do You Go To My Lovely — Peter Sarsted
Mrs Brown, You've Got a Lovely Daughter — Hermans Hermit
Toast and Marmalade for Tea — Tin Tin
Movie Star — Harpo

Where Did Our Love Go — Diana Ross & The Supremes
Hurdy Gury Man — Donovan
I Go To Pieces (chorus) — Peter & Gordon
Get It Over With — Angie Gold
Sad Sweet Dreamer — Sweet Sensation
Down Town — Petula Clark
Easy — Oakridge Boys
Only You Can Do It — Francoise Hardy
Costafine — Splinter (Chorus)
Where Did Our Love Go? — Phil Collins

It's A Heartache — Bonnie Tyler
I Don't Like Mondays — Boomtown Rats
My Angel Baby — Toby Beau
Land Of Make Believe (verse) — Bucks Fizz
I'm In The Mood For Dancing — The Nolans
What's In A Kiss — Gilbert O'Sullivan
My Baby Loves Love — Joe Jeffries
Dreamin' — Jonny Burnett
Cruel To Be Kind — Nick Lowe

READING SHEET MUSIC

You should try to work from sheet music as much as possible. Nearly all sheet music is arranged for piano and this presents problems for guitarists. Piano music uses three staves thus:

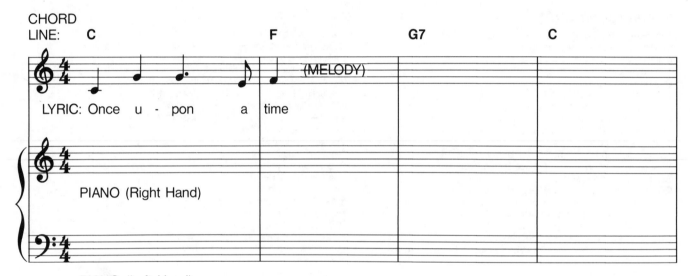

A guitarist need only look at the top stave which contains the melody line (the tune), the lyrics and the chords. Sheet music does not indicate what rhythm the guitarist should use. This is where your creativity and background rhythm playing must be put to use. **SEE PROGRESSIVE RHYTHM GUITAR** by Gary Turner and Brenton White.

APPENDIX THREE

CHORD SYMBOLS

In sheet music notation, there is a lack of uniformity in writing chord symbols. For example, the C major seven chord can be written as "Cmaj7" (used in this book), "CΔ7" or "CM7". The table below outlines the symbols used in this book, together with correct pronunciation and alternative symbols used for each chord type.

SYMBOLS USED IN THIS BOOK	NAME	ALTERNATIVE SYMBOLS
(None)	Major	Maj, M
sus	Suspended	sus4
-5	Major Flat Five	♭5
add9	Major Add Nine	
m	Minor	min, mi,
+	Augmented	♯5, +5, aug
6	Major Six	Maj6, Δ6, M6
6/9	Major Six Add Nine	6(add9), $\frac{6}{9}$, Maj6(add9), M6(add9)
m6	Minor Six	mi6, min6
m6/9	Minor Six Add Nine	mi6(add9), min6(add9), m6(add9)
7	Dominant Seven	Dom7
7sus	Seven Suspended	sus7, 7sus4
m7	Minor Seven	mi7, min7
m7♭5	Minor Seven Flat Five	∅7, ½dim7, mi7♭5, min7♭5, m7-5
°	Diminished Seven	°7, dim7, -7, dim
7♯5	Seven Sharp Five	+7, 7+5
7♭5	Seven Flat Five	7-5
maj7	Major Seven	Δ7, M7
m(maj7)	Minor Major Seven	m(Maj7), m(Δ7), m(+7), mi(+7), min(+7)
7♭9	Seven Flat Nine	7-9
7♯5♭9	Seven Sharp Five, Flat Nine	7+5-9
Maj9	Major Nine	Δ9, M9
m9	Minor Nine	mi9, min9, -9
9♯5	Nine Sharp Five	+9, 9+5
9♭5	Nine Flat Five	9-5
9♯11	Nine Sharp Eleven	9+11
m9(maj7)	Minor Nine Major Seven	m9♯7, min9♯7, m9(Δ7), m9(Maj7), m9(M7)
m11	Minor Eleven	mi11, min11, -11
13	Thirteenth	M13, M7(add6)
13♭9	Thirteen Flat Nine	13-9
13♭5♭9	Thirteen Flat Five Flat Nine	13-5-9
m13	Minor Thirteen	mi13, min13, m7(add6), -13

In sheet music, chord symbols which indicate the bass note to play are sometimes used. For example, C/G indicates a C chord with a G bass note (it may also be written C/Gbass). The bass note will not always be a note of the chord; for example, Am/G is an A minor chord with a G bass note, which could also be called Am7.

GLOSSARY OF TERMS

ACCENT — a sign, >, used to indicate a predominant beat.

ACCIDENTAL — a sign used to show a temporary change in pitch of a note (i.e. sharp ♯, flat ♭, double sharp ✕, double flat ♭♭, or natural ♮.) The sharps or flats in a key signature are not regarded as accidentals.

ADDITIONAL NOTES — a note not belonging to a given scale, but can be used for improvising against most chords in a progression without sounding out of key.

AD LIB — to be played at the performer's own discretion.

ALLEGRETTO — moderately fast.

ALLEGRO — fast and lively.

ANACRUSIS — a note or notes occurring before the first bar of music (also called 'lead-in' notes).

ANDANTE — an easy walking pace.

ARPEGGIO — the playing of a chord in single note fashion.

BAR — A division of music occuring between two bar lines (also call a 'measure').

BAR CHORD — a chord played with one finger lying across all six strings.

BAR LINE — a vertical line drawn across the staff which divides the music into equal sections called bars.

BASS — the lower regions of pitch in general. On guitar, the 4th, 5th and 6th strings.

BASS NOTE RUN — a series of single notes played on the bass strings, used to connect two chords.

BEND — a technique which involves pushing a string upwards (or downwards), which raises the pitch of the fretted note being played.

'BLUES' SCALE — consisting of the I, ♭III, IV, V and ♭VII notes relative to the major scale.

CAPO — a device placed across the neck of a guitar to allow a key change without alteration of the chord shapes.

CHORD — a combination of three or more different notes played together.

CHORD PROGRESSION — a series of chords played as a musical unit (e.g. as in a song).

CHROMATIC SCALE — a scale ascending and descending in semitones: e.g. C chromatic scale:

ascending: C C♯ D D♯ E F F♯ G G♯ A A♯ B C

descending: C B B♭ A A♭ G G♭ F E E♭ D D♭ C

CLEF — a sign placed at the beginning of each staff of music which fixes the location of a particular note on the staff, and hence the location of all other notes. e.g.

◄ G note

Treble Staff

◄ F note

Bass Staff

CLICHES — small musical phrases that are frequently used.

CODA — an ending section of music, signified by the sign ⊕

COMMON TIME — an indication of 4/4 time - four quarter note beats per bar. (also indicated by C)

COMPOUND TIME — occurs when the beat falls on a dotted note, which is thus divisible by three, e.g. 6/8 9/8 12/8

D.C. AL FINE — a repeat from the beginning to the word "fine".

DOT — a sign placed after a note indicating that its time value is extended by a half. e.g.

♩ = 2 Counts   ♩. = 3 Counts

DOUBLE BAR LINE — two vertical lines close together, indicating the end of a piece, or section thereof.

DOUBLE FLAT — a sign (♭♭) which lowers the pitch of a note by one tone.

DOUBLE SHARP — a sign (✕) which raises the pitch of a note by one tone.

D.S. AL FINE — a repeat from the sign (indicated thus ٭) to the word 'fine'.

DURATION — the time value of each note.

DYNAMICS — the varying degrees of softness (indicated by the term 'piano') and loudness (indicated by the term 'forte') in music.

EIGHTH NOTE — a note with the value of half a beat in $\frac{4}{4}$ time, indicated thus ♪ (also called a quaver).

The eight note rest indicating half a beat of silence, is written: ⅞

ENHARMONIC — describes the difference in notation, but not in pitch, of two notes; e.g.

F♯ or G♭

FERMATA — a sign, ⌒, used to indicate that a note or chord is held to the player's own descretion (also called a 'pause sign').

FLAT — a sign, (♭) used to lower the pitch of a note by one semitone.

FORTE — loud. Indicated by the sign f.

GLISSANDO — to glide the pick slowly across the strings of a chord. Indicated by a wavy line placed immediately before the chord notes.

HALF NOTE — a note with the value of two beats in $\frac{4}{4}$ time, indicated thus: ♩ (also called a minim).

The half note rest, indicating two beats of silence, is written: ▬ third staff line.

HAMMER-ON — sounding a note by using only the left hand fingers (also called a 'slur').

HARMONIC MINOR SCALE — a series of 8 notes in alphabetical order based on the interval sequence; T, S, T, T, S, T½, S

HARMONICS — a chime like sound created by lightly touching a vibrating string at certain points along the fret board.

HARMONY — simultaneous sounding of two or more different notes.

IMPROVISE — to perform spontaneously; i.e. not from memory or from a written copy.

INTERVAL — the distance between any two notes of different pitches.

KEY — describes the notes used in a composition in regards to the major or minor scales from which they are taken; e.g. a piece 'in the key of C major' describes the melody, chords, etc., as predominantly consisting of the notes C, D, E, F, G, A, and B - i.e. from the C scale.

KEY SIGNATURE — a sign, placed at the beginning of each stave of music, directly after the clef, to indicate the key of a piece. The sign consists of a certain number of sharps or flats, which represent the sharps or flats, found in the scale of the piece's key: e.g.   indicates a scale with F♯ and C♯, which is D major; D E F♯ G A B C♯ D. Therefore the key is D major.

LEAD-IN — same as Anacrusis.

LEDGER LINES — small horizontal lines upon which notes are written when their pitch is either above or below the range of the staff, e.g.

LEGATO — smoothly, well connected.

LYRIC — words that accompany a melody.

MAJOR PENTATONIC SCALE — a 5 tone scale based on the interval T, T, T½, T, T½.

MAJOR SCALE — a series of eight notes in alphabetical order based on the interval sequence tone - tone - semitone - tone - tone - tone - semitone, giving the familiar sound do re mi fa so la ti do.

MELODIC MINOR SCALE — a series of 8 notes in alphabetical order based on the interval sequence T, S, T, T, T, T, S ascending, and T, T, S, T, T, S, T descending.

MELODY — a succesion of notes of varying pitch and duration, and having a recognizable musical shape.

METRONOME — a device which indicates the number of beats per minute, and which can be adjusted in accordance to the desired tempo. e.g. **MM** (Maelzel Metronome) ♩ = 60 indicates 60 quarter note beats per minute.

MINOR PENTATONIC SCALE — a 5 tone scale based on the interval sequence T½, T, T, T½, T.

MODE — a displaced scale e.g. playing through the C to C scale, but starting and finishing on the D note.

MODERATO — at a moderate pace.

MODULATION — the changing of key within a song (or chord progression).

NATURAL — a sign (♮) used to cancel out the effect of a sharp or flat. The word is also used to describe the notes A, B, C, D, E, F, and G; e.g. 'the natural notes'.

NOTATION — the written representation of music, by means of symbols (music on a staff), letters (as in chord and note names) and diagrams (as in chord illustrations).

NOTE — a single sound with a given pitch and duration.

OCTAVE — the distance between any given note with a set frequency, and another note with exactly double that frequency. Both notes will have the same letter name;

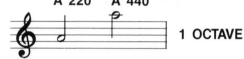

1 OCTAVE

OPEN CHORD — a chord that contains at least one open string.

PASSING NOTE — connects two melody notes which are a third or less apart. A passing note usually occurs on an unaccented beat of the bar.

PHRASE — a small group of notes forming a recognizable unit within a melody.

PITCH — the sound produced by a note, determined by the frequency of the air vibration. The pitch relates to a note being referred to as 'high' or 'low'.

PIVOT FINGER — a finger which remains in position while the other fingers move, when changing chords.

PLECTRUM — a small object (often of a triangular shape) made of plastic which is used to pick or strum the strings of a guitar.

POSITION — a term used to describe the location of the left hand on the fret board. The left hand position is determined by the fret location of the first finger, e.g. The 1st position refers to the 1st to 4th frets. The 3rd position refers to the 3rd to 6th frets and so on.

PURE MINOR SCALE — a series of 8 notes in alphabetical order based on the sequence T, S, T, T, S, T, T.

QUARTER NOTE — a note with the value of one beat in $\frac{4}{4}$ time, indicated thus ♩ (also called a crotchet). The quarter note rest, indicating one beat of silence, is written: ⌡

RITARDANDO — Gradually slow down (abbreviated to 'rit').

REPEAT SIGNS — in music, used to indicate a repeat of a section of music, by means of two dots placed before a double bar line:

In chord progressions, a repeat sign ✕, indicates an exact repeat of the previous bar.

REST STROKE — where the finger, after picking the string, comes to rest on the next string (for accenting the note).

RHYTHM — the aspect of music concerned with tempo, duration and accents of notes. Tempo indicates the speed of a piece (fast or slow); duration indicates the time value of each note (quarter note, eighth note, sixteenth note, etc.); and accents indicate which beat is more predominant.

ROOT NOTE — the note after which a chord or scale is named (also called 'key note').

SCALE TONE CHORDS — chords which are constructed from notes within a given scale.

SEMITONE — the smallest interval used in conventional music. On guitar, it is a distance of one fret.

SHARP — a sign (♯) used to raise the pitch of a note by one semitone.

SIMPLE TIME — occurs when the beat falls on an undotted note, which is thus divisible by two.

SLIDE — a technique which involves a finger moving along the string to its new note. The finger maintains pressure on the string, so that a continuous sound is produced.

SLUR — sounding a note by using only the left hand fingers. (an ascending slur is also called 'hammer-on'; a descending slur is also called 'flick-off').

STACCATO — to play short and detached. Indicted by a dot placed above the note.

STAFF — five parallel lines together with four spaces, upon which music is written.

SYNCOPATION — the placing of an accent on a normally unaccented beat. e.g.:

 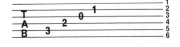

TABLATURE — a system of writing music which represents the position of the player's fingers (not the pitch of the notes, but their position on the guitar). A chord diagram is a type of tablature. Notes can also be written using tablature thus:

Music Notation   **Tablature**   Each line represents a string, and each number represents a fret.

TEMPO — the speed of a piece.

TIE — a curved line joining two or more notes of the same pitch, where the second note(s) is not played, but its time value is added to that of the first note.

 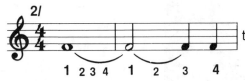

In example two, the first note is held for seven counts.

TIME SIGNATURE — a sign at the beginning of a piece which indicates, by means of figures, the number of beats per bar (top figure), and the type of note receiving one beat (bottom figure).

TONE — a distance of two frets; i.e. the equivalent of two semitones.

TRANSPOSITION — the process of changing music from one key to another.

TREBLE — the upper regions of pitch in general.

TREMELO (PICK TREMELO) — a technique involving rapid pick movement on a given note.

TRIPLET — a group of three notes played in the same time as two notes of the same kind.

Quaver triplet

VIBRATO — a technique which involves pushing a string up and down, like a rapid series of short bends.

WEDGE MARK — indicates pick direction; e.g.: **V** down pick, **Λ** up pick.

WHOLE NOTE — a note with the value of four beats in $\frac{4}{4}$ time, indicated thus ○ (also called a semibreve). A strum equivalent of the whole note is written: **V**

1 2 3 4

The whole note rest, indicating four beats of silence, is written: ▬ 4th staff line.

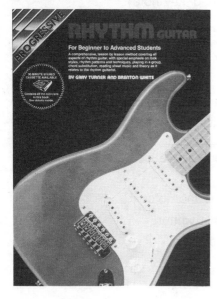

Progressive Rhythm Guitar
Beginner to Advanced

"I have seen few books containing such a skillful blend of practical guitar playing and music theory." AUSTRALIAN MUSICIAN MAGAZINE.

- No previous knowledge of the guitar or music required.
- Lesson by lesson, carefully graded introduction to playing rhythm guitar in a Rock group.
- Uses the simplest most logical rhythm notation V = down strum, Λ = up strum.
- Separate sections on open, bar and jazz chords.
- Teaches how to read music with basic elements of music theory including time signatures, note values, sharps, flats and scales.
- Over 130 chord progressions with suggested rhythms.
- Tips for playing in a band.
- Special sections on tuning, reading sheet music, transposing, major and minor keys, chord construction and a comprehensive glossary of musical terms for the guitar.
- Contains many photos of popular rock groups and guitarists.
- 144 pages, over 133 exercises, 84 photos. Color cover.

 ## 90 minute cassette

A 90 minute stereo cassette containing all the exercises in this book.
Left Hand Channel — rhythm guitar exercises.
Right Hand Channel — bass guitar and drum backing (to play along with).

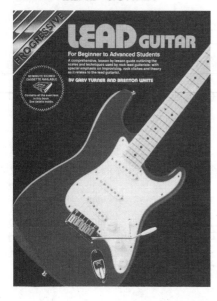

Progressive Lead Guitar

"A Godsend to the beginning player . . ." GUITAR PLAYER MAGAZINE.

- Discusses rock and blues scales used by EVERY lead guitarist.
- Music and tablature notation.
- Riffs, rock cliches, hammer-ons, slides, bends and every important lead guitar technique in a lesson by lesson format.
- Pick and scale exercises for speed and dexterity.
- Jamming progressions and tips for playing in a group.
- Special sections on scale theory, chord construction, improvising, playing by ear, modulation, harmonics and a comprehensive glossary of musical terms for the guitarist.
- Contains many photographs of popular rock groups and lead guitarists.
- 104 pages, 65 exercises, 45 photos. Color cover.

 ## 60 minute cassette

A 60 minute stereo cassette containing all the exercises in this book and featuring a full backing band to play along with.
Left Hand Channel — contains the lead guitar by itself.
Right Hand Channel — contains the backing band (to play along with).

Progressive Fingerpicking Guitar

" . . . bridges the gap between the old-time folk methods and the contemporary playing styles of today."

- Music and tablature notation.
- Fingerpicking patterns covering folk, claw-hammer, ragtime and classical styles of playing in a lesson by lesson format.
- Bass note runs, hammer-ons, flick-offs, moving bass lines and other important picking techniques.
- In depth analysis of arranging styles featuring some of the world's most popular classical, folk, blues, ragtime and Spanish pieces.
- Special sections on tuning, basic music theory, transposing, capos, reading sheet music and a comprehensive glossary of musical terms for the guitarist.
- 136 pages, 80 exercises and pieces, 28 photos and color cover.

60 minute cassette

A 60 minute stereo cassette containing all the exercises in this book.